Debi Marshall is a freelance jo
Tasmania. She started her caree
now writes extensively for nat
in crime. She is also an exper
reporter. A qualified teacher (BA, Dip Ed), Debi also teaches
Media and English at college and university.

the DEVIL'S GARDEN

The Claremont Serial Killings

DEBI MARSHALL

RANDOM HOUSE AUSTRALIA

Random House Australia Pty Ltd
Level 3, 100 Pacific Highway, North Sydney NSW 2060
www.randomhouse.com.au

Sydney New York Toronto
London Auckland Johannesburg

First published by Random House Australia 2007

National Library of Australia
Cataloguing-in-Publication Entry

   Marshall, Debi.
   The Devil's garden: the Claremont serial killings.

   ISBN 978 1 74166 4669

   1. Serial murders – Western Australia – Claremont. 2. Serial
   murderers – Western Australia – Claremont. I. Title.

364.1523099411

Cover photo reproduced courtesy *The West Australian*
Cover design by Darian Causby/www.highway51.com.au
Typeset in Minion by Midland Typesetters, Australia
Printed and bound by Griffin Press, South Australia

10 9 8 7 6 5 4

To my precious daughter, Louise, and lovely mother, Monica

In memory of the girls who didn't come home:
Sarah, Jane and Ciara

I will show you fear in a handful of dust.
T.S. Eliot, 'The Waste Land'

Preface

February 2006. After five years of research and writing, my two true-crime books, *Killing for Pleasure: The definitive story of the Snowtown serial killings* – the macabre, terrible story of South Australia's 'bodies in the barrels' murders – and *Justice in Jeopardy: The unsolved murder of baby Deidre Kennedy*, were published. I felt drenched in blood, exhausted. But another story was tugging at me, one that had been making the news on and off for a decade. Perth's Claremont serial killings: the longest, most expensive and most secretive unsolved murder investigation in Australian history. Between 1996 and 1997, three girls went missing; only two bodies were ever found. A decade on, and still no one has been charged. But I sensed there was more to this story. Much more. As my research was to prove, I was right.

Just how many victims has this serial killer claimed? Police have admitted that Julie Cutler, who disappeared in 1988, could well have been the first victim. Sarah Spiers went missing in summer. Jane Rimmer in winter. Ciara Glennon in autumn. Coincidence, probably. Or was the killer, in his perverse way, working to nature's pattern? Whatever the truth, this laidback city – and particularly its affluent heart, Claremont – was, as one journalist described it, being 'king-hit by a menace it couldn't see'.

With police refusing to release modus operandi, the public would have to be content with the findings of the final independent review, in 2004. But there is a catch. Beyond generalisations, the details of those reviews cannot be released. The public is again kept in the dark and victims' families continue to wait for answers. At least a few innocent men have their reputations in tatters. And the investigation remains secretive, police and killer locked in what one newspaper calls a 'deadly stalemate'.

Not since the Ivan Milat backpacker serial killing investigations, where police had abundant crime-scene evidence, have police been so under the pump to solve a case. But it is not easy. Homicide investigation by its very nature is challenging, complex, sensitive and political. And serial killers – cunning, clever chameleons – are, by *their* very nature, notoriously difficult to apprehend. The length of time the girls were missing ensured deterioration of evidence – if there was any. There were no eyewitnesses to the abductions or murders. No definite abduction point. No known crime scene. No murder weapon. No known motive. No confession. And no victim to verbalise what happened. In this atmosphere, a hothouse of pressure from inside and outside the police force, the investigation becomes a battle of wills and power play.

When I started writing this book, the murders had been unsolved for ten years. Why so long? Has the killer simply stopped for fear of apprehension? Died? Or is he – or they – still operational in another area, another state or another country? As the years slipped by without a resolution Dave Caporn, the former head of the Macro taskforce, formed after Jane Rimmer went missing, admitted that as more time passed, the tougher it would be to secure a conviction. This would prove to be unerringly accurate. This, in Western Australia, a state which averages 34 to 40 murders a year and where police boast a 95 per cent 'solved' rate.

The Claremont serial killings have become a story that has seared itself into the Western Australian psyche; a bleak chapter in Perth's history and one steeped in scuttlebutt and urban myths. It is a case that has damaged some reputations beyond redemption and on which some investigators have staked their careers.

In writing *The Devil's Garden*, I drew on my 20-year experience as a journalist, biographer and true-crime author, in particular the extensive research and writing I have done about murder and serial killers. I also drew on the findings of experts in this field. From the outset, I kept an open mind on known suspects. Frustratingly, for legal reasons some of the information I gathered from both inside the Macro taskforce sources and outside cannot be included.

Despite plainly setting out a list of questions for police and meeting them in Perth for the first time in February 2006, they refused to speak to me for eight months on the grounds that the Claremont killings are an 'ongoing investigation'. Confronted with the so-called 'blue wall of silence' – and not having been made privy to the reasons why – it was impossible for me to check their version of events or to apply the balance they expected to receive. At times – though thankfully by no means always – their attitude to me bordered on outright hostility; at other times I felt patronised by a pervading male culture, the boys club. At all times when they were confronted with questions they did not wish to answer, they could – and frequently did – take refuge in the line that Claremont was an 'ongoing investigation'. There were a few occasions when I had cause to heed the warnings of journalist colleagues from the eastern states that Western Australia was indeed still the 'Wild West'.

Six weeks before the book's deadline, after negotiation with the police commissioner's media adviser, former journalist Neil Poh, the police agreed, with restrictions, to talk. Better to do it now, they reasoned, than to wait until publication and then have to defend themselves, if necessary.

While the breaking of the police silence so close to deadline brought with it the challenge of integrating the interviews into the manuscript, it also brought with it many pluses. Not least of these was that for the first time former high-ranking Macro insiders, fed up with constant media harping about their actions, revealed staggeringly intimate details, born from covert and overt surveillance, of their prime suspect's psyche. For the first time, they explain why they cannot risk eliminating him from the inquiry and why, unless someone else confesses and is proven to be the killer, they never will.

This book is not just about the tragedy of missing and murdered girls; it also explores the particular police culture in Western Australia and the stain that a proportionately large number of miscarriage of justice cases, over several decades, has left on the judicial and social landscape. What is going on in Western Australia that so many cases have been botched? And if that culture has not changed, what does it say about the police handling of the Claremont serial killer case? The two issues seem inextricably linked, and the truth perhaps more frightening than we would care to realise. The question is a stark and simple one: how do we trust they got investigations into this lengthy, unsolved case right when they have got so many others wrong? As the law journal *Justinian* noted of the often spectacular legal bungles in Western Australia: 'The number of miscarriages is reaching endemic proportions.' As a result, the Western Australian police force is often forced to defend itself against a highly critical media. In one of the miscarriage of justice cases, Andrew Mallard, wrongly incarcerated for 12 years for the murder of Pamela Lawrence, a crime he didn't commit, was finally released from jail. The Corruption and Crime (CCC) is reviewing the police investigations into the case and, at the time of completing this manuscript, the CCC findings had not been released. This, police hoped, would give them some room to manoeuvre in interviews for this book and a platform from which to do it. Those manoeuvrings were often transparent. 'I hope you appreciate that your book is scheduled to be published very close to [potentially in the middle of] the Corruption and Crime Commission's public hearings into the conduct of the original Pamela Lawrence investigation,' a police media spokesman wrote to me. 'We can't say anything that might come even close to being in contempt of the CCC (and neither should anyone else I'd suggest!)'

I forwarded further questions to the police. Most were given the okay; some were met with seething indignation. 'Why the focus on miscarriages of justice in a book on the Claremont serial killer?' they demanded. 'Miscarriages of justice happen everywhere.' They do – hence the mushrooming of Innocence Projects around Australia and worldwide. But Western Australia, as shown by comments from many senior legal counsel around the country, seems to have a particular problem. This was often expressed in colourful language. 'Some of these cops couldn't find their own bum with their hands tied behind their back,' one lawyer told me. And why, some police demanded to know, 'talk to disgruntled, bitter ex-coppers?' Because, I responded, it is not my role to play police PR and they, too, have a right to offer opinions. Some of these police officers, disenchanted by the hounding they received from the system in spite of their loyalty, requested anonymity because of the opinions they expressed. Some – but not all – of these people are the 'sources' to whom I refer. Where I have recreated what has been said to people by police, I use the word 'alleged'.

Critics of the Macro taskforce claim that the investigation was and is a catalogue of disasters overlaid with compounded errors, dominated by white male culture and overseen by a 'protected species' – career police officers; a murky collision of lack of evidence and tunnel vision. I wanted to find out if that was correct. Macro supporters claim the investigation – despite the murders being still unsolved – has been brilliantly executed and the investigators nothing short of strategic warriors. Whatever the truth, for many officers on the Macro team, the sense of disappointment that they have so far failed to apprehend the serial killer is acute and a failure they take personally. What is the truth? Is the fact that these dreadful killings are still unsolved due to police incompetence, the sheer brilliance of the killer to escape detection, or just plain bad luck? Is it a combination of all three?

With the stench of the WA Inc scandal still lingering in the Perth air, there have also been rumblings of a sometimes unhealthy relationship between some sections of the media, government, police and judiciary. Given the size of the city, and its accessibility, it is easy to overlap social or sporting activities with work.

And that, says a former police officer, can lead to cronyism. 'You know the old saying, "Fish stink from the head down." That has certainly been evident here at times. Some journalists have taken a middle line with the Claremont story to ensure their sources don't dry up.'

Some family members chose not to talk. The most notable was victim Ciara Glennon's father, Denis. We exchanged several phone calls during which he asked me why I was writing this story. I answered that after a decade, the investigation appeared no closer to reaching a conclusion and I believed it was time to collate the information into one cohesive piece. He did not agree, but did concede that I was at liberty to use any statements made by him and on public record. This I have done. It soon became apparent that beyond Mr Glennon's inconsolable, protracted grief was also biting anger that I might criticise the police operation. Sarah Spiers's father, Don, did speak to me, but he too was angry that the story may be less than flattering toward the police involved. They were, he said, always a great support to himself and his family. Not all victims' parents share his viewpoint, including Jane Rimmer's family.

If this story causes further anguish to already grief-stricken families, that was not the intention. But perhaps this story will pierce a conscience. If not the killer's, perhaps a partner, a parent, a friend? *Someone* knows *something*. The abduction and dumping sites suggest someone who is suave in the city and adept in the bush. But who?

The longer I researched this terrible story and the more people I spoke to, the more alarmed I became. So many men with the inclination and the opportunity. So many sick, sexual deviants. For all the sunshine and carefree lifestyle, Western Australia – and particularly Perth – has not escaped the scourge of all big cities. It is crawling with possible suspects.

A journalist described this case as a 'multimillion-dollar, three-ring circus' – three victims, three people investigated and three detectives heading an investigation that has been reviewed 11 times. *Sunday Times* investigative journalist Colleen Egan, who was instrumental in reopening the Andrew

Mallard case, wrote to me in June 2006 in reply to an email I had sent her. The Claremont story, she opined, was both fascinating and complex. Just how complex, I was about to find out.

The Devil's Garden was a harrowing book to research. It was not just that I was constantly confronted by the anguish of the victims' families who have no answers about their murdered or missing daughters nor, for the first eight months, the bewildering silence of the WA police, but I also had to wade into other areas that are dangerous, defamatory and murky. The hysterical ravings of people anxious to incriminate former partners; allegations not backed up by any hard evidence of tightly organised paedophile rings in the big end of town and the scary, sordid stories of sacrificial occult offerings. Some stories I believe but couldn't, for legal reasons, run. Others I scotched as nothing more than the warped imaginings of sick people. Others still I took with a small grain of truth and have reproduced in this book. These decisions were not purely subjective; on each occasion I sought advice from people well versed in the particular area about how I should treat the material.

This story in no way attempts to pinpoint my own theories as to the identity of the Claremont killer. Rather, it is an overview of the tragic events and other cases in Western Australia.

In a heartbreaking eulogy to his daughter, Ciara Glennon, her father, Denis, told the congregation that 'God has come into our garden and picked the most beautiful rose.' These girls were *all* beautiful roses – young, fresh, in first bud. It became a metaphor for how I thought of the killer: a monster who stalked the innocent yet to blossom and who, when he was finished, tossed away their bodies as nothing more than human compost for the earth. Planting them in the Devil's Garden, around which the death lilies grew.

Mindful of the fact that the Claremont serial killer has not been caught, I was necessarily cautious about whom I met and where. From the outset, I worked by my own rule: when you chase a serial killer, you need to be very careful that the serial killer doesn't start chasing you. And I was never tempted to forget the wisdom of the Malay proverb, 'Don't think there are no crocodiles because the water is calm.'

Part One
The Devil's Garden

'God has come into our garden and picked the most beautiful rose.'
Denis Glennon, in his eulogy to his daughter, Ciara

1

The taxi driver circles the phone box from where Sarah Spiers had called requesting a cab. That's odd. There is no one here. He checks his watch. 2.06 am. The radioed request had only come in six minutes ago and he had driven straight to the pick-up site at Claremont. It is dark; virtually no street lights illuminate the phone box on the corner of Stirling Highway and Stirling Road. He circles again. There is definitely no one here. It's bloody odd. And bloody annoying. The girl must have changed her mind and got a lift with someone else. He curses to himself: now he will have to take his chances with a random fare from one of the young partygoers leaving the nightclub up the road.

They spill out from Club Bayview into the balmy January night. Girls in short dresses and perilously high heels, flushed from dancing, too much alcohol or party drugs, giggle as they drape themselves around their friends and walk unsteadily up the street. Many are continuing the party from yesterday – Australia Day, 1996 – in the languid first month of the New Year. Claremont, the well-heeled heart of this gentle city where a violet sky winks to ruby sunsets that wash over the Swan River, is home to the ritzy clique; the big end of town where upmarket boutiques with upmarket prices nestle alongside trendy cafés. Perth's wealthy citizens – playboys in sporty BMWs and young women boasting platinum credit cards and solarium tans – shop here during the day and cruise, carefree at night.

Shaped by its status as the most isolated city in the world, Perth is more than remote. Sequestered from Australia's eastern states by time and distance – its closest city, Adelaide, is a three-hour flight – it is bordered by the vast Nullarbor

Plain, Simpson Desert and the Indian Ocean. Up north, the Pilbara – a place of blistering heat and ochre rock – churns out vast wealth for mining companies, and the Kimberley, famous for its port town, Broome, and its pearling industry, attracts tourists to its beautiful, rugged coastline.

They party on Bayview Terrace while the rest of Claremont, with old houses built on old money, sleeps. The nearby Stirling Highway is virtually deserted, the odd car heading east toward Perth, ten kilometres away. Perth's aquatic playground, the Swan River is inky black in these pre-dawn hours, lapping gently on the shoreline.

2

Don Spiers started with nothing, leaving school at 14 and working relentlessly to ensure his family never wanted for anything. His daughters, Amanda and Sarah, were educated at a private school, Iona Presbyterian, and stayed close, sharing a flat after they left home. The family lives in an apartment in salubrious South Perth and Don runs a highly successful shearing company in Darkan. It's a tight ship: blokes who apply for a job at his outfit know better than to mess with him. No grog. No drugs. No brawls. Many a time he has stood toe to toe with tough shearers half his age who haven't abided by his rules. 'Get this through your head,' he warns them, 'or you'll come off second best. Either shape up or ship out.' He works the men hard but expects no more from them than what he delivers himself, shearing up to 200 sheep a day. An old man who had lived in Darkan all his 80-odd years paid Don a compliment just before he died. 'I've lived in this district all me life,' he said, 'and I've never seen a man work as hard for his family as you do.' Life in the Spiers household is simple, and happy.

The road is glistening with summer rain. Don stares out the window, struck by a bleak thought. This weather can only hinder any search for his daughter Sarah, who has now been missing for more than 12 hours. The windscreen wipers move rhythmically like a metronome as he flattens the accelerator, barrelling along the country roads on the three-hour drive home to Perth from his shearing contracting business in the rural town of Darkan. His wife, Carol, had left an urgent message with an employee that morning for Don to return her call, immediately. There was panic in her voice. 'Sarah is still not home. You had better come back.'

Don nervously drums his calloused shearer's fingers on the steering wheel. Sarah, their ebullient, affectionate daughter, would never go anywhere without notifying them. Her flatmate and sister, Amanda, two years older than Sarah, is distraught. Sarah hasn't contacted her since she went out to Claremont with friends on Saturday night. It is completely out of character: extremely close, the sisters have not had one fight in their life. Sarah was in fabulous spirits, excitedly planning Amanda's forthcoming twenty-first birthday party before she went out. Amanda had dropped Sarah at a Cottesloe hotel before she took her to Club Bayview around 12.15 am. The area was teeming with young people, celebrating the Australia Day long weekend.

Amanda peeked into Sarah's room on Sunday morning and noticed her bed had not been slept in. 'Sarah hasn't come home,' she tells her mother. 'She doesn't love me!' It is said tongue-in-cheek. Sarah adores her, she knows.

Her bed remains empty on Sunday night. Don churns through the possibilities of where she might be as the car swallows up the kilometres on his way home. Did she impulsively decide to go for a trip to the country? She hasn't got a mobile phone; has she lost her purse and can't call home? Has she been assaulted and is too ashamed to show her face? She has no boyfriend; has she met a bloke and is simply preoccupied?

Sarah. A Hebrew name meaning 'princess', Sarah is responsible and loving, virtually running the household, doting on her family, cooking meals for them even after she had moved out. She was, Don recalls, a giver not a taker. On weekends, she would snuggle up with him and watch the footy, cheering on their team. It bonded them closely but now raw fear binds the family in a vice. Where the hell is she?

The police arrive, cognisant of the family's grief but wary, too. All too frequently, the perpetrator of a crime is a person close to the family, or a family member. Don is quizzed closely but ruled out. He was nowhere near Perth the night his daughter went missing. They run through the normal questions. Could she have run away with a boyfriend? Was she suicidal? Did she have enemies? Any problems at home or work? They draw blanks at every turn.

The investigation falls under the command of the Major Crime Squad. Sergeant Mal Shervill is the case officer. By Sunday, police have all the relevant details. Name. Age. Last seen by friends leaving Club Bayview. Last call made from a phone box near the corner of Stirling Highway and Stirling Road to a taxi company. Sarah Spiers is now, officially, a missing person. The family mounts a 24-hour vigil, monitoring the phone at all times, snatching to answer it as soon as it rings. An army of volunteers distributes her photograph on 35,000 posters around the city. 'Have you seen this girl? She is 18 years old. A secretary for an engineering consultancy. She disappeared from a roadside telephone box in Claremont. Have you seen her?' Up to 35 people a night, roaming the streets of Perth, endlessly asking questions.

Post newspaper proprietor and journalist Bret Christian recalls that time. 'What is often forgotten is that Sarah Spiers was treated as simply a missing person for two weeks. Her friends, family and journalists worked bloody hard to prove that she hadn't just simply taken off somewhere. It's a major problem in investigations; until police realised she wasn't going to turn up, it wasn't prioritised.'

The Spiers family is appointed a liaison officer with whom they can direct concerns or information and who helps bear the burden of their grief. The responsibility falls to OLC of Major Crime Paul Coombes, who walks the tightrope between the family and the media,'When a body is located, we immediately contact the family. But sometimes the reporters get to them first.' One journalist rings Don Spiers informing him that a female body has been found in the bush. Not knowing if it is Sarah or not, he is devastated until he speaks to Coombes. 'Police had already briefed the media off-the-record that they knew it wasn't Sarah,' he says. 'That irresponsible search for the big headline didn't help anyone in those early days.'

The phone jangles in the darkness. Don Spiers, instantly awake, snatches it from its cradle, magnetised by the voice on the other end. That voice: smooth, precise, confident. He quickly hauls himself up on the pillow.

'Is that Mr Spiers?'

'Yes.'

'Mr Don Spiers?'

'Yes.'

'You are Sarah's father?'

'Yes.'

'Sarah's dead, and her body is at Gnangara Pine Plantation.'

The caller hangs up.

Don replaces the phone on the hook, lying in the darkness trembling and distressed. He glances at the clock. Just after 2 am. He has not recognised the male caller's voice, but he would know it again, instantly. Educated. Modulated. So confident. He has slept only fitfully for weeks, from that terrible moment when he was told Sarah went missing. He knew then, with a father's instinct, that something was horribly wrong.

Gnangara Pine Plantation: more than five-and-a-half thousand hectares of inhospitable, desolate scrub. A graveyard for stolen cars, wrecked and dumped. A place of stunning fauna and birds, and of ticks and snakes and spiders. A place of winds and shadows and impenetrable parts. Don wills the male caller to ring again. To clarify information. To tell him all he knows. To be specific about her whereabouts. *Ring back. Ring back. Please, ring back.*

Sarah's disappearance tips the family's axis. But they can't know, in those early days, just how bad it will get.

The police will theorise that Sarah was abducted within two minutes of making the phone call for a taxi – the amount of time it takes for a cab to travel from nearby Eric Street, Cottesloe, where the taxi logged the job-call. But when the scene is checked in a re-enactment scenario at the same time of night as the phone call was made, the police discover that the caller could barely be seen from the roadway, if at all. This raises a disquieting, though distinct possibility: that Sarah could have been in the vicinity of the phone box for a lot longer than just two minutes, and that her presence was simply missed by the taxi driver. The taxi drives away; someone else pulls up.

But who? Some taxi drivers come forward with leads on people they have had in their cab. One is Steven Ross. An unsophisticated, slovenly man whose vehicles are notoriously untidy, in 1996 Ross volunteered to police that he had picked up Sarah Spiers in his taxi the night before she disappeared. In the taxi was another woman, who was dropped off in the next suburb and a man – apparently unknown to Sarah – who had indicated he wanted to go to the city. Sarah got out of the cab, Ross said, at the hip Windsor Hotel in South Perth, close to where she lived. The man, having changed his mind about going to the city, paid the fare, unceremoniously pushed her out of the taxi and followed her. Ross forwarded his theory to police that the following night, the man had returned to Claremont, found Sarah Spiers and murdered her.

Ross was not unknown to police. In the early 90s his partner, a former Austrian beauty queen, housebound after being severely injured in an accident, died. Ross inherited her property and during the police investigation into her death was extensively questioned until it was proven she died of natural causes.

3

Despair and hope render the Spiers family pitifully vulnerable and clairvoyants hover like crows at a feast. Don Spiers does not believe in clairvoyants, but for years he will continue to take their calls, locked in a vicious circle. One of them, he reasons, one day may just have the answer. Or they may be his daughter's abductor, offering cryptic clues as to where she is.

One offers a vision of Sarah, her body entombed in marshy reeds at Salter Point, a small distance from the family's Perth home. Don should search this area, the clairvoyant suggests. He must search tonight. He drives to Salter Point immediately, thrashing and fumbling around with a torch in the darkness, alone and knee-deep in rushes and mud. Parting the reeds, looking for a sign, crying softly at first and then sobbing, calling out her name. *Sarah, Sarah.* He struggles home after a few hours in the water, soaked, distraught, empty-handed.

Up to 300 clairvoyants contact Don, all with their peculiar, specific visions. One advises that Sarah is in a house with a tree in the garden and a 'For Sale' sign out the front. Don becomes obsessed, driving around Perth suburbs, peering up at houses. But there are so many with a tree in the garden and 'For Sale' signs out the front that he becomes disorientated, distressed, his car his place of solace where, away from his family, he buries his head in his hands and weeps.

The clairvoyants' obscure visions weary him. One couple has him driving all over Perth with them in the car for two days. Every time their 'vision' is proved wrong, they change the location. After days of fruitless driving, the last insight they share with Don is that Sarah is at a weir where there is a flock of wild geese. The geese are there, but nothing else. 'There's the geese,' Don points upwards. 'And this is a wild goose chase.' He returns home, dismayed.

The family has nothing to go on. Nothing but the mystery of Sarah vanishing without trace. Don angrily taps a finger on the table as he recalls the clairvoyant who described himself as 'No. 1' in Western Australia. 'He charged into our home without invitation, stood in our living room and started blurting out statements as though they were facts,' he recalls. ' "Sarah is deceased," he said. "Her head has been smashed in with a rock." We just stood there, amazed and disgusted. And then his mobile phone rang and he started doing business! "I charge $50 a session," he told the caller. When he hung up, he volunteered that there was normally a fee for his services, but under the circumstances he wouldn't charge me. We were so outraged at his insensitivity, we were all speechless.'

Thousands of different leads pour in from the public. Information about a stranger offering lifts to young women in Claremont the night Sarah vanished; calls from people who want to assist the inquiry but only serve to hinder it further. Two weeks after Sarah disappears, Detective Senior-Sergeant Paul Ferguson, who heads the inquiry, is circumspect about her chances of being found alive. A popular copper with the press who avoids corporate-speak, he has a determined lack of ego and an approachable air that belies a sharp mind. 'Reality must take effect eventually that this young lady has come to harm,' he says. 'But we say to the parents, "don't give up hope, we're trying our hardest". The inquiry team is still working to try and find the lady alive.' From hard experience, Ferguson knows that this is unlikely. He reads and re-reads the motto stuck on his wall. 'Thoroughness + Persistence = Success.'

If anyone knows about persistence, it's Ferguson. He is going to need it.

4

Western Australia is the largest police jurisdiction in the world, covering often remote and barely accessible areas of 2.5 million square kilometres. The population of almost 5000 uniformed and non-uniformed officers is a far cry from the fledgling colonial service that from its earliest days developed in isolation. A fresh-faced copper in 1972 when he joined the force, Paul Ferguson was seconded to the CIB in 1976 and attained the pinnacle – officer in charge of the Homicide Squad – in 1994. Through the years, his personal motto hasn't changed. It is, he says, an absolute privilege to work in homicide and to speak on behalf of murdered victims who cannot speak for themselves. In 1986, Ferguson was handed the file on a case that defied description. The unrepentant killers would later be identified as husband-and-wife serial killers, David and Catherine Birnie.

What David Birnie, an angular, thin-faced man, did to his victims was depraved enough. That he sought – and received – willing help from his wife, Catherine, in his debauched perversions was beyond comprehension. In early autumn 1987 the pair, both 35, pleaded guilty to the abduction, rape, torture and murder of four women in suburban Perth the preceding year. Three were strangled as they begged for mercy, their bodies tossed into scrub at Glen Eagle Forest, 30 kilometres southeast of Perth. Another was stabbed and axed to death, her body buried at a pine plantation north of Perth. The Birnies' murderous spree had lasted four weeks; the court hearing just 30 minutes. Details of the crimes are so horrific that, decades later, police who worked on the case still shake their heads in horror.

Both highly dysfunctional adults with appalling backgrounds, the Birnies met in their teens, forming an intensely intimate relationship during which they embarked on a series of domestic burglaries, crimes that would become an ominous precursor to the serial killing spree that would follow years later. After they separated, David Birnie married and Catherine worked as domestic help in a house, marrying the owner's son. Despite having five children, Catherine yearned for David; when they reconnected in their 20s, she walked out of her marriage, leaving the children behind. Theirs was a volatile, highly sexual relationship in which David Birnie demanded intercourse or other sexual acts up to six times a day. As a twenty-first birthday present for his brother, James – who would also serve time for sexually molesting his 6-year-old niece – David offered Catherine as a sexual gift. In 1984, during a temporary separation from Catherine, David climbed into his brother's bed, demanding and receiving sexual gratification.

The Birnies had planned to abduct and rape girls a year before they took their first victim, 22-year-old Mary Neilson. The student had ventured to the Birnies' house to buy tyres; instead, she was forced to submit to a brutal rape, which Catherine watched after David steered the petrified young woman into the bedroom at knifepoint. Raped again in the forest where they had planned to bury her, Mary was mutilated after death and then buried.

The Birnies' next victim was 15-year-old Susannah Candy. Imprisoned for days, during which time she was repeatedly raped, Susannah was finally strangled by Catherine Birnie, who had grown tired of her husband's sexual obsession with the teenager. Their next victim, Noelene Patterson, a 31-year-old airline stewardess, had met the Birnies prior to her abduction. After helping push her car to a nearby service station for petrol, Noelene endured the same terrifying ordeal as the other women, raped repeatedly at the Birnie home before being murdered days later at Catherine's demand. Jealous of the attentions David had shown the attractive woman (he would later describe to Paul Ferguson that it was not rape, but that he and Noelene had 'made love'), when Catherine showed police where Noelene was buried, she vented her contempt by spitting on her grave. 'That's where we got rid of the bitch,' she told police.

The final victim was 21-year-old computer operator Denise Brown. As the wind howled through the pine plantation, she was raped for days, and finally stabbed while being sexually violated where she was murdered. Frustrated that her death was taking so long, Catherine expedited the process by handing her husband a larger knife.

The Birnies' reign of terror finally ended three days after Denise Brown's murder when a 17-year-old, semi-naked and hysterical girl ran into a supermarket, screaming that she had been raped. Dragged into the Birnies' car the evening before from where she was strolling near her home in the elite suburb of Nedlands (near Claremont), the girl had been tied to a bed in chains and subjected to repeated rapes by David. Either deliberately or through carelessness, Catherine left her alone and unchained when David went to work the following morning. The girl seized the opportunity to escape through an open window. Within the hour, police had the Birnies in the station for questioning.

Paul Ferguson led the gruelling eight-hour interview. Near the end, he appealed to Birnie to confess for the sake of a victim's mother. When Birnie asked if he could see Catherine, Ferguson knew he had him. 'How many are there?' Ferguson asked.

Birnie shrugged his shoulders, nonchalantly. 'Four.'

'But why did you kill them?' Birnie's response was typically psychopathic.

'Well, if you kidnap someone and rape 'em, you've gotta kill 'em, dontcha?'

Catherine Birnie – a cold-faced sexual monster with an icy demeanour – sickened investigators when she calmly recounted details of what was done to the victims, including her taking photographs as David raped them. While the defence painted a picture of Catherine as a subversive woman who desperately needed to satisfy her husband's insatiable sexual desires, Ferguson saw this 'witch', as he would dub her, very differently. Women, she had told Ferguson, were put on earth to satisfy men. Regardless of what men did, that was a woman's role. Each sentenced to life imprisonment, Justice Wallace showed the court's disgust at the premeditated, shocking crimes. David Birnie, he ruled, 'should not be let out of prison – ever'.

But despite the judge's warnings, it is not the last time Paul Ferguson would see David Birnie.

If the Birnies' deplorable crimes riveted Western Australia, other murders and attempted abductions, equally as heinous, made the news for a short time before sliding off the front page. In 1991, 18-year-old Kerry Turner was last seen hitch-hiking to a girlfriend's house in a Perth suburb after partying all night at a city nightclub. With no money to pay the fare, a taxi driver first dropped her at an all-night café; shortly after revellers described to police a woman fitting Kerry's description climbing into a Datsun sedan. One month later her clothed body, still adorned with jewellery, was found by picnickers near a gravel track off an access road at Canning Dam, 15 kilometres from where she was last seen. Her church-going family, frustrated at their daughter's classification as a missing person, organised their own desperate searches. Police refused to let them see her body, leading to rumours that she had been mutilated. As they would later do with taxi drivers in the Claremont case, police home in on all drivers of blue Datsun 240c cars.

In March 1996, two months after Sarah Spiers disappears, a 21-year-old woman is bashed and indecently assaulted in a lane behind Claremont's Club Bayview. The assault is investigated and no one charged. Police would ask themselves if this, too, was the handiwork of the Claremont serial killer, desperate to strike again.

On 12 January 1996 Detective-Sergeant Dave Caporn – whose name will shortly become synonymous in Perth with the Claremont investigation – is assigned to a murder in

Geraldton that will lead to the exposure of a large-scale organised crime syndicate whose currency is cannabis crops, illegal guns and explosives and which will end, sensationally, with the acquittal of a man who was provided with the perfect alibi: another man's confession to the shooting.

While Wayne Tibbs' murder led to the establishment of one of the biggest police taskforces ever seen in Western Australia, police juggle the inquiry into Sarah Spiers's disappearance at the same time. The victimology between the two people could not be more different, but with the clean-up rate for major crime high – about 60 per cent of murders in WA are crimes of passion – in 1996 police can boast that there are only two unsolved murders on file over the past four years.

With the Claremont killings, that is about to spectacularly change. Of equal importance, the West Australian Police Service is about to enter a protracted and uncomfortable period during which they will fight with everything at their disposal to protect their reputation. It is the Pamela Lawrence murder.

5

In 1994 the Major Crime Squad investigated another brutal murder in the suburb of Mosman Park, near Claremont. By the time this case finished, most people had heard of Andrew Mallard. Of more importance to WA police, they also knew the names of those police officers who had investigated him. This will become one of the most talked about police stories in a decade, involving the top echelons of lawyers, police and politicians.

On 23 May 1994, 45-year-old Pamela Lawrence was found dying in a pool of blood, violently bludgeoned with a blunt object at her chic jewellery store in wealthy Mosman Park. She died soon after and her apparently motiveless murder, with no eyewitness and no murder weapon ever found, would set in place events that would expose serious flaws in the police investigation into her shocking death and have ramifications far beyond it.

Claremont Criminal Investigation Branch (CIB) started the investigation into Pamela Lawrence's death. Maverick lawyer turned MP, John Quigley would take a keen interest in the Mallard inquiry. 'I am told' – he elongates and leans hard on the word *told* – 'but have been unable to confirm – that according to high-up police sources there was huge political pressure to get a result in the Lawrence murder. If that is the case, would it be because it fell within the elite electorate of Nedlands – then Premier Richard Court's electorate?'

The Major Crime Squad appointed five investigating officers to the case: supervising officer, Detective-Sergeant Mal Shervill; principal investigator, Detective-Sergeant Dave Caporn; assistants, John Brandham; and detectives Mark Emmett and Alan Carter. More than 130 possible suspects fell under suspicion but by 10 June – less than three weeks after

Lawrence's murder – the team singled out 31-year-old Andrew Mallard for questioning. Mallard, an awkward delusional man with drug-induced psychosis, had come to their attention with his odd behaviour. Discharged on 10 June from a psychiatric hospital to attend a court hearing on another matter, he was taken to the police station and subjected to an eight-hour, unrecorded interview – then legal – by Dave Caporn. During this interview Mallard offered bizarre theories on who may have committed the murder, and how. At his trial, he commented that during that interview he had been in 'total confusion to the point where anything that Caporn suggested to me I would adopt'. He was not cautioned or charged during or immediately before the interview.

At the end of the interview, a tussle took place between Mallard and Caporn. 'Mallard's story was that he was attacked by Caporn, and Caporn said that he was the victim of an attack by Mallard,' Quigley would later submit in parliament. 'In any event, Mr Mallard was charged with a minor assault and admitted to bail. It is remarkable that the police let him loose on the streets of Fremantle given they thought he had confessed to murder.' Seven days later, Mallard had a second, unrecorded interview with Brandham, now Detective-Sergeant. To the detective's knowledge, Mallard had spent most of the previous evening at a nightclub where he had been assaulted, and he had had little sleep. After recording the end of this interview, Mallard was formally charged with Lawrence's murder.

However, the police realised there were inherent difficulties in the prosecution case, which was outlined to then-Director of Public Prosecutions (DPP), John McKechnie QC. Not least of this was part of Shervill's report, where he noted that, '. . . the rambling admissions made by the accused during interview left doubt in the minds of some investigators as to whether the accused had in fact murdered Pamela Lawrence'. Another problem was the state pathologist's view that the murder weapon – a wrench – that Mallard had hypothesised would have been used to kill Lawrence, could not have caused her injuries. But at no stage during the trial was this mentioned by either police or the crown prosecutor. 'The police must have known . . . that if the evidence went before the court, there was a real chance that the prosecution case would fail,' Quigley said. He also outlines how, prior to the trial, the investigating police changed or excised parts of the witness statements.

Found guilty in 1995, Mallard was sentenced to life imprisonment. Determined to prove his innocence, his family sought and received help from a team of people, including Perth journalist Colleen Egan and highly respected Perth lawyers. While Mallard languished in prison, the case picked up its own steam. By the time the appeals finished, it had claimed more casualties than a wrongly convicted man and exposed faultlines that placed extreme pressure on the investigating police officers and the DPP.

6

Police target rogue taxi drivers, getting them out of business and off the road. Cut-out stickers and two magnets slapped together on the roof with the 'taxi' sign could convert a vehicle into something that resembles a cab within 15 seconds. Demand for taxis from people spilling out of nightclubs in Claremont is always high, creating a perfect cash industry for people prepared to take the risk and pose as a reputable driver. With women making up more than 50 per cent of the user group, it could also prove a lucrative killing field. The order comes from both the taxi industry and the police: shut down every rogue driver, right now.

Don Spiers descends into a black hole of chronic depression, from which he has to fight and claw his way back, over and over again. He resorts to anti-depressants to reduce his stress, requiring 32 times more than the medication usually prescribed for a patient to feel normal. The crank calls are just as bad as clairvoyants. Anonymous people with malice in their voice call and accuse him of murdering his own daughter. Letters sent to the police from armchair detectives offer bizarre theories.

Life is a torment of unanswered questions and a bottomless, aching emptiness but the family are also the recipients of random acts of kindness from strangers. Shortly after Sarah goes missing, a man knocks on their door and gives them his mobile phone. 'Take it,' he says. 'It will give you more mobility in your search.' The Spiers family tries to adjust, taking counselling, advice and help but nothing alleviates their pain. In an open, full-page letter in *The West Australian* two months after she disappears, headed 'Please, tell us where Sarah is', they open their hearts to the public.

It is eight weeks since Sarah went missing and our lives have been absolute hell . . . Sarah was part of a close and loving family and showered us with her love. We miss her so much . . . The lack of information is worse than the worst possible news . . . We don't know what to do other than to hope someone comes forward and is willing to say what happened to her. At least one person knows and I urge that person, if they have any feeling for the anxiety and suffering they have caused us and Sarah's friends, to please ease some of it . . . This is the worst feeling any parent could have – being absolutely helpless and not being able to do a single thing for our daughter.

The phone rings incessantly following publication of the open letter, but none of the calls take the family any closer to finding Sarah's whereabouts. Perth remembers Sarah, shock and sympathy spilling out in letters to the press and warnings to take special care. And the young people do. For a time.

Summer turns to autumn, leaves turn russet and gold and temperatures plummet as the hot, still nights become clear and chilly. But as autumn passes the baton to winter, memories fade.

And another girl goes missing.

7

The Rimmer family has lived in their modest, spotlessly clean home in leafy, politely affluent Shenton Park, ten minutes from Claremont, for 35 years. Jane, 23, was the youngest: her sister, Lee, is six years older; her brother, Adam, is three years her senior. Family pictures jostle for supremacy on the sideboard: the entire family at Adam's wedding; Jane as a young girl; Jane with her siblings. They are a close-knit family who always gathered at home every Sunday for an anticipated roast lunch or dinner. Protected and adored, Jane was a quiet girl, placid by nature who became a popular scallywag as she grew older. 'Janie', as they called her, finished her mandatory education at Hollywood High and never wavered in what she wanted to do. Her dream was to work with children, babies through to toddlers. And she fulfilled it. Bouts of depression dogged her in her early 20s, born of a lack of self-confidence, but by the time she disappears she is living independently in her first flat and driving her first car. She loves her car, with its natty sunroof.

Jane calls in to see her parents, Trevor and Jenny, every night after work. On the weekends her beloved West Coast Eagles play football; she barracks so hard her head often hits the overhead light. Generous spirited, she empathises with Sarah Spiers's disappearance, fretting about the young woman who simply vanished into the night. She worries so much for the girl who never came home that she pays her girlfriends' taxi fares instead of allowing them to risk getting into a car with a stranger. Jenny and Trevor also warn Jane to take care. They talk at length about Sarah Spiers, how they are grateful it is not their daughters who are missing. How shocking it must be for Sarah's family to endure this pain.

In between boyfriends, Jane rings her brother, Adam, on

9 June 1996 to ask if he would accompany her to the movies. They are extremely close; Jane lived with Adam and his wife for a short time after first leaving home, before she moved into her first flat. But Adam can't make it. It is a refusal that sets in place the first chain of events that will lead Jane – buoyant, fun-loving with a cheeky approach to life – to Claremont and for which Adam will never forgive himself. From this time on, he will live in the netherland of 'if only'. 'If only I had gone with her . . . If only I had said yes.' He is constantly reassured it is not his fault, but guilt plagues him.

Jane phones another friend, who is also too busy to go to the movies. However, she hears that some girlfriends are heading into the Continental Hotel for a few drinks. The Conti: its architecturally designed bar shaped like an unburnt match, the decadent décor evocative of the Garden of Eden. It sits opposite the post office and across from the railway line; Club Bayview is nearby. *The* places to go in Claremont. The young people know the rules, plastered on the Bayview's front door. 'A neighbourhood cocktail bar for those who look over 25. If you're turned away, please do not be offended but rather fade away quietly only to return another night, dressed to kill and looking very, very mature.' Jane changes her mind about the movies. It's Saturday night after all. She'll head out to party instead.

Trevor picks her up from her flat and drops her at the Shenton Hotel for a drink with her mother before she heads into Claremont by taxi with her friends. She is in high spirits, looking forward to a night out. Trevor is proud of his daughter. Since she has moved out of home, he has got to know her again as a young woman, as opposed to his baby. 'See you tomorrow for lunch,' she says, as she gives him an airy kiss goodbye.

She doesn't turn up. Jenny is worried sick; it is so unlike Jane not to let them know she can't make it. She calls Jane's flat and when it rings out, she and Trevor take the spare key Jane has given them and go over. Her bed has not been slept in.

Jenny traces patterns on the table with her fingers as she discusses her daughter. There is a feeling in the room, like sombre background music, a feeling that pervades all. As though Jane's spirit hovers over us as we talk, gently whispering to us. There is an acute sense of something missing in this neat, suburban home; a void that no other person can fill. Jenny gives up the pretence at calm, covers her eyes with her hands. 'Sorry,' she stumbles. 'Sorry. I didn't mean to break down.' She inhales a shaky breath. 'We knew Sarah Spiers was missing and that she had last been seen in Claremont. I had a feeling of dread that something was wrong.' By 9 pm, they report Jane as a missing person. Basic details: age, description, clothes she was wearing. Jenny, sighing and restless throughout the long night, calls Jane's employer at the child care centre as soon as it opens to see if she has turned up. They draw another blank.

By morning, harried police are on their doorstep, trudging through the gate and walking up the few steps, a walk that will become all too familiar in the following months. Shifting from foot to foot and looking ill at ease, they take down further details. Sarah Spiers's disappearance, albeit treated as a missing persons case until then, had essentially been a local inquiry. But by lunchtime, because both girls have gone missing from the same area, police privately link the disappearance of Sarah and Jane to a serial predator. It is knowledge they do not share with the public. What they do declare publicly is the formation of a special taskforce: Taskforce Macro.

As the officer in charge of Major Crime, Paul Ferguson's face and personality are well known to the public. He will continue to front the press as head of Macro, a huge task given his other responsibilities. Dave Caporn will remain as case officer, driving the investigation. He allocates teams and people on the ground. It is frantic. In the early days, they juggle 140 people with all the other tasks that have to be dealt with on a daily basis.

There are not enough trained detectives to make up the teams Macro needs. With the intense pressure for a resolution to the case, they start internal training of uniform staff – used to responding to task questions and low-level crises – to teach them basic investigative skills. 'Prior to Macro,' Ferguson says, 'the force was divided into different squads, such as homicide, drug and vice. This was a whole new concept. It was a rocky road to change, because it was unfamiliar. We had to rape and pillage other districts to get what we needed. And we didn't have the luxury of time to do it.' The teams will be rotated into other areas within Macro every six months to keep them fresh. For the pressed officers, it is akin to Pharaoh's orders – to 'make as many bricks without straw as you've been making with straw'.

The secrecy rules are also set early. All officers sign confidentiality agreements and under no circumstances is any information to be released to the public. Officers are not to discuss the case, apart from with their Macro colleagues. Even if they leave the force, they are not to discuss the case. They are not to talk about it whenever an outsider is within earshot. Cause of death, weapon used, time or place of death, the condition in which the clothing was found: their mouths are zipped up tight as a body bag. Don't invite copycat killings by leaking any details. Shut up. It is the police version of the military saying, 'Loose lips sink ships.'

The enforced secrecy stuns officers working in other units – and other states. 'In all my years in the job – and I was there a long time – I had never heard of this before,' a former officer said. 'They actually "used" it to expel two detectives who got pissed and started talking about some facet of the investigation in a pub. They made the fatal mistake of talking within earshot of another copper, who reported them.' The secretive nature of the investigation is also not welcomed by all its officers. Grumbles are frequent: this particular job is hard enough, without the added stress of command heads who keep a stranglehold on information leaks and a tight controlling hand over all aspects of the case.

The former hostage negotiator believes Caporn squandered precious opportunities to make the most out of bad situations with the team. 'It was a proud team, and people were happy to be on it,' he says. 'It was an important case and, on another level, it also offered opportunity for a truckload of overtime, which is always appreciated.'

Despite WA Police assurances that confidentiality agreements are the norm, outside the state police are also amazed at the agreement Macro officers had to sign. A retired Assistant-Commissioner from the eastern states expressed incredulity when he heard of it. 'I was in the job 40 years, in the Major Crime area,' he said, 'but that was never done. Never. It's unusual, to say the least.'

Paul Ferguson muses that it is vital not to stamp out the natural, inquisitive nature of police officers, vital that they are allowed to talk to each other, exchange information. 'It's that that keeps them on their toes, keeps them hungry. It's ludicrous to take that away.' The Macro team, he says, was so focused on their task, they could have sworn on *anything* – a dictionary or copy of the criminal code – and they would have stayed silent. They were hot-wired to do that.

The Rimmer family is appointed two liaison officers to answer any inquiry: Peter Norrish and John Leembruggen.

In June 1996 police circulate up to 100 copies of a questionnaire to select people that pointedly asks where they were when Sarah Spiers disappeared from outside the nightclub. The questionnaire is given to those people who have, in some way, attracted police interest. But there is a problem. The question 'Describe in detail what you did from midday Saturday, 26 January to midday Sunday, 27 January 1996' is incorrect. Sarah disappeared on the 27th. Embarrassed by the error, the police scrap the questions and start again. But it is the second part of the quiz and the questions 'Did you abduct or murder Sarah Spiers?' and 'Should we believe your answers to these questions?' that creates controversy and no little hilarity.

Paul Ferguson was quick to point out that the people who were asked to fill in the questionnaire were not suspects, but could have information that would help their inquiries. And individuals could refuse to fill in the quiz. Police would know if they did.

The questionnaire is based on the Scientific Content Analysis (SCAN) technique, which changes a verbal interview into a written form. This then is assessed by the interviewer, to ascertain whether a face-to-face meeting with the person is required. The writing of answers can be done in the interviewees' own time and place and saves unnecessary time in interviewing people who are clearly telling the truth. Supporters of the questionnaire claim success in solving numerous cases in Australia and overseas. Developed in 1984 for the army, it was first used to survey soldiers who had failed urine analysis tests for traces of drugs in their bodies. Requesting a lie-detector test to show there was some error in the test results, the soldiers were asked to also fill out the questionnaire. The results were forwarded to headquarters without the polygrapher knowing the questionnaire results. Twenty-eight per cent of the people who filled out the questionnaire showed incriminating responses.

But many in the legal profession regarded the questionnaire as a ludicrous waste of time. How likely was it that a guilty person would either fill it out or tell the truth? Lawyer Richard Bailey encapsulated the general feeling. 'You're hardly going to get somebody writing in and answering the question "Did you abduct or murder Sarah Spiers?" with a "Oh yes, I've done it" reply, then sign it "Merv" or whatever and send it back to police. The concept is absurd.'

Overt criticism of the questionnaire was met with serious admonishment. An academic at a Western Australian university whose work was funded by the police was warned that unless he stopped publicly criticising the form, his funding would be withdrawn. Unchastened, he chose another path. He left the state.

WA Council for Civil Liberties President Peter Weygers – a distinctive-looking man in his mid-60s, with a stocky build and standing 192 cm tall – was Claremont mayor between 1985 and 1997. A man of means with a substantial property portfolio, including a unit overlooking the street where Sarah Spiers was last seen, and a reputation as an eccentric, he was known as the 'Super-mayor'. Depicted in press cartoons wearing a red and blue suit, complete with cape and a huge S on the front, nothing in his career could compare with the publicity he received when he, too, was outed as a person of interest by the Macro taskforce. He was also the only individual publicly named in *The West Australian* newspaper as having received the questionnaire. His refusal to fill in the form was accompanied by a gruff admonishment that the whole tactic was 'ridiculous'. Weygers had warned Steven Ross not to insert his name into the investigation by telling police Spiers had been in his cab. Both would come to rue the day Ross ignored that advice.

Commissioner Bob Falconer, driven by media perceptions, keeps a hawk eye on the Macro taskforce. Any adverse media comments require an immediate explanation. The media, too, become an integral part of the 'think-tank' sessions. Police ask their advice on the best way to get the message out to the public. They need all the help they can get. And they need to manage the media, before the media start managing them.

The media are relentless, acting like starving hordes foraging for news scraps. Ferguson is cognisant of what police call the 'Three Cs' when dealing with the press. First, Cooperation, when there is enough in the news stories to ensure fresh headlines every day. Second, Competition, the cut-throat jungle journalists inhabit in the desperate rush for exclusive news angles. Third – and most dangerous – Controversy, when the pickings are lean and the media start feeding on each other and investigators, criticising management and pecking at the case like vultures.

In his easy way of dealing with the press, Ferguson earns their respect. 'They could have chopped me up,' he admits. 'There was so much going on, I didn't have time for the pompous tone some officers take, telling journalists that "this is an operational matter".' Instead, Ferguson chooses a more relaxed style. 'If a reporter came close to something that

I couldn't release, I'd tell them, "I can't let that out of the bloody bag and you know I can't. I can confirm that it's correct but I'm asking you, please don't release this detail." ' Most didn't. 'Occasionally a reporter would overstep the mark,' he recalls. 'The suburban *Post* newspaper was one that sometimes ran with assumptions. My appeals to them not to do this were met with the response that they were journalists with an obligation to give their readers the truth. It wasn't always helpful.'

8

Three days after Jane's disappearance, her parents front a press conference. Looking drawn and gaunt but still hopeful that Jane will return home, their confidence is shattered by the first carelessly constructed question. 'Trevor, can you tell us what sort of girl Jane was?' from a young reporter. The question, phrased in the past tense, sends Jenny into a paroxysm of tears.

The madness begins. The Rimmers endure the same endless procession of people as the Spiers family. Police. Friends ferrying food. Clairvoyants. Psychics. They have little patience for the seers and rarely return their calls. One psychic with a divining rock stands on the pavement outside the hotel at Claremont before moving to the beach, 15 minutes away, and pointing to a nondescript house. 'Jane is here,' she tells Trevor with authority. 'Or she has been here.' It is useless information, all so obscure. But the Rimmers pass the information on to police, anyway. Who knows? But Jane isn't there.

The family put hundreds of flyers on lamp posts, beseeching help. *Have you seen Jane Rimmer? Phone Crime Stoppers.* Jane's face is at every corner. A person calls Jenny's relative with news that they know what has happened to Jane and who has abducted her. It is an anonymous call; always anonymous. The second last sighting of Jane, outside the Continental Hotel, is captured on the hotel's security camera. She is grinning as she swings around the pole outside the pub. The final poignant sighting of her is standing alone on the pavement for a few minutes, on the corner of Bayview Terrace and Gugeri Street. The camera moves to another area of the hotel. When it pans back, Jane is gone.

Paul Coombes, who started as an investigator and was later promoted to Detective-Sergeant on the Macro taskforce, recalls, 'Police made public statements that they would take all information. The result was that we were flooded with calls from the public, receiving many, many more than even the Milat backpacker investigation. And the case still attracts calls from clairvoyants. But research doesn't back up their claims. There isn't one where it's been proven they have solved a case. In Claremont, no one ever linked any information they gave us with fact. They usually homed in on Sarah, because she is still missing. In the end, we would tell them, "If you know where she is, go out there, take your mobile with you and if you find her, give us a call." We never got that call.'

Police install a second telephone line to free up calls that may lead to information and are compassionate, gentle in their dealings with the Rimmer family. Peter Norrish and John Leembruggen, the Rimmers' liaison officers, call in frequently, keeping them up to speed.

A relentless rain teases and taunts the Rimmer family. Trevor continues to go to work, staring at a photo of Jane on his desk. 'Where are you, Janie?' he asks her. 'Tell us where you are.' Jenny pretends normality, returning to work at the Shenton Hotel and telling herself Jane will come home. It is a mantra, and one she knows is nonsense. 'She's probably gone overseas or met a guy. She'll be back soon.' She knows they are feeble excuses. Jane has no passport and no ambition to travel. And she always lets them know where she is.

9

Hard rain has fallen for months, a lashing, cold rain that daubs her naked body. A canopy of trees protects her; branches thin as whips bow in mourning. It is lonely here, through the winter months of June to August 1996, as the body of a 23-year-old lies hidden from the world in a sodden roadside verge, lightly covered with foliage. Elegant snow-white flowers with elongated leaves and vibrant lemon tongues grow tall around her, surrounding her in a macabre guard of honour. Arum lilies – *death* lilies.

A lashing rain has fallen for months, forming stagnant pools that wash the evidence away. Pools in which the death lilies grow.

10

Jane Rimmer's foot peeks from her rough blanket of foliage. The Arum lilies have kept her disposal site secret. A woman, picking water lilies with her children on the dirt Woolcoot Road in rural Wellard, 40 kilometres south of Perth, pauses, then looks again. It takes only a moment to compute what she sees lying on the roadside verge, sprawled pitifully in death. *Oh, God*, she thinks, her stomach somersaulting as she turns her children's heads away. *It's a body*. Within an hour, the area will swarm with police officers.

Fifty-four days of exposure to the filthy weather have rendered Jane unrecognisable. From the moment of her death, nature started its inexorable march toward decomposition. Within 24 hours of her death the insects, working in their rhythmical, cyclical way, zero in, in successive waves, colonising her corpse, laying their eggs in the body's orifices or wounds. The internal tissue begins to decay, turning into gas and liquids, and after just one week the flesh under the skin is of liquid consistency and skin sloughs off it when touched. As the body moves through its ritual of decay, a month after death hair and nails can easily be removed, the trunk is bloated to twice its size and the tongue protrudes. By six weeks, the body resembles what is described in the trade as a 'soup'.

Wellard, in the shire of Kwinana, houses Casuarina Prison and the mockingly named Hope Valley. Tucked away here, out of sight in the verge that captures water like a dam, lying for almost two months in nature's shallow bath at the mercy of the tiger snakes and wild animals that inhabit the area, Jane is so putridly decomposed that only dental and fingerprint records can prove identification. But while she can't tell investigators what has happened, her body can, offering clues to the forensic scientist to calculate the circumstance and time of her death. Using the insects' life span as a barometer, they count back from the age of the bug or larvae to determine how long they have lived on the corpse.

Jane is naked, her clothing, handbag and some jewellery items missing. Police delay broadcasting details of the missing jewellery to prevent the killer panicking and disposing of them. The only piece of jewellery found, much later, is Jane's watch, a small distance from her body. The rain, relentlessly pounding her for 54 days, has turned the crime scene into a quagmire, such a washout that Dave Caporn, with pursed lips and extreme understatement, will describe it to the press as being 'not fertile'. It does not provide any clues. But the lilies surround her, tall as a picket fence.

Trevor Rimmer knows straightaway. Jane has been missing for almost two months and now the police are standing on his doorstep, looking intently at him. They always say 'no news', so as not to get his hopes up, but they don't say this tonight. A handsome man with a gentle face, Trevor says nothing as the police follow him inside. He turns away from them to continue cooking his rack of lamb. The police are used to odd reactions to bad news: shock and overwhelming grief kick the brain into a dull numbness and will keep Trevor buffeted from the pain for a short time, at least. 'Do you want to come with us while we go and tell your wife, or should we just bring her home?'

Trevor stares at them, unseeing. 'Bring her home,' he says.

Jenny Rimmer is at the Shenton Hotel where she works, sharing a drink with friends before they return to the house for dinner. The past two months have been so harrowing that she and Trevor have tried to pretend some semblance of normality. Anything, the small rituals, to pretend Jane will return home to them safely.

Jenny, sitting in the alcove off the main bar, watches as the police walk toward her. An obscene inner voice starts taunting her: *This isn't going to be good, this isn't going to be good.* She feels the police are moving toward her in slow motion. She knows these police officers who have liaised with the family over the months but wants to cringe from them as they approach. She stumbles to her feet. 'Can we speak to you outside please, Jenny?' The bar has fallen silent, drinks and conversation poised mid-air. She feels insensate and cold and her chin starts quivering; from somewhere a hand reaches out to catch her lest she falls. 'Can we have a quick word please, Jenny?'

'You've found Jane, haven't you?'

They didn't want to tell her here, in a bar with people watching, but they now have no choice. They keep their voices calm and low. 'We're sorry. We have found a body. We believe it could be Jane.' A fog has fallen, shrouding her in darkness and she can't hear anything now but a muted scream in her head. She follows the police outside, not noticing as people stand up as a mark of respect for her as she walks past.

Jenny recalls pieces of the conversation, small trivialities the police tell her but mostly she sees their mouths move, and she feels numb and ill.

They want to know cause of death, nod mutely when police tell them what happened to Jane. Her throat, it appears, had been slashed. Nature has betrayed the indignities visited on her, swarms of ants rushing to the site of her jugular vein to feast. It is, as a forensic officer will note with grim irony, a 'dead giveaway'.

Jane's belly button ring is still on her body, and the amethyst ring she wore. But her clothing is gone. Jenny and Trevor brace themselves for the inevitable that they are sure is to follow. Do they want to know? Yes, they do. They can take some consolation, they are told, that it does not appear Jane has been sexually assaulted. It is heartening, a small relief, but one that will haunt them. Are police telling them the truth or simply trying to shield them from further grief? They don't want to dwell in a world of ifs and maybes. They want to know what happened, gritty and sordid as the detail may be. It is their daughter, they say. They have a right.

The police agree. As far as they can tell, there was no sexual assault and definitely no mutilation, dismemberment of the body or bondage. And Jane was not left in a staged, set pose.

At home, they eat in silence the rack of lamb Trevor has prepared, tasteless and chewed over and over in their mouths. By morning, Jenny Rimmer will assume a foetal position, and stay curled that way until her daughter's funeral and for months after.

Jane – meaning 'God is gracious' – comes to Jenny in dreams. Not as the young woman heading off to Claremont for a night out clubbing with friends, but as an 8-year-old child, swinging androgynous hips as she dances to Abba and sings into the broom handle. She wakes and tells Trevor, 'Jane has been here again,' and he knows not to ask. He knows she would only be eight years old. In Jenny's dreams, Jane never grows up. She never goes to Claremont.

Woolcoot Road is meticulously searched, media choppers flying overhead as every object from cans, cigarette butts and hairs are picked up and sealed. An infra-red scanning system is employed to search the bush around the disposal site, detecting objects and other materials foreign to the area by heat radiation. Forensic teams vacuum the bush and tracks near Jane's disposal site, using gauze pads that they repeatedly change. Entomologists, who calculate the time of death from the life cycle of insects and the age of flies that have gorged on the body, go about their grisly task.

Police are also quietly briefed to look for Sarah Spiers, who has now been missing for seven months. They have no doubt she has been murdered and reason the killer would feel comfortable returning to the Wellard area. Sarah's body hasn't been found. He may have dumped her there, and later Jane, believing he would not be caught.

The taskforce goes over and over the 'points of fatal encounter' as geographical profilers call it – the area from where the victim is abducted. Very often it proves to be close to the killer's home, always much closer than the disposal site. The more victims the killer murders, the cockier he – or they – becomes, dumping bodies increasingly closer to home.

Trevor and Jenny have been married 40 years and still touch hands tenderly as they discuss their murdered daughter. They move effortlessly around each other, as couples do after years of intimate familiarity, but they cope very differently. Jenny, brown eyes set in a face chiselled with grief, is not afraid to cry and does so, often. Trevor, quiet and circumspect, is more controlled. Look closer and his heart is splintered into tiny shards, like the spidery lines that criss-cross his gaunt cheeks.

Trevor borders on angry when the police ask him pointed questions about his relationship with his daughter, and when they take blood samples for possible DNA testing. But he understands their reasons. Everyone is under suspicion. Still the phone calls flood in to police, thousands of people offering clues to the killer's identity. Mothers nominate sons. Wives point the finger at husbands. Bisexual men suggest former partners. Early on police form a list of names whose calls should be ignored. They don't have time for crackpots. Prostitutes are asked to go through their 'ugly mugs' file, the photos and names of clients who they know to be sexually perverted or violent.

It is a simple symbol, on a tiny badge: the Arum lily, chosen after Jane's body is found. Underneath, there is an equally simple, one-word inscription. Macro. Normally, the names of taskforces are spat out of a computer at Canberra's Australian Bureau of Criminal Intelligence. Not this time. 'Macro', meaning 'to look at everything', was chosen by taskforce members themselves. 'To look at everything'. Every possibility.

The taskforce officers choose the symbol as a sign of respect, to honour Jane Rimmer and Sarah Spiers, to keep them focused on the girls' disappearances. Each officer – around 100 at the peak of the investigation – will wear it discreetly on their lapel.

11

If police know anything about serial killers, it is that their cooling-off period is followed by an overwhelming need to kill again. It has been five months between Sarah Spiers's disappearance and Jane Rimmer's. Odds are, he will strike again soon – if he hasn't already. Mother nature has loosened her grip on the normal controls that balance conscience and fear, has 'stuffed up, badly' as one psychiatrist noted. What police don't know is *when* they will kill again or the motive, the underlying reason why this person is killing women at all. Are they strangers to the killer, or have they met before? Is their murder an act of revenge against women in general? Is he targeting women who remind him of someone else: a dominant mother, a former girlfriend who rejected him, a hated sister? Do the murders, afforded front-page headlines, satisfy some perverse longing for celebrity? Are the killings born out of resentment against a society that the killer perceives does not recognise his worth? What is known of the victims?

Police examine what they know of the girls, the similarities. They are the same *type*. Both young women, aged between 18 and 23. Decent. Well heeled. Well groomed. Both employed. Both out in the same area late at night. Both drinking. Average build. Sarah Spiers: shoulder-length fair hair. Slender. Open, attractive face. Jane Rimmer: Similar hair colour and length to Sarah. Taller at 167 cm. Well proportioned, though slim figure. Open, attractive face.

The police work through the possibilities. Was the killer, or killers, targeting a type? Was it the case, as with American serial killer Ted Bundy, who murdered 23 women and chillingly remarked that 'the victims have to be worthy of me'? Had he watched them in the club or hotel, loitering at a distance, observing their movements, following them as they left? Or was it random, opportunistic as he stood outside his vehicle ready to use a rehearsed line – *I wonder could you help me?* Did he attack them from the shadows and throw them in the car? Did he lie in wait inside the vehicle, dragging them in as they walked past, or wind down the window to engage in casual conversation? Did he monitor taxi radios, know that a woman is waiting for a cab, cruise along and offer her a lift?

How did the women get into the vehicle? How much alcohol had they consumed? Police will not release that information, but concede each woman was highly intoxicated. Jane Rimmer, caught on security camera outside the Continental Hotel swinging around a lamp pole, a young woman with a zest for life after a night out with friends. A young woman just having fun. The memory of that last glimpse of her daughter makes Jenny smile. Jane loved a good time. Sarah Spiers? Her father, Don, is defensive on the subject when it is raised, and emits an unspoken warning not to delve too hard there. It is a protective mechanism, to shield his beloved daughter's memory from prying reporters. Back off. This is hallowed ground.

Alcohol would render the women more vulnerable, less inhibited, impair their decision-making. And the killer would know that. Would know that they are more likely to be approachable, more likely to be at ease.

The team theorises that the girls got in the car of their own free will; that the chances of forcibly abducting a female on two separate occasions, without one person seeing them or without something going wrong, are too remote to be credible. They work on three areas: that it is probable, possible, or unlikely.

Were they forced into a vehicle? Possible, but not probable. If they had not been forced, what made them enter the car? Their ability to assess risk was diminished by alcohol. They have a driving need to get home and have no alternative transport. Would they, under those circumstances, get into a stranger's vehicle? Were they seduced, cajoled or beguiled into the car by someone smooth, well-educated and plausible? Probable or possible? *Both.* Was it possibly someone they knew? *Both.* A trusted stranger, such as a taxi driver? *Both.*

Without lucrative crime-scene evidence, strong leads or eyewitness material, police are locked in a deadly game of Blind Man's Bluff. The vastness of their task is more than daunting. The clock is ticking as they shadow box with a deadly stranger.

12

Serial killers. Their names litter the pages of criminal histories, sadistic, psychopathic individuals whose abominable crimes are driven by sexual fantasies or a compulsive, overwhelming desire to watch their victims suffer. Without the normal neural circuitry that characterises a balanced mind, they are deaf to the victims' pleas to stop hurting them, to spare their life. And when their violent fantasies are played out – torture, rape, mutilation – and the victim is finally killed, the body is simply a carcass to be thrown away. They have had their fun; there is no further need for them.

The statistics are frightening. Most serial killers are white, from middle-class backgrounds and with a higher than average IQ. They generally start killing in their mid-20s, long after their apprenticeship in minor crimes – house break-ins, voyeurism – has begun. There is usually abuse in early childhood – physical, sexual and/or emotional. They often wet their beds into adolescence, deliberately light fires, torture animals and fail to bond with other people closely. In childhood, it is often the father who plays the pivotal role; he will usually hold down a steady job but is erratically inconsistent with discipline.

They may be in and out of jail, perfecting their techniques from hardened crims, coming out and practising what they have learnt. Usually cowards, when picked up by police they often cry, but the tears are not for their victims. They are for themselves. Remorse is not in their vocabulary. The more sadistic the torture and murder, the more they cower in jail, often taking their lives to escape.

There will be pre-crime stressors, factors that tip this person into a killing frenzy. Perhaps loss of a job or added responsibility at work; marital break-up; money problems.

Usually it is a fatal combination – the straw that breaks the camel's back – that is the main contributor, the key to their warped motivations. Recent events may be triggering memories from childhood. His partner leaves, he is driven to kill. Did he feel helpless as a child when his parents separated? Is he determined not to feel helpless again?

Serial killers initially appear friendly and easygoing with their victims, their voice and mannerism changing as the psychopath comes to the fore. They have a script for their victims, telling them what they want them to say, forcing them to use foul, sexually explicit language. *I am a dirty whore. I want you to fuck me.* Now she has admitted she is a slut, a whore, he can kill her because she deserves it. And he has to kill her, because she can identify him. The only protection she may have is to fight like hell, to scream, kick and get on top of the situation. 'You don't play like you're ill or defecate or throw up,' criminal profiler John Douglas advises. 'That just further degrades you in the eyes of the subject. You've got to fight with everything you've got.'

A serial killer rarely uses guns; they are too impersonal. He or she wants to watch their victim suffer, likes to watch them die. Stabbing, followed by strangulation and suffocation, is their preferred method. Death up close.

Creatures of habit, they generally – though not always – go for type. Prostitutes: easy targets who willingly go with strangers. Old women. Homosexuals. Young children. Blacks. The idea is cemented in their sick psyche, and they trawl for victims with the same dedication and planning that others use in normal pursuits. They do not advertise their work. Ritualistic and repetitive, their modus operandi often changes from those that characterise their early murders. As they become more sophisticated, more confident, so their 'signature' – based on their fantasies – emerges. While their pick-up area, method of entrapment, choice of weapon and the disposal site are all important elements in the jigsaw puzzle, the key to their modus operandi is the killers' ritual signature, the aggressive fantasy that is endlessly imagined prior to the first

murder and finally played out on the victim, before death or
post-mortem.

Serial killers fall into two categories – organised and disorganised – although the categories can sometimes fuse. The
planning and murder themselves can be organised, the
frenzied mutilation of the corpse the opposite. But if their
targeted type is not available, they won't pass up an opportunity to kill. It is more important to them to see their victim
suffer.

The 'organised' serial killer – more ruthlessly violent than
their disorganised counterparts – is never hindered by conscience. They know what they are doing, and they know what
they are doing is wrong. The concept of right and wrong is
nothing more than an academic exercise: ego-driven and
highly manipulative, the coldly planned and executed
murders are his trademark. This killer usually uses a vehicle
for a fast getaway and constrains his victims with handcuffs,
gags or terrifying threats.

Their victims are usually targeted strangers – a person the
killer has stalked during his stake-out of his chosen territory.
Like a wild beast hunting its prey, targeting the victim involves
a carefully planned reconnoitre of both the pick-up and disposal sites. Streets and highways are memorised, driven or
walked hundreds of times before the abduction, and all
entrances and exits mentally marked. Given the seemingly
flawless way in which the Claremont serial killer lures his
victims into his vehicle, police are in no doubt he fits this type.
A chameleon, easily able to blend into his environment, control
is his catchword: able to glibly seduce a victim, often with just
conversation, to do his bidding. It is the planning that most
excites this killer, using his logical mind to act out his fantasies.

The level of organisation will be evident in his taking the
weapon of choice to the crime scene and disposing of it afterwards. He will also not leave victims where they are killed;
instead, their bodies are moved after death. From that point,
he develops an obsession with keeping track of news items or
police reports to see whether the body has been found.

Outgoing and charming in the entrapment phase, the killer's real personality quickly asserts itself once he is alone with his victim. If rape is involved in the murder, the organised killer needs his victim to be submissive. Resistance heightens his rage and sense of indignation; women are the hated, worthless sex, for whom he feels contempt. If he fails to gain an erection during the rape, this killer will likely blame the woman for failing to ignite his sexual interest. The crimes are always driven by sex, even if the act itself is not completed. Sex equals power and control. They take trophies, grim mementos of their crime. Jewellery, clothing, hair, body parts. Items to salivate over, to fondle and view when they celebrate the murder in their memory.

In contrast, there is no apparent rhyme or reason to the disorganised killer's choice of victims. He has no interest in personalising the people he chooses and when caught, finds it difficult to explain rationally to others the fractured logic he used to target his high-risk victims. His vehicle, like his mind and home, will be dirty and his personal appearance slovenly. Mutilation of the corpse and a chaotically frenzied crime scene are pointers to this killer's state of mind: the body is often found quickly as the disorganised type is not in possession of the clarity of thought required to move a body without being caught. The disorganised offender is very often raised in a household where the father's work patterns are haphazard, discipline is tough and there are external pressures: drug addiction, alcoholism or mental illness. As a child, he is virtually silent at school, retreating behind the mask of shyness but as an adult, he can disrupt his workplace by not getting along with his colleagues. Normal emotions – fear, rage, hurt – are internalised; the disorganised type is incapable or unwilling to express himself. Often physically unassuming or unattractive, they are serial loners, with no social skills at all. Finding it impossible to discourse with others, this type very often lives with their parents, or parent.

Instead of planning the crime, the disorganised killer will strike impulsively, without warning, an attack that may be precipitated by mental illness. Their victims are usually, though not always, females and after, he has virtually no interest in what he has done. This type does not take trophies.

Profilers have divided serial killers into distinct types who engage in either slow or fast kills. The Visionary, often a psychotic, hears voices or sees visions that order him to commit murder. The voices are variously that of Satan or God, and the victims are strangers. The Missionary is driven by a misguided, warped sense that it is his duty to eliminate certain people – often prostitutes or those of certain religious persuasions. Both engage in fast kills – the urgent need to enact their violent thoughts. The Hedonist kills purely for pleasure, and often gains financially from the murder; the Lust-driven Hedonist gains pleasure from the anticipatory and real association between sex and murder. These killers will often return to the disposal site to sexually violate a corpse, experience erotic pleasure while fantasising about murder or become sexually aroused while in the act of killing. The Thrill-driven Hedonist experiences a sensational 'rush' when killing, exulting in the mix of control and excitement he feels when a victim is powerless in his hands. The Control Freak takes extreme pleasure in dominating and manipulating his quarry. The latter types will frequently tape their victims' screams or pleas for mercy or photograph them – as was the Birnies' wont – in varying stages of their capture and death.

Which category does the Claremont serial killer fit? Visionary? This type rarely has a controlled crime scene, moves the body from the murder site or targets a specific victim. What can point to the signature of this killer is penetration of the body using an object, and necrophilia – having sex with the corpse after death. Missionary? Though the crime scene is controlled, this type of killer does not move the body and targets a specific victim. Like the visionary killer, the missionary will not indulge in aberrant sex, use weapons of torture and will not have a prior relationship with the victim.

Unlike the former, there will not be penetration with an object or necrophilia. Comfort? These killers like a controlled crime scene, often have a prior relationship with the victim and will leave a weapon at the scene. Lust? This type of killer has a controlled crime scene, may torture, targets a specific victim, engages in aberrant sex and does not know the victim. Thrill? He will move the body, target a specific victim and use penile or object penetration. And the killer with a need for power and control? The crime scene is controlled, torture is possible, a specific victim is targeted and necrophilia is often practised.

From the way in which the Claremont victims vanish into thin air, it is likely that the killer is organised, social and clever, with an IQ that is probably above average. A person who is used to dealing with intelligent women and able to hold his own in social situations. If single, he will have a history of dating women. If married, he will maintain the façade of being a good husband and father. He could have a history of some form of abuse in childhood but is also possibly well educated and mobile in his work and leisure. His hygiene levels would be high and he would not drive an old car. Before discovery of the body and after, he would very possibly return to the crime scene as an onlooker or participant, and may contact police to offer help.

But regardless of how the serial killer – usually a white male, between the ages of 25 and 35 – acts, one thing never changes. It is never his fault. He is adept at abrogating responsibility, blaming society or someone else. And by shifting the blame, he feels no requirement to examine his behaviour.

It's not his fault. So he will do it again.

13

Macro taskforce investigators engage in official, formal debates. Police on one side, police on the other. Airing ideas and possible scenarios. 'How often do these debates occur?' I later ask a Macro insider. He can't tell me, he says. I will have to talk to Dave Caporn, but he may not wish to answer. It becomes a frequent mantra, bordering on the absurd; the squirrelling of information that could not in any way hinder the investigation if it was made public. 'Why?' I persist. 'Why would Caporn not want to discuss this?' He does not answer.

The Macro taskforce has twice daily briefings, at 7 am and 7 pm, which everyone, from the youngest constable to senior detectives, must attend. No one can plead ignorance or shyness. It is a dynamic strategy that pays dividends: by checking and cross-checking information gained during the day, it is often the younger team members with vibrant, fresh ideas that bring the best results. The need to look after the health and safety of the Macro team is also paramount. Everyone is encouraged to have counselling, whether they feel they need it or not. For the older officers the concept is often regarded as 'soft', but they are told to set an example. If someone is not coping, their superiors cut them loose early, putting them back into other areas. The needs of the investigation override those of the individual.

The taskforce adapts the American version of VICAP – Victim Identification of Violent Crime – to help organise the overwhelming amount of data. A comprehensive recording of all details of violent crime, including murder and sexual assaults, it creates a searchable database which is interrogated to find a link between old recorded cases with new cases. It is a quantum leap forward; pre-VICAP, officers who worked the modus operandi section physically examined offence reports and wrote up cards on each particular characteristic of the offence. Time-consuming, it also wasted space: Sergeant Tony Potts, who started at Macro in February 1997 in the role of media officer, recalls there was a drawer full of index cards that identified offenders who had a cobweb tattoo on the elbow alone. Computers could easily store and search that information; however, it was still time-consuming.

Macro officers set about the arduous task of identifying and linking known facts about the Claremont victims to any previous offence in WA, the rest of Australia and overseas and any known or recorded modus operandi. To do this, they need a system that can expedite the feeding of that information.

In conjunction with VICAP, they settle on the HOLMES system – Home Office Large Major Enquiry System – developed by the UK Home Office in response to identified failings of several British police jurisdictions when investigating the Yorkshire Ripper murders in the 1980s. Murders that changed the face of policing.

The most notorious serial killer in Britain since Jack the Ripper, the Yorkshire Ripper, as he was dubbed by the press, first attacked a stranger in 1969. It was the start of a maniacal killing spree that would stop only with his arrest. Police failures to identify the Ripper's modus operandi started early, when they did not notice similarities between attacks and murders. As late as 1996, the Chief Constable of West Yorkshire, Keith Hellawell, theorised that judging by the weapon used and other similar indicators in a large number of unsolved murders and attacks, 20 murders could have been the handiwork of the Ripper. For six years, Peter Sutcliffe terrorised Yorkshire residents. Of his 13 victims, eight were prostitutes and other women who had made the simple fatal decision to go out after dark. Sutcliffe's weapon of choice was the knife: the signature of his murders was repeated slashing in the area of his victims' stomachs and vaginas. Many were mutilated after death. By 1978, the hunt for the Yorkshire Ripper was the biggest in British criminal history.

Frustrated by the lack of strong leads and with the killer not leaving behind evidence that offered clues to his identity, the UK police were forced to resort to slow, mechanical means: sifting through the huge number of suspects, checking the car registration numbers of vehicles regularly seen in the red-light districts and pulling the drivers in for questioning. Then, a breakthrough. A murdered street worker was found in possession of a new five-pound note, and police started the laborious task of tracing the destination of the batch of notes. At one of the 23 factories traced, Peter Sutcliffe calmly answered police questions about his whereabouts on the night of the murder, offering an alibi that police believed. He would again call on his sangfroid the following year when questioned as to why his car had been seen numerous times in a red-light district, coolly answering that he had to drive through the area to get to work. Sutcliffe again walked away from the questioning and continued to kill for another two years.

It was this, in hindsight, where police recognised they had made their biggest mistake. While Sutcliffe's vehicle registration number was in the computer at police headquarters, there was no corresponding information to link that he had also been interviewed with regard to the five-pound note. The sheer number of suspects' names that had been fed into police computers ensured that cross-checking was laborious. The errors compounded. Reducing the number of factories that could have been recipients of the five-pound note from 23 to three, Sutcliffe was again questioned. The evidence was literally at the policemen's feet: during this questioning, Sutcliffe was wearing the boots he had worn when he murdered his tenth victim. An imprint of the boot mark had been taken, but police did not think to look at his boots.

Something had to give. Public disquiet had reached a frenzied pitch and a fresh approach needed to be taken. A team of examiners was established to take a fresh look at the entire evidence and the sites at which the women had been murdered. Dr David Canter, Professor of Psychology at the University of Surrey, applied his skills in locating what he termed the 'centre of gravity'. It was this that brought another breakthrough: with the aid of a computer centralising the murder areas, investigators homed in on Bradford as the city in which the killer lived. They only needed now to join the dots: Bradford; known suspects; five-pound note; evidence.

Despite the manhunt and the heightened risk of being discovered – or because of a subconscious desire to be caught – Sutcliffe went trawling for another victim. He gave police a false name when he was interrupted sitting in his car with another prostitute he planned to murder, but this time a check of his name proved that the car also had false number plates. Asking to relieve himself before he was taken in for questioning, Sutcliffe disposed of the hammer and knife behind a storage tank. He had been committing murder for six years; finally in 1981, the identity of the Yorkshire Ripper was about to be revealed. Returning to where Sutcliffe had relieved himself, an astute young police officer found the weapons he had secreted behind the tank. When Sutcliffe confessed, he gave police an insight into the disturbed psyche of a serial killer. Driven to avenge a prostitute who had ripped him off for ten pounds, Sutcliffe targeted prostitutes as his victims. In his warped state of mind, any woman walking along the street at night was fair game. After his first murder, revenge intertwined with blood lust. He could not stop.

The lessons from the Yorkshire Ripper case led to a significant shift in the way British police tackled evidence and suspects in major crimes. Dr Canter had described to police how people use 'mental maps' to centre themselves in an area, marking out their territory with their own idiosyncratic memory of that place. '. . . Each person creates a unique representation of the place in which he lives, with its own particular distortions,' he wrote. 'In the case of John Duffy [serial rapist], journalists recognised his preference for committing crimes near railway lines to the extent that they dubbed him the "Railway Rapist". What neither they nor police appreciated was that this characteristic was likely to be part of his way of thinking about the layout of London, and so was a clue to his own particular mental map. It could therefore be used to see where the psychological focus of this map was and so specify the area in which he lived.'

It was a salient lesson that their police counterparts in Western Australia would need to heed – that, and the wisdom of Friedrich Nietzsche: 'Whoever fights monsters should see to it that in the process he doesn't become a monster.'

14

Despite the fact that Sutcliffe had been identified by several different police jurisdictions, a lack of appropriate data storage and a workable case management system meant British police had failed to recognise that he had already come under police scrutiny multiple times. To prevent the embarrassment of this reoccurring, HOLMES was created. The WA Major Crime Squad purchased HOLMES in 1989. Applied to Macro as its case management system, it has provided a database for all information gained during the investigation, identifies common denominators and allows priorities to be noticed and actioned. It also provides a case management tool that identifies how many lines of inquiry are currently active, how long particular information has been with an investigator and the current workload of investigators. With more than 60,000 pieces of information that need to be assessed and prioritised for 'action' or 'information only', it also quickly eliminates people from the investigation. Taking each step at a time, HOLMES picks over the known data. Starting with the capture of information, it moves through priorities, allocation of resources, investigation, suspects' alibis and quality control before it finally archives material.

The system is linked directly to the UK police via a telephone link, which allows the HOLMES system experts access to the data for quality assurance purposes. 'This was 1996, pre-internet days,' Tony Potts says. 'It was an innovative use of breaking technology aimed at ensuring we were doing it right. We averaged around 2000 calls per day to Crime Stoppers for the first few weeks after each disappearance. All that information was channelled into HOLMES.' But if it proved helpful, it didn't provide the one thing police desperately needed. A breakthrough.

Pre-HOLMES, police relied on three prongs to solve a crime: the crime scene, doorknocks and media. The Macro taskforce inveigle the press for help and they receive it. Reporters call in to identify ways in which to keep the case alive in the public eye and to offer clues on what can be packaged as a story. With a background of more than 30 years in journalism, veteran Channel 10 reporter Rex Haw recalls it was a time when the lines between police and the media were deliberately blurred for the sake of the community's safety. 'It didn't mean we didn't kick them if we needed to, but we did work very closely with them. The media is always ravenous for a new angle on a story this big, so that helped.' On one occasion, his cameraman had captured the name of a person of interest penned on the Macro headquarters board. 'The coppers knew we were shooting the image, but this bloke was so litigious, he'd have used every avenue he could to attack the police. We chose to reshoot instead.'

But Haw's efforts weren't always appreciated. Known as a gentleman in an industry that has more than its fair share of unscrupulous reporters, Haw was approached to run a news item regarding the mystery caller whom Don Spiers had desperately willed to call back. The upcoming news item was advertised in television news breaks for it to gain maximum effect, and Haw was startled when confronted later by a furious Spiers at an outdoor concert, accusing him of ruining Don's chances of hearing from the man because advertisements for the story had scared the caller away. It was a verbal attack that stung. 'I was trying to do the right thing, getting maximum exposure for the story,' Haw recalls, 'but it wasn't perceived that way. I wanted to write Don a letter trying to explain that, but I decided against it. He is so full of intense sorrow that it takes nothing to upset him and I didn't want to make it worse. It was a volatile time for police, media and, most particularly, victims' families.'

15

Shortly after the discovery of Jane Rimmer's body, criminal profiler Claude Minisini is invited to Perth by the Macro team to decipher any clues found at the scene of her disposal site. Minisini, a colleague of Commissioner Bob Falconer and founding member of the Victoria Police Rape Squad, had undergone a 12-month fellowship at the FBI's Behaviour Science Unit in Quantico, Virginia, made famous by the movie *The Silence of the Lambs*. During his sojourn in the United States, Minisini interviewed notorious serial killers Ed Kemper – who, amongst his other victims, murdered his mother and put her voice box in the blender to finally 'shut her up' – and Jeffrey Dahmer, who killed at least 15 men and on whose character Hannibal Lecter was partly based. Returning to Australia after 13 years in the police force, Minisini left and co-founded the Forensic Behavioural Investigative Services (FBIS).

Criminal profiling is based on behaviour clues that are left behind at the crime scene and offers pointers to the offender's personality and the relationship, if any, that they had with the victim. It analyses the victim, why and how they may have caught the attention of the offender, and the similarity between each serial crime. Carefully studying the crime scene, the criminal profiler then layers the clues to put together a composite picture to help police. But profiling never replaces the hard investigative slog of good police work.

The profile that started the technique was that of New York's so-called 'Mad Bomber' in the 1950s. In open letters to a newspaper, he taunted police with clues to his identity. Psychiatrist Dr James Brussels examined both the bomber's handwriting and the bombs, shaped like a penis, to draw conclusions about his personality. This man, he advised police, was obsessively neat. He went further. When the bomber was caught, he said, he would be dressed in a buttoned-up, double-breasted suit. Brussels's profile proved uncannily accurate: as he walked out of his home on the day of his arrest, George Metesky wore a buttoned-up, double-breasted suit.

Minisini – a meticulous dresser who favours white shirts and cufflinks and sports an Inspector Clouseau moustache – flies into Perth with the city's expectations resting on his shoulders. The stakes are high, as are the public's hopes for a speedy arrest. Examining the site where Jane Rimmer's body is found, he maps out a profile of the killer. This person, he tells police, is organised and the murder was controlled, careful, planned. This is not the work of a disorganised killer with a dishevelled mind.

Paul Ferguson calls a press conference to spell out to the public the profile of the type of person the police are seeking. He asks Perth residents to help, by watching closely anyone who had a strange response to the media reports that Jane's body had been found. These signs could include 'absence from work, an inability to remain at work for the entire day, a sudden deterioration in work performance, an inability to concentrate, experiencing headaches, sudden changes in plans . . .' Ferguson also outlines other profiling clues picked up by Minisini. The killer would drive a late-model car that he keeps spotlessly clean, hold down a job and be of unremarkable appearance. Police release no further details, the lack of information inviting sharp criticism and no little incredulity. Minisini stands his ground. They did find enough evidence to deduce strong and incisive conclusions, he says. But he can't say any more than that.

Advertisements based on the profiling are shown on prime-time television, using the familiar faces of actor John Wood, from *Blue Heelers*, and singer Kate Ceberano. 'Like Sarah's family and friends you're agonising over the events of that weekend, because you think someone close to you may be involved in her disappearance,' Ceberano says. 'You're worried because you've noticed a change in their routine or behaviour. Whatever it was, ease your mind.' The ads work, seducing people into coming forward with information.

Criminologist Paul Wilson, from Bond University, watches the unfolding profiles on television with more than a passing interest. 'This is all very general and quite superficial,' he says. 'Just because, for example, someone is showing signs of anxiety at work or decides to go off and wash their car, doesn't make that person a serial killer. The accuracy rate for the FBI profiling is less than 90 per cent and the whole technique is not scientifically based.' Minisini is used to the flak. If police don't perceive that profilers are doing a good job, he says, they are the first ones to say so.

Not so Dave Caporn. 'They left here winning the respect of the force,' he beamed. 'They did excellent work.'

Although the work of profilers in Australia has received a welter of publicity – it was profiling that targeted where Frank Denyer, who committed Victoria's Frankston murders, lived – it has never directly solved a case. So while profilers command huge sums for their services and boast they have worked on high-profile cases, they can never point to a result. 'Dave Caporn said that Claude Minisini did excellent work,' a former police officer says. 'Well, no doubt he did. But all we – the public – know is that he told us that the killer likes driving, keeps his car clean and is of neat appearance. Now that's all very fascinating, but does it take Einstein to work that out? Everything else he deduced is kept under wraps, in order, they say, to be able to tell the difference between a true and a false confession. But with the greatest respect to all concerned, without public scrutiny and without an arrest, it's a bit like farting in the wind.'

Minisini's generalisations about the killer's profile also exacerbate the rumblings of discontent heard after it was announced that FBIS had scored the lucrative one-year contract with the WA Police Service. Digging for background, and confirmed by documents released under the Freedom of Information Act, *The West Australian* journalist Luke Morfesse found that despite written advice to the deputy commissioner from the acting assistant commissioner that the $40,000 cost of their services could not be justified, it was awarded to FBIS regardless. 'The deal,' Morfesse wrote, 'included an option to pay FBIS . . . $350 an hour for each extra hour after the first 100 hours.'

The West Australian newspaper was originally denied access to any documents pertaining to FBIS. Requesting a review by the office of the information commissioner, they were only then disclosed. 'The whole thing was like a scene out of *Yes, Minister,*' Morfesse recalls. 'We were told that we couldn't get our hands on the FBIS documents because the internal affairs unit, exempt under the FOI Act, had created them. They also told us that if Falconer had created any documents they were also exempt because as head of the police department he was also head of the internal affairs unit. So when the whole story came out, it didn't look great.'

16

Five hundred people attend Jane's funeral at Karrakatta cemetery on a sunny August morning, seven days after the discovery of her body. Her white coffin is adorned in pink, mauve and white flowers, her favourite song, 'Distant Star', played as mourners leave the church. Macro taskforce officers move unobtrusively through the crowd, blending in and watching to see who attends the funeral. All too often, the killer himself will move amongst the mourners, taking ghoulish pleasure from their grief, feeling momentous joy at his power to take a life. The Rimmers take no comfort in a religious faith, but they are nurtured by the speeches Jane's friends give about the generous-spirited, loving young woman who always had a ready smile.

After the service they adjourn to their local pub, inviting everyone, including Macro officers, to join them. Trevor puts $1500 on the bar for drinks. Tortured with grief, Jenny unashamedly drinks to her daughter's memory, alcohol numbing the pain as the evening wears on. She smiles wistfully. Jane was her best friend, she says. She would have understood. She would not have judged her for drinking too much that night. Shattered with grief, Jane's siblings, Lee and Adam, mingle amongst the crowd of mourners, trying to keep a brave face.

The rain has waterlogged Jane's car. It has sat outside her flat, water pouring through the warped sunroof and drenching the seats. A few days after Jane's funeral, Trevor climbs in to return it to the car yard. Here, alone in the quiet of the car's interior with water sloshing around his ankles, he puts his head on the steering wheel and sobs.

Christmas 1996. There is no family celebration, just an overwhelming realisation that Jane is not present at the table.

The phone rings. It is Don Spiers, the first time, before or since, that he has approached the family. His voice is choked with emotion. 'I'll keep this brief,' he says. 'We are thinking of you all. We know you must miss Jane as much as we miss Sarah.'

17

Every year on Jane's birthday, 12 October, Jenny and some friends make the pilgrimage to Karrakatta, sitting in front of the plaque they erected for her in front of a baby pine tree. The plaque is simple. 'In loving memory of Jane Louise Rimmer. Taken from us on 9th June 1996, aged 23. Precious daughter of Trevor and Jenny, dearly loved sister of Lee and Adam. Our distant star, in our hearts forever.' They celebrate her life with Blush champagne, flowers and cake. Trevor goes alone every Saturday to talk to his daughter. It is, he smiles ruefully, the only chance he gets to see her. The questions never go away. She had had a fair amount to drink. Did she get into a car, thinking it was a taxi? Was she dragged into a vehicle as she walked down a dark street? Was she seduced in by a smooth talker who appeared to be on the level? What the hell happened to their Janie? It drives them mad, not knowing.

Jenny's mother tries to give them comfort. 'She's in a better place, now. She'll never get sick, never get any older, never be unhappy.' Jenny sees the flip side. Trevor will never walk her down the aisle. She will never have children. She loved life; she would have embraced getting older. They have mountains of cards and letters from friends and strangers, offering their prayers and support. They treasure one from Jane's friends, which arrives shortly after she is found. 'I remember once, not long after Sarah Spiers's disappearance, we were going to catch a train home late one night after having drinks at the Shenton Hotel. Jane offered to pay for a taxi for us both because she didn't think it would be safe after what had just happened to Sarah Spiers. Jane was a very caring person who always brought a smile to our face . . .' They treasure a lock of hair, too, that the police gave to them after they found her body. It stays in a keepsake chest with other precious mementos of their daughter.

As distraught as the family is that Jane has been murdered, her sister, Lee, recalls feeling a sense of relief that she had been found, that they can start the grieving process and lay her to rest with dignity. Jane's murder has strained Perth women's sense of safety, their personal boundaries. Lee will later march in 2001 with hundreds of others through Claremont streets, to reclaim the night and the space as safe. It is a small gesture, but important. Jenny joins in the march that starts at the Continental Hotel where she huddles in the warm safety of friends and family. It breaks her heart to be there, and she will never return.

The police are puzzled by questions they can't answer. Why did Jane leave her friends at the hotel? She was standing outside the Continental for a few minutes on her own – was she waiting for someone? If so, who? Was it a taxi and, if so, why would she choose such a bad spot to get a cab? What they don't tell the public is that after Sarah Spiers disappeared, a secret video was installed to monitor girls' movements outside the hotel. But a transport desk to arrange taxis home or to escort girls to the nearby Club Bayview is highly visible.

The taxi industry in Perth is intensely feeling the pressure. Parents pick up their daughters instead of allowing them to risk getting into a cab with a stranger, and drivers' backgrounds are scrutinised. Within a short time, for a variety of reasons, 78 drivers lose their jobs.

The police presence at the Rimmers' home dwindles off. Days turn into weeks, weeks to months. The family, police later say, asked that they receive visits only if there was important news. It is not a conversation Jenny recalls. Dave Caporn's visit – months after Jane's body is found – leaves Jenny nonplussed. 'He walked around with a huge radio phone, explaining he hadn't visited before as he hadn't wanted to get too close to the case,' she says. 'But he was the *head* of the case! Why *didn't* he want to get too close?' It seems ludicrous, and all a little too late. 'Why has he waited until now to visit us?'

The Rimmers are fair in their judgements of how Macro handled Jane's murder. 'I guess they did a good job,' Jenny murmurs. 'I guess there wasn't much more that they could have done?' It's a question, not a statement and one that hangs limply in the air. What she is most upset about, she continues, is the lack of communication. 'We never hear from them anymore, unless it's to tell us something that gets our hopes up and amounts to nothing.'

Anger for Trevor Rimmer is a wasted emotion. He is a gentle, private man, given to reflective comments. What does it matter, he shrugs, if they find Jane's killer or not. Punishment will not bring her back. He sees his daughter's murder as some perverse, reverse lotto: wrong place, wrong time, right type. A million people in Perth and a million-to-one chance it would happen to them. But he would like closure, that nebulous, grey concept that families cling to in situations like this. Closure, so that at least his daughter's killer doesn't strike again.

It is nine months since Jane's abduction, long enough for young women to tentatively hope that the disappearance of Sarah and the murder of Jane is simply an aberration. Shock and sympathy still spill out in letters to the press and the media, though police continue to warn women to take special care. And the young people do. For a time.

Winter turns to spring, denuded branches are now in blossom and the cool, clear nights become warmer, seducing people outdoors. And as the long, hot summer passes the baton to an unseasonably warm autumn, memories fade.

Then another girl goes missing.

18

Terror now replaces fear. It is unbelievable. How could *another* beautiful young woman simply vanish into the night when there is such a strong police presence in the area? Ciara Glennon, a feisty, spirited Irish woman with a gentle lilt, her face framed by a mass of dark curls streaked with blonde, had only returned a week before from a year-long backpacking trip around the world. It was dangerous, at times, but this willow-limbed, petite woman – only 152 cm tall – who hitchhiked through Egypt, North America and Europe, had the gift of the gab, a way of engaging people with a smile. Born in a Zambian bush hospital when her parents worked for a Catholic mission, even as a young child Ciara drew people to her.

A lawyer who had majored in and spoke fluent Japanese, Ciara was friendly, fun-loving and extremely popular with her peers. Sporty, she excelled in ballet and had been excited about being the bridesmaid at her sister Denise's wedding the following weekend – a black-tie affair with 200 guests at the Royal Perth Yacht Club. Just five days before Ciara had started back with the law firm she had worked with prior to going overseas. At a quarter to five on Friday afternoon, her mother Una speaks to Ciara. She is feeling tired, Ciara says, but is expected to go for after-work drinks. 'Do you have to go?' Una asks. Ciara pauses, briefly.

'Oh yes, I'd better.' Una doesn't ask her what time she may be home: a 27-year-old who has been around the world can make that decision herself. But she is *expected* home.

'Have a good time,' Una says. 'And be careful.'

Ciara had done her law articles at the firm in which Neil Fearis is a partner. He has known Ciara's father, Denis, for 16 years and it was always understood that Ciara would practise in corporate and commercial law at Fearis's firm when she became a fully-fledged lawyer. She proves herself acutely intelligent, a gift to the firm. Six months earlier, whilst Ciara was travelling overseas, Fearis had met up with her in London for dinner. Travelling hasn't changed her, he notes: she is as engaging as ever and over drinks after work that first Friday night back, she proves to be still the same. But Fearis, a conservative man who is the Western Australian chairman of Australians for Constitutional Monarchy, is tired. He has returned from Singapore only late that afternoon and is not up for a late night.

At 10.45 pm Ciara and her group, including Fearis, move to the Continental Hotel in Claremont for drinks. The Continental; two blocks away from the four-lane Stirling Highway and 150 metres from the next Claremont nightclub, Club Bayview. It is St Patrick's Day, time for a traditional Irish celebration, but Ciara is also weary. The Continental is only the next suburb from her home and she drifts around the crowd, chatting to people she knows. Neil Fearis yawns and looks at his watch. It is just after 11 and he needs to get some sleep. He slips out of the pub quietly without saying goodnight.

Ciara's bed is empty Saturday morning. Una calls one of Ciara's best friends, who promises to ring around and call her back. She also calls Fearis. 'What time did Ciara leave the hotel? Have you seen her since she left?' He hasn't, he assures her.

It is Denise's bridal shower that afternoon and Ciara has a hair appointment in the morning in preparation. She and Denise are very close friends; she would not miss today. There is an edge of panic in Ciara's girlfriend's voice when she calls Una back. 'Ciara went to Claremont and left the hotel around a quarter past eleven last night,' she says. 'She was only there for about 20 minutes.' Her voice is wavering, and she tries to control it with a deep breath. She has read the papers, knows what has been happening in Claremont. Everyone in Perth knows what has been happening in Claremont.

Una knows instantly, with the innate, sick feeling that mothers possess, that her daughter is not going to be found alive. Claremont. Something evil is happening at Claremont.

Reported as a missing person, by nightfall family and friends are frantically searching for Ciara. The last confirmed sighting of her is at 12.15 am on the southern side of the Stirling Highway, between Bayview Terrace and Stirling Road. Striding down the road, a confident young woman determined to get home.

Paul Ferguson hears about Ciara's disappearance around 4.30 that afternoon. The station is buzzing with the news he is dreading as he calls senior command. *He's got another one. The bastard's got another one.* Macro taskforce officers take the news hard. It is bad enough that another woman has been taken. But this one has been taken on their watch, right under their nose. Paul Coombes remembers it as a 'where were you when?' moment – one that no one could ever forget. At his children's primary school function, he has his mobile switched off. A message is sent to him via another person. 'I was notified that I needed to get into work ASAP,' he recalls. 'We all knew how serious it was.'

Stage three of Macro has begun.

Stephen Brown, a Detective-Sergeant in the Organised Crime Squad, has kept abreast of the Claremont investigation since its inception. He is stunned when he hears news of Ciara's disappearance on television. It is, he knows, not only crystal-clear confirmation that there is a serial killer working in Claremont, but also the impetus for him to want to immediately join the Macro taskforce. He rings a colleague. 'Let's get in there,' he says, 'and make a difference.'

Within 24 hours, the number of core investigators on Macro has blossomed to 70. Unknown to the general public, there is a chilling reality underpinning the taskforce's need to beat the clock. After their third victim, a serial killer's level of violence escalates with frightening speed. Having escaped detection three times, they now feel indestructible. The next victims will be targeted hard and fast.

***

Jenny and Trevor Rimmer are taking a break at Rottnest Island, seven months after Jane's funeral, when police call. They have some bad news, the police warn them. Trevor squeezes his eyes shut in preparation for what he may hear; Jenny buckles at the knees, and cries.

Police circulate a press release to all media. 'Police hold grave fears for the safety of a woman who was last seen leaving the Continental Hotel in Claremont at approximately midnight on Friday March 14, 1997 . . . Given the circumstances of the disappearance of Sarah Spiers and Jane Rimmer and the similarity of this incident, the Macro taskforce has commenced immediate investigations. We have an assurance from police services state commander Deputy Commissioner Bruce Brennan that every resource will be made available to ensure a successful and speedy resolution.' Within four days they announce that as part of an increased allocation of resources to Macro, Superintendent Richard Lane – formerly in charge of the personal crime division – will join the Macro taskforce. They are bringing in their big guns.

By 16 March, Perth media are again saturated with headlines about a missing girl. News bulletins alert the public to the harsh realities in stark language. 'The police are almost convinced a serial killer is at large in Perth following the disappearance of a third woman from outside a popular nightspot over the weekend,' ABC Radio Perth announces. *The West Australian* is equally blunt. 'Woman Missing: Serial Killer Fear'. The headline represents a chilling, though seismic shift: it is the first time that WA police publicly acknowledge their belief that a serial killer is operating in the city.

19

The government wades in, with Premier Richard Court – a personal friend of Denis Glennon's – offering a quarter of a million dollars for any information that may lead to Sarah Spiers or Ciara Glennon or to the arrest of the person responsible for the murder of Jane Rimmer. News of the reward – the biggest offered in the state – is greeted with cynicism in many quarters. Would that amount of money, many people ask, have been offered if Ciara had come from a less privileged background?

The Glennons go through the motions, consumed with numbness but clinging to some vague hope that she will be found alive. Una has little if any faith that Ciara is safe, but Denis – proud, private and extremely well connected in the Liberal Party and Perth society – launches an immediate appeal to the public. Pale with shock, he articulates the family's grief in his soft Irish brogue. 'We are a strong family and I don't cry easily but Ciara's alive, we believe that and we are confident that the way she's been brought up she will fight on, and we are hopeful that she will be found at this stage even. Only now do I even begin to understand the terrible trauma that the parents of Jane and Sarah went through and the degree of empathy that I have with them now is just enormous and my final comment is that no parent who loves their child, even a child of 27 like Ciara was, can even begin to comprehend the devastating pain that this is in any family.' His voice breaks throughout his appeal for help. 'Somebody in Perth must have noticed something unusual around that time outside the hotel. They may not remember it, but if they were in Claremont that Friday night around that area, could they please come forward and talk to the police. Una, my wife, she is numb with shock and she has asked me to appeal to the mothers, the wives, the girlfriends, the ladies in the community who may have some husband or partner that they notice is doing something different now or did on Saturday morning and Una says, please help her, we are just distraught and we just need your help and your prayers.'

Rainstorms are deluging Perth, rivers of rain that drench the city and the bush. Ciara Glennon has now been missing for 36 hours. Jenny and Trevor Rimmer try not to articulate what they are thinking as the rain pounds on their roof, demanding attention. Across the river, Don Spiers stands bleakly at his kitchen window watching crystals of water slide down the pane as the night closes in. This rain. It is an omen. A terrible, desolate omen.

Neil Fearis is questioned by police for seven hours immediately following Ciara's disappearance. He had organised the drinks at the hotel, he was one of the last people to see Ciara, he had caught up with her months earlier in London. Fearis understands. They are just doing their job. A young detective-constable quizzes him in detail about his movements from early Friday evening to Saturday lunchtime, when concern was first raised about Ciara's whereabouts. They also speak to his wife, Jasmin, to corroborate details: what time he got home from the hotel, what time he got up the next morning. The minutiae of policing. Fearis remembers the small moments in that ghastly time. The detective-constable is highly amused that Fearis corrects his spelling and grammar on the transcript of interview provided to him for checking. Obviously, he muses later, he has never interviewed a lawyer before.

Police are courteous, solicitous in their dealings with him, thank him for coming to the station as they walk him to the door.

Neil Fearis is under fire in the weeks following Ciara's disappearance. Perth's talkback radio airways are jammed with scuttlebutt about the nature of his relationship with

Ciara. Everyone, it seems, has an opinion. *The relationship must have been improper.* Fearis shakes his head. He knows it wasn't, and this can only serve to upset Ciara's family further. The calls continue. *He was a senior partner and she was a young woman. He should have seen that she got home safely.* What can he say? He knows this is true. He *should* have seen that she got home safely. But what they don't know is that, as it transpires, Ciara had left the hotel five minutes before he did. But it is what he calls the 'extreme lunatic fringe' who upset him most. The rabid, strident rednecks with their rabid, strident opinions. *If that girl has been murdered, I reckon he did it. He must have.* Thank God, Fearis thinks, that the Glennons don't subscribe to that view.

The city has descended into the twilight world of outright panic and bedlam. The shockwaves are felt throughout Perth, permeating the press, taxi service, politicians and police. Dave Caporn, charged with the unenviable task of keeping Macro staff on track and placating the powers that be, is in the office as dawn rises over the city and leaves after 10 each night. Stricken with grief, Denis Glennon demands that his family not be given a junior liaison officer to work with them. Caporn, too, gets that role.

The West Australian prints 5000 Help Find Ciara posters as a grim Paul Ferguson plays his hand. 'This is an appeal to the mothers and fathers of the young people who might have been in the area at the time. We don't want to see any other person or family go through the heartache that these families have gone through.' The appeal works, perhaps too well. Within weeks of Ciara's disappearance, 35,000 people phone police with information. Most of it is useless and none leads to an arrest. Ten teams comprising six investigators are on the floor, each with its own persons of interest. In the first weeks following Ciara's disappearance, there are up to 50 Persons of Interest that they can't eliminate. They need a breakthrough.

While women avoid partying in Claremont, they are only too aware that this killer could be anywhere. Throughout the city, in pubs and clubs, signs warning young women to be careful are placed in toilets and bars. 'Don't walk alone to your car. Don't trust strangers. Don't take risks.' Perth has reverted to the horrific, dark days when serial killer Eric Cooke indiscriminately ran amok in suburbs near Claremont, killing its beautiful young women. And as with Eric Cooke, they don't know when this one will turn up again.

20

When scrawny, two-bit criminal Eric Edgar Cooke started his murderous rampage in Perth's wealthy inner-western suburbs on Australia Day weekend, 1963 – ironically, the same weekend Sarah Spiers disappeared – he targeted complete strangers. Cooke's killing spree changed the heartbeat of the city: once coddled in innocence and with a low crime rate, its carefree air changed virtually overnight to one of unimaginable terror. Cooke's modus operandi changed at whim, his eight victims variously stabbed, shot, strangled, or run over – changes that police later asked the public to believe had attributed to the ill-informed judgements they made about the identity of the killer.

Finally caught, Cooke – who had a cleft palate and was bullied as a child – confessed to all the crimes he had committed: 8 murders and 14 attempted murders. All but two of the 22 confessions were accepted.

As Western Australians prepared for Christmas in 1959, beautiful 21-year-old Jillian Brewster, socialite and granddaughter of millionaire chocolate manufacturer Sir MacPherson Robertson, was slaughtered in her bed. Brewster was butchered with an axe and scissors, sustaining shocking wounds to her upper body, breasts and genital area. The scene of her murder – her Cottesloe flat near Claremont on the Stirling Highway – would resonate years later as the same vicinity from where the Claremont women went missing. As the city's residents recoiled from the details of the senseless death, the cry went out for someone to be charged. Despite his confession to Brewster's murder, that someone was not Eric Cooke. Neither did authorities accept his confession for the hit-and-run murder of 17-year-old Rosemary Anderson. Cooke, they said, was an inveterate liar seeking glory for a crime he didn't commit. Cooke's confession, clothed in stark language, was ignored. 'I, Eric Edgar Cooke, now of Fremantle Prison, say on 10 February 1963, between 9:00 pm and 10.00 pm, I stole a Holden sedan car . . . I drove the car straight at her [Anderson]. At the time I struck her, I was doing about 40 miles per hour . . . She was scooped up onto the hood for a couple of seconds and then thrown over the bonnet.' As authorities did not believe Cooke's confession for these two murders, someone would have to take the fall.

True to form for serial killers, Cooke had also led up to his murderous spree with hundreds of smaller offences, including peeping through women's windows at night, burglary and theft. Seven women who lived in similar areas were attacked in identical ways; five survived, two did not. After breaking into their flats and stealing the door key, Cooke later returned, watched them while they slept and then made his move. In the Brewster and Anderson murders alone, Cooke's modus operandi was identical to 14 other crimes he had committed. He was finally caught when police found the gun he used for his last murder. They waited until he returned for it and arrested him.

Faced with the police not accepting his first confession, Cooke retracted it, but stood steadfastly by his second. As Peter Ryan, former editor of Melbourne University Press who published *The Beamish Case*, wrote of Cooke's hanging, 'His second confession was made at the very step onto the gallows, and was sworn on the Bible in the presence of a clergyman. No matter; he was turned off, and carried his confession with him into the drop.' Cooke, the last man hanged in Western Australia, was buried at the Fremantle prison cemetery on top of child killer Martha Rendell. But if Cooke had gone, his legacy lingered. It would return to haunt authorities years later in ways they could never imagine.

21

The Macro taskforce officers do a quick mental check. Sarah abducted in summer, Jane in winter, Ciara in autumn. Is there some pattern in this? All disappeared on long weekend holidays. Sarah on Australia Day; Jane, the Queen's birthday (not celebrated in WA) and Ciara, Canberra Day in the ACT. There is five months between Sarah and Jane. Nine months between Jane and Ciara. *Nine between Jane and Ciara.* Why has the killer's cooling-off period become longer, instead of shorter as is their usual pattern? Has the police heat kept him lying low? Or has he, God forbid, acted somewhere else in the meantime, moving back to Claremont out of a desperate, uncontrollable urge to return?

The Commissioner, too, is highly visible. A hush descends on the normally rowdy crowd at a night football game at Subiaco Oval, near Claremont, when Bob Falconer makes an unscheduled, emotional address for them to help police solve the Claremont mystery. He also makes a plea through the press. Alarmed at the 'panic, paranoia, fear and mistrust' that have gripped the city, he urges the community 'not to self-destruct'.

The taskforce implements a location register to identify persons who were present in the Claremont area on the night Ciara went missing. Through extensive media coverage, potential witnesses are asked to register if they had been in Claremont, the time they were there, their movements within the area, their observations and a description of themselves with the clothing they had worn on the night. While it allows the taskforce to build a picture of Claremont on that night, it also eliminates suspects from witness accounts by referencing the register. 'If, for example, a witness had contacted the taskforce and advised they were at a particular location at a set time and were wearing a red dress,' Tony Potts says, 'and another witness had already mentioned they had seen a woman in a red dress, we could then cross-reference that information to identify and eliminate persons from the inquiry.'

Within days of Ciara's disappearance, a new fundraising arm takes shape: the Secure Community Foundation (SCF). Denis Glennon has clout – serious clout. If he rings the police commissioner, Falconer takes Glennon's call. And if he wants to start a fundraiser, the heavyweights will come on board. They need no persuasion. Terry O'Connor QC, Chairman of the Anti-Corruption Commission and a close personal friend of Denis Glennon. Julie Bishop, who will later become a Federal MP. Michael Chaney, Wesfarmers boss. Top number-cruncher Peter Middleton and Neil Fearis. 'The Secure Community Foundation,' Fearis admits, 'was unashamedly pitched at the big end of town. This was no rattling of tins on street corners.' But it cauterised opinion as nothing else to date had done.

Denis Glennon's company, Environmental Solutions International, chipped in $50,000; law firm Blake Dawson Waldron, where Ciara worked, another $100,000. Big names in the Perth business community provided the rest. 'We went straight to those people with power, connections and money,' Fearis says. 'It was a corporate fundraiser, targeting captains of industry and all those who sport Armani suits in St George's Terrace. Our plea was simple. "Get on the phone to 20 of your wealthy mates and send us a cheque." But despite that, total strangers also walked in off the street, offering money to help. It was very humbling.'

It was also urgent. Behind the phone calls was the raw desperation that if they hurry and bolster police resources they might, just might, get to Ciara, alive. And every day, Fearis wades through the flowers and cards from well-wishers left in the foyer of his law firm. Ciara Glennon's disappearance has galvanised the city, linking the rich with the poor.

Police media liaison has the task of convincing the media that the foundation has not been set up to supplement a lack of police funds. The structure of the foundation is clear. From the start, police fund any required outlays and the money is then reimbursed. The structure is designed for transparency, to sidestep any possible allegation from the public that the powerful private figures on the board have any undue or improper influence on the police investigation. But for all their intentions, the transparency does not work.

Within a few weeks the initial fundraiser has secured $600,000 – money that pours out as quickly as it pours in. Not one of the eight proposals put before the SCF committee was rejected. An upmarket media campaign, including commercials with the theme, 'You may have a suspicion. Act on it now,' appeals for information from the public. Ten thousand responses flow in. Perth's Forensic Laboratory, the Path-Centre, which handles DNA profiling, was equipped with a quarter of a million dollars worth of genetic analysing equipment. Now used at Sir Charles Gairdner Hospital, the state government – the taxpayer – also put in a substantial amount toward the machine. This would become a bone of contention in scientific circles: a decade on, the centre has still not used the equipment for the Macro investigation.

The SCF and Macro officers also looked overseas for innovative, sophisticated means to investigate the case. The use of lie detectors – not admissible in any Australian court – was one avenue. The foundation would fund several trips to Perth for international experts, including polygraph operator, Ron Homer – twice – and criminal psychiatrists. The tactics used didn't always appear credible. The average punter on the street looked at the international maestros waving their credentials at Perth airport and the whiz-bang technology and asked: all well and good, but where are the results?

Within weeks, the foundation funds a haunting re-enactment of Ciara's last movements as she breezes around the Continental catching up with friends before moving outside. Her friends, including Neil Fearis, agree to play their own roles in the re-enactment. An eerie silence hangs over the actors in between takes, but some revellers at the pub, fuelled by booze and bad manners, start heckling. They stop abruptly when a furious and distraught Fearis warns them to shut up.

Critics of the foundation start baying early. Civil libertarian and defence lawyer Terry O'Gorman slams the use of private money as funding 'Mickey Mouse' techniques, such as the lie detector, that would never stand up to serious legal scrutiny. Worse, he says, it blurs the lines between what is kept secret in the investigation and what is told to those who are injecting the money. The premise of a fair trial must balance on police investigations independent of private funding.

Paul Ferguson is also initially critical. 'Ciara's murder changed the axis of the investigation,' he recalls. 'Prior to this it had been community based. But Denis Glennon – himself a victim – had barbecues at Premier Richard Court's house and the political connection was undeniable. Suddenly, there was another arm of the investigation that we had to deal with, like a hungry octopus. I raised objections but it achieved nothing. Falconer left us to do our job, but the reality was, it was his way or no way when it came to dealing with people in power. And Falconer was incredibly media savvy.'

But Dave Caporn doesn't flinch through the onslaught. The use of private funds, he says, is welcomed. Whatever it takes. Denis Glennon is unsurprisingly defensive of the money being used to help bolster Macro's coffers. He doesn't agree that any of the techniques are controversial. It is, he says, a cooperative approach to tackling the investigation, a means of involving the community in the fight. It is his daughter out there, missing.

Whatever it takes.

22

Nine days after Ciara vanishes, an editorial in *The West Australian* encapsulates the public fears.

> ... It is the predatory nature of the disappearance that shakes the foundations of the community. The thought that there is someone out there who is biding his time, waiting for the right moment to strike. Someone who possibly is not what he appears ... three women have disappeared but police do not appear soon to be any closer to solving the mystery. Everyone has a theory – but theories are not hard to find in Perth at the moment. The only certainty is that we are uncertain, the only established fact is that we don't know – or to be more precise, most of us don't know. The nightmare can't continue.

The clairvoyants circle again with wild, fanciful ideas. Denis Glennon – tough, grief-stricken – does not suffer fools, but they come at him from all angles, sorrow attracting them like moths to a flame. He dispatches them, curtly and quickly. Unless they have real information, they are of no value to him.

They are not all clairvoyants and soothsayers. Neil Fearis receives a visit from Perth GP Dr Andrew Dunn. He has information to pass on, he says, that has been given to him by a female patient whom he does not name. He has gone to the police with the information, he tells Fearis, but they have not taken him seriously. This patient has told him that Ciara is being held captive in a house where black magic rituals will take place to appease the gods at the autumnal equinox. Come the Easter long weekend, she will be offered up as a human sacrifice, like the sacrificial lamb. Fearis, too, passes the information to the Macro taskforce. 'We were all so desperate to get Ciara back,' he recalls. 'But they didn't take the information at all seriously, so unbeknown to Denis Glennon, whom we knew did not need this extra stress, we hired private detective Mick Buckley to keep watch on the house in the hills for three days.'

After leaving the police force, Buckley became a private investigator in 1983. 'I got a phone call around 6 pm on Easter Thursday,' he recalls, 'asking me to start surveillance on this female patient. The information was that Ciara Glennon's murder would take place at The Spot in Yanchep. I rotated with two private investigators, tailing the woman when she came out of her house.' Keeping around-the-clock surveillance, Buckley reports back. There is no sign of anything odd, he says. Nothing at all.

'Who knows why this information was passed on in the first place?' Fearis shrugs, weariness showing in his voice. 'Maybe the woman was simply a crackpot, maybe someone wanted to insert themselves into the investigation for their own reasons. Who knows?'

Another female caller rings to advise that her husband has information about the Claremont offender that he wants to pass on. Fearis requests that the man call him when he has finished work. 'Oh, he doesn't work,' the woman says. 'He hasn't worked in years.'

'Well, in that case,' Fearis adds politely, 'could you ask him to call me now, please?'

'He can't do that, neither. He's at Casuarina.' Accustomed to moving in select social circles, Fearis doesn't understand what she means. 'Casuarina,' she repeats in an exasperated tone. 'Casuarina Prison.'

But they are not all strange calls from strange people. An Irish woman sends a CD of Irish lullabies to the Glennon family. They may, she hopes, be of some comfort to them. Denise's wedding goes ahead, but not as planned. No black-tie reception, no bridesmaid; just a quiet ceremony, private and sacred. Denis thanks the guests for attending, and the bride and groom go home. This is a time for prayers, not celebrations.

***

Fear is paralysing commonsense and women react in different ways. Petrified of strangers, one who lives in Claremont is chased by police after refusing to stop at a roadblock on a country road. An intoxicated teenager walking alone through Claremont late at night gives police a spray of abuse when they warn her she should take more precautions. They let her walk, following her from a discreet distance.

Radio station Triple M kicks off a personal safety campaign for women. 'The best plan is to have a plan. Decide before you go out how you'll get home.' They keep hammering the messages. 'Meeting Mr Wonderful is every girl's dream, but sometimes connecting in a smoky nightclub can cloud your vision. If you think you want to go home with someone you've just met, tell your friends, and if he won't give his name or phone number, go no further! Don't walk alone. Tell your family and friends where you are going. Write down the taxi number if a friend gets in. Key an emergency police number into your mobile phone. Be alert. Be careful. Take no chances.'

And the young heed the warnings. For a time.

23

3 April 1997: four days after Easter. There is a body lying in the scrub, slushy in death. Jason, a 24-year-old labourer, is wandering through the bush, jarring to a halt as he sees her. It is not yet lunchtime but the sun is high and the sharp, hard light morbidly illuminates the pitiful scene. Despite being concealed by branches and twigs, he can just make out a partly naked body. He turns away, fearful and distraught, and runs to the nearby house of his former boss, George Kyme, to call the police. He can barely articulate what he has seen, shaking and gibbering that there is a dead woman out there. He splutters it out the best way he knows how. 'Whoever did this,' he blurts, 'is one sick fuck.' Taken into the station where he is questioned by police, he is made to sign a confidentiality agreement that he will not divulge to anyone what he has seen. Ever.

Telstra workers in the area had smelt the decomposing body days earlier but had reasoned it was a dead kangaroo. Ciara Glennon has been missing for 19 days. This time, it is Assistant Commissioner Bob Ibbotson himself who knocks on the Glennons' door.

If ever the family need to call on their faith, it is now.

Don Spiers's family hears the news through the media, his wife, Carol, hears it via a friend. A woman's body has been found in the bush and police are yet to identify who it is. Within a short time Don is told it is not Sarah, but the shock elicits a heartbreaking response from him. 'Every time I hear of a similar case, I know what those parents are going through and I relive it. It's an endless, endless torment.' But he is angry, too. It's not good enough, he grimaces, to hear news like that through the press. The media should consult first with police to see whether the victims' families will be distressed by the reports. They are pariahs.

Across the river, the Rimmers watch and listen to the news on radio and television, silently uniting with the Glennons in their despair. Is it Ciara?

Driving back from the funeral of a business partner who had died of cancer, Neil Fearis hears that a body, believed to be Ciara's, has been found in the scrub. He calls the police and offers to identify her body. 'That won't be necessary, Mr Fearis,' they tell him. 'Thank you, anyway.' He has the impression there is perhaps little left to identify.

He calls to see the Glennons two hours after they have received the news. There was, he remembers, a heartbreaking sense of loss in the room, a mixture of sadness and resignation but relief, too, that the uncertainty was finally over. Denis is composed, grateful for the visit. It is a composure that will not last.

The forensic team know only too well what they will find. Ciara has been here for 19 days, dumped to become a banquet for foxes, crows and other wild creatures: dogs, cats, rats, pigs. Lying here through an uncharacteristically hot March, with autumn temperatures in the mid-30s and torrential thunderstorms that drenched her semi-naked body. Her flesh will be fetid and decomposed; insects would have started feasting within 20 minutes, laying eggs within 12 hours. This weather is a perfect incubator for nature's creatures. The hideous sight of Ciara in situ will return again and again to haunt the police officers who are first at the scene, turn their stomachs and make them determined to find whoever did this to her.

Ciara's disposal site, on a sandy track off the unsealed Pipidinny Road, is isolated, remote, the nearest house 500 metres east. Acacia trees and a sudden drop conceal the area from traffic that passes day and night on the track. Police know that, on average, offenders travel 27 kilometres to dump their first body, a distance that becomes shorter as the murders continue. Ciara's killer has travelled even further:

40 kilometres. He would have turned his car onto the track and dumped her, not hanging around the area unless he wanted to.

Mick Buckley recalls the information passed on from Dr Dunn's patient, that Ciara's murder would take place at Yanchep. 'When they found Ciara's body, she was only a few kilometres from Yanchep. That was very, very odd.'

The media are camped two kilometres from where Ciara's body was discovered, held back by a strong police presence. A television crew desperate to break from the pack and get exclusive images sneaks around another way, walking on sand tracks and getting within 70 metres of Ciara's body before they are spotted and told by a ropable Tony Potts to piss off. The reporter, spying a blonde hair on a tree trunk, feeds the public the story that police are searching for a suspect with blonde hair. It is not only frustrating for police; the information is dangerously wrong, leading the public in a scattered direction and giving the killer further confidence. A confident killer will strike again, soon. It isn't human hair. It is horse hair.

The tension and pressure are so palpable, Tony Potts – media savvy and usually placid – threatens to arrest Rex Haw when the reporter swears at him for wanting to call a news conference in the city at 4.30 pm. They are 40 kilometres away; it will take them at least an hour to get back to the city. And they have a news broadcast to get out by 6.30 pm.

Forensic pathologist Karen Margolis and Macro officers Richard Lane and Paul Ferguson attend at the scene. By six o'clock, when their sad business is done, Ciara's body is taken to the city morgue.

24

Jane and Ciara's disposal sites follow a pattern. Eighty-six kilometres apart, but both around 30 minutes drive from Perth's centre and both not far from a major arterial road. This killer is cocky, arrogant. He knows the bodies are going to be found, probably sooner rather than later.

Eglinton. Bordered on the Indian Ocean and named after the barque *Eglinton* that violently smashed on nearby rocks, Aboriginal legend claims the Pipidinny swamp was created from the meat and blood of crocodile tail. Covered in banksia woodland, scrubland and heath, it is so lonely that the area registers a nil population. There is a beach at the end of the road, and the track that passes where Ciara is dumped is a popular route to a fishing spot. Who uses this area? Who would know it? Swimmers, anglers, divers, surfers, bush-walkers, 4WD enthusiasts. It doesn't narrow the field. But the fact that access is only available via Pipidinny Road – meaning the killer could not have got out any other way – may help.

The incessant rain over the Easter long weekend has eroded tyre tracks and footprints and a strong sea breeze has deposited fine layers of salt and sand around the scene. Like Jane Rimmer's disposal site, the area is afforded the same critical care as an archaeological dig, a radius of five kilometres sealed as police spread out in sections searching for minute detail.

After the family has been briefed, Paul Ferguson does a live cross to the media from police headquarters. Without forensic proof, police cannot yet publicly acknowledge the identity of the body, but the media have guessed and are told, unofficially. It gives them time to prepare tomorrow's headlines.

Perth wakes to the headline splashed on the front page of *The West Australian* on 4 April 1997. It is personal, poignant.

'Ciara's body found in bush. A state mourns.' There is no need for surnames, now. The entire city is on a first-name basis with these women. Sarah. Jane. Ciara. The entire city is in mourning.

The hours and the stress are taking their toll. Driving home, Paul Ferguson's thoughts are consumed by Ciara's murder. *The bastard's got another one. Right under our nose. The media will crucify us. And another family is left to pick up the pieces.* Normally a careful driver, he doesn't notice the speedo accelerating to well over 100 kilometres an hour as the car barrels over a causeway and runs straight through a red light. An oncoming car screams on the brakes a second before they collide.

In his quieter moments, away from the hurdy-gurdy of the station, Paul Ferguson thinks about the families. It is his way to go to homicide scenes or disposal sites, to sit reflectively and try to reconstruct the moments, to make some sense of what was done to the victim and to put himself in the mind of the killer. He admits he can't cope at traffic accident scenes, the sudden deaths of people trapped in vehicles or spewed onto the road, but years of working the 'whodunits' have taught him to always expect the unexpected, to keep an open mind.

The families are all so different. The Spiers: country people with organised lives, open, naïve and trusting. The Rimmers: easygoing, suburban, accustomed to the city, more broad-minded in their approach. And the Glennons: private, wealthy, empowered, accustomed to a life of privilege. Three families, joined by a tragedy outside their control. Three families, suddenly rendered powerless.

The disappearances and murders are taking their toll on all the investigators. With robberies or non-violent offences, police can afford to sit back and wait until the offender makes a mistake. They can't do that with this maniac on the loose.

By the following day, police have pulled out their big guns, Commissioner Falconer giving a lengthy, convoluted message to the public. Paul Ferguson's message is simpler. 'As terrible as this discovery is,' he says, 'it is a major breakthrough for investigators. Offenders of this nature have been found to be compulsive drivers who spend a lot of time with their cars and are concerned with the appearance of their car.' Did anyone, he continues, arrive home agitated between the hours of 3 am and dawn? And did they clean and polish their vehicle? The questions hang over police like a dark shadow. If they can answer them, they have some hope of getting close to this killer. If they can't, they are back to praying he – or they – make a mistake. Even the smallest slip-up can bring them undone.

From which exit did Ciara leave the Continental Hotel? Where was she, and with whom during a 25-minute gap in her whereabouts at the hotel? Did she reach the Stirling Highway? Was she aware the other girls were missing? How did she plan to get home? Was she headed somewhere else when she left? Did she plan to meet someone? What are the similarities with Jane Rimmer's abduction? They know that Jane, like Sarah Spiers, was educated at Iona Presentation College at Mosman Park – near Claremont. Is there a link?

25

With limited information forthcoming from police, Perth residents resort to rumour-mongering, engaging in a game of Chinese whispers that is further embellished as time goes on. Fear and ignorance drive the gossip, and rumours that gross mutilation was visited on Ciara's body lead police to an early frontal attack, carried on the front page of *The West Australian* on 15 April. 'The fact that we keep under our hat what caused the death enables us to ID where a person is telling fact or fiction,' Caporn said. But the swipe at the public did not work. The rumours keep circulating, driven by the simple reality that facts can't be checked with police.

Everyone knows someone who knows someone who knows who the killer is. Urban myths spring up like mushrooms: a teacher knows a woman who got into a taxi that turned out to be suspect; Sarah Spiers's wallet has been found in a car in Port Hedland; the killer dresses as a woman in order to seduce the victims into his car; police officers know the killer is a cop and protect him. Everyone is an armchair detective, the case endless fodder for dinner party conversations. The killer has removed the door locks from inside the car so the girls can't get out. They are trapped, ready for his next move. A gun or knife is held to their head and they are silenced with fear. They are injected with a sedative and wake later, tied and captive. They are knocked on the head with a blunt object and instantly disabled. Always conjecture, no facts. And the saddest, most damaging rumours of all: that the girls' bodies were dismembered and mutilated after death, their killer a doctor, a cop on the Macro taskforce, or a debauched couple seeking thrills through murder.

'Channel 9 television had camera footage of where Jane Rimmer was found, and of her body,' Luke Morfesse says.

'There was a lot of speculation about dismemberment. Obviously they didn't air footage of her body, but my understanding is that there was no gross mutilation.'

But Macro insiders believe the girls could well have been kept alive after the abduction, used as a plaything for the killer to satisfy his macabre lusts before he decided he had had enough of the game and moved up a gear. Perhaps he held them at his house, where he feels safe, or at a house he knows, if there is no one else home; in a caravan or deserted building, where no one can hear their cries. And perhaps he held them, too, after death, revelling in his power, relishing the chance to humiliate them, moving their limbs into different positions, keeping them close, like debauched mannequins, before tiring of this and tossing them away in the scrub.

In the first instance, Morfesse recalls that all the Perth media understood that the cops had a job to do. But it wasn't always plain sailing. 'Early in the piece, Bob Ibbotson had a go at me, calling me irresponsible after we called the murders the work of a "serial" killer. The concern seemed to be about the fallout from the public, the drama it would cause in stirring up fear, more so than the fact that there was a serial killer out there. But they did some great things, went to painstaking lengths, like after Ciara disappeared when they plotted a street map of the Claremont area and spoke to every person who was in the area the night she vanished.'

Mick Buckley becomes involved in checking other theories forwarded to him regarding suspects. 'I received a call from a woman who nominated her former husband, a taxi driver, as the serial killer,' he says. 'He was originally from Victoria, and she claimed he was responsible for the so-called "Lover's Lane" murders in the early '80s and that of another two females – a woman and a child. He then left Victoria and spent quite a lot of time in Queensland, driving into New South Wales. In one particular area there, there were a few unsolved murders, which she also believed was his handiwork. He then moved to Western Australia, living very close to where the prostitutes at Northbridge were murdered.' Buckley forwards the man's name to the Macro taskforce. 'They investigated him, but what they came up with I don't know. But they definitely tipped him over for a look.'

Buckley tells of another informant who nominated three men and a woman as responsible for the killings and who passed the information to a university professor. 'One of the men was a taxi driver and the woman used to travel in the car with him. She had been a patient at a drug rehabilitation centre two kilometres from Wellard, where Jane Rimmer's body was dumped. The cabbie had been driving the night Jane went missing and couldn't explain his movements between critical hours late that night. The professor passed the information to police, but to my knowledge nothing was done about that. They ignored it.'

Buckley also has dealings with psychics regarding the case. 'One woman actually paid us $3000 to go with her to a place she nominated. It was an old deserted flour factory, three-storeys high near Karrakatta Cemetery. We spent three days with her, looking through the place. We found nothing.'

Another psychic told Buckley after Sarah Spiers disappeared that police should be looking for a serial killer. 'A journalist from the now defunct newspaper *Vincent Times* did a story on the murders I had covered and also interviewed the psychic. He gave the tape of that conversation to Major Crime,' he says. 'They didn't want to know about it and they certainly made no contact with me to see if I could throw any further light on anything. A week after they were given the tape, Jane Rimmer went missing.'

Buckley is adamant that there should be an inquest into the disappearance of Sarah Spiers. 'Why hasn't that been done? I am very concerned about that. Western Australia police have stuffed up so many murder cases that victims' families often come to us, asking for our help. Do I think they have stuffed Claremont as well? I certainly do.'

In his line of work, Buckley has encountered a lot of deviant people. 'You know, the worst thing about this whole story is not just that these crimes are unsolved. It's the amount of people in Western Australia who could be responsible for the crimes. So many people with form who could have done it. Educated, uneducated, it makes no difference. Taxi drivers. Police. Criminals. Sexual psychopaths. Doctors. Lawyers. When you start to investigate these sorts of horrific crimes, the sickos who crawl out of the woodwork are truly frightening.'

Psychological profilers wade in. The finding of the body, they say, will have a significant impact on the killer's demeanour. That person may suddenly start missing work or leave early; lack concentration; change their plans; develop headaches, mood swings or display reclusive behaviour. Employers are asked to be vigilant, particularly of employees who can't account for their movements. Do they live alone? Have they had a recent emotional trauma such as a marriage break-up? Does their work ensure them flexibility and mobility? And, they warn, the killer may also revel in the notoriety, hoarding souvenirs or press clippings about the murders.

It becomes something of a public debate. Criminologist Professor Paul Wilson, from Queensland's Bond University, disagrees with the profiler's assessment. Signs of anxious behaviour, he says, and people who have clean cars could create a false idea about what constitutes a serial killer's characteristics.

Tony Potts stands by the assessment. 'We are confident that the information we have released will bear fruit and is relevant,' he says. 'The point is, these serial killers trawl around a lot, looking for victims. And while they're doing that, their car gets dirty so they need to clean it. The thing that many people overlook is that the car, really, is secondary: the issue is that they are on the move, actively trawling for victims.' Dave Caporn shows more than a flash of impatience at the misinterpretation of the message about the clean car. It is just commonsense, he says, that the killer would make sure his vehicle was clean. Just commonsense.

While the parents grieve, the debate continues.

***

Una wants to die with her daughter. The sharp, searing pain she felt when she heard Ciara was dead is now replaced by a anaesthetised, listless disinterest in even the smallest things. Panic attacks overwhelm her, and even leaving the house is a trial. Her former staunch faith in God shattered, Una begs for answers. Why did He not help Ciara? Where is she, now, in the universe? Is she safe? She prays for a sign – any sign – that her daughter is at peace.

Ciara's family make the lonely trek to pay their respects at her disposal site, leaving broken and distraught. Her friends and colleagues also come to the site, laying sprays of carnations and roses at the base of the cross wrapped with police crime-scene tape. They sense that her killer has spent time here, preparing the ground, snapping limbs from trees now weeping sap and using them later to cover her body. One leaves a card at the scene. 'Ciara – truth and justice will prevail.'

Ciara Glennon's memorial service at the cathedral is packed inside and out with two thousand people and those who can't fit inside watch its relay on video screens. Ciara Glennon's murder has touched a raw nerve in this mellow city. The premier, dignitaries, the Anglican archbishop, Roman Catholics, rabbis and the man in the street: everyone wants to pay their respects. Many shops close their doors while the service is underway. Flanked by family and each clutching a single red rose, Denis and Una enter the cathedral. Ciara, the priest tells the congregation, has been a victim of naked and brutal evil. Neil Fearis and Denise read the lesson, and Una leads the Prayers of the Faithful. The congregation listens as Denis Glennon, in his lilting West Coast Irish brogue, delivers the heartbreaking eulogy to his daughter. He recalls her sense of justice, the loyalty she showed to her friends and her love of ballet.

'To this day we can only link your love of dance to your Irish heritage and some mysterious intrusion of rhythm from your African nanny and others during the first five years of your life. Your best dancing friend, Denise, is endowed with the same gifts. One day you two friends will dance again.' When his heart and soul can endure no more anguish, he says he remembers Ciara standing radiant in the bridesmaid's dress that Una had made for her. Ciara's dignity and courage, he continues, has helped the family cope with their most 'horrific ordeal'. 'God has come into our garden and picked the most beautiful rose.' His chin wavers, but he does not stop. This moment belongs to Ciara.

'Many women are now petrified and angry. Many men feel a fury and a feebleness that is impossible to convey. We all want to stop this killing of our children . . . You were our daughter, our pride, our joy. You were a bright and healthy young person with the prospect of a successful career with lots of friends and a sunny outlook on the world.' He wipes his eyes, pauses for a fraction and concludes the eulogy in his native Gaelic. 'Goodbye for now, my friend, and God bless you.' There is silence, then tears, before the mourners break into applause. This moment belongs to Ciara.

Pallbearers carry the coffin from the cathedral, preparing it for its final journey to Karrakatta cemetery. Ciara Glennon is sent to her God in a private service. Buried behind the children's cemetery, her coffin is adorned with her graduation photograph and favourite fluffy toys from childhood. Distraught and inconsolable, Denis cannot place the traditional piece of soil on his daughter's coffin.

For many years, Denis Glennon will visit his daughter's gravesite every day. Without fail.

26

The Macro taskforce adds another name to their mission statement, written after Jane Rimmer disappeared. 'Mission: to identify, apprehend and prosecute the person or persons responsible for the disappearance of Sarah Ellen Spiers and the murders of Jane Louise Rimmer and Ciara Eilish Glennon.' In fulfilling that mission, over the next three years alone, the taskforce will track 30,000 separate lines of inquiry.

The investigation is now at its most intense stage, the activity frenetic. Paul Ferguson returned to Major Crime in April 1997. Dave Caporn – from January 1996 the lead case officer on Macro – now assumes overall command of the taskforce and is its public face. With a third victim, the department needs a fresh structure, one that reflects the requirements of a long – potentially very long – inquiry. Tony Potts, a former Major Crime homicide investigator, now assumes sole responsibility as media spokesperson and strategist, handling day-to-day inquiries while Dave Caporn is rolled out for major developments: startling new evidence, the advice of profilers and, God forbid, any further victims. This structure allows Caporn to continue at the coalface of the investigation and not be drawn continually to answer media inquiries as Ferguson had done before Potts. The intent is for the public to have faces they know, trust and recognise instantly as Macro taskforce members. From this time, they will see Potts, Caporn and occasionally Ferguson on television, or hear them on the radio.

With Ferguson returning to his duties as officer in charge of the Major Crime Squad, Caporn fronts his first press conference for Macro in April. Outwardly tougher than his predecessor, and despite being in the force since 1976, Caporn is the new breed of officer: a politically ambitious man, steeped in the minutiae of administrative policing, frugal with information he doesn't want the press to know. Hawk-eyed, with large glasses that dominate his face, he can be charming, charismatic. But gone is the easy banter that Ferguson employed with the press, replaced by the implacable mask and arrogant air that reporters come to recognise as Caporn's media style. He nods to the cameramen and sits down, getting straight down to business. The way the killer operates, he says, shows adaptability that is a common trait in organised, intelligent offenders. The headline in *The West Australian* spells it out: 'Killer will strike anywhere: police'.

Perth journalists have a plethora of stories to tell about the way in which Dave Caporn likes to keep his finger on the pulse. One recounts that he requested the contents of a high-profile story, due to run in the next day's edition, be recounted to him prior to publication. When the reporter suggested that he instead spend a dollar and buy the paper, Caporn called the chief-of-staff. When the story duly appeared, television and radio stations were asked not to repeat it. They, too, ignored the request. Caporn, known as a great networker, has the nickname 'Gurkha' – 'take no prisoners'. To both his supporters and detractors, it seems well earned. He also has a reputation for maintaining an obdurate demeanour in the face of the harshest criticism.

'There was a press conference not long after Ciara Glennon's body was found,' Paul Coombes recalls. 'The usual commotion, reporters screeching questions, flashbulbs going off everywhere. "Mr Caporn," one journalist said, "do you feel personally responsible for these deaths?" What sort of question is this? We were furious but Dave stayed calm. "No," he said. "I don't feel personally responsible. I know we're doing everything possible to resolve and apprehend this person."'

Every day there is a full briefing by the ten team leaders, bringing Caporn up to speed on all aspects of the investigation. Paul Coombes, who sat next to Caporn for three years, recalls he led by example. 'No one can ever overestimate just how bad it was in those early days. Absolute, utter pandemonium. There was so much pressure from all sides and, even then, officers were caving in, taking sick leave and mentally falling over. Caporn didn't. He was – and has remained – an easy target, but he was always incredibly focused.'

Desperate for information, 15 weeks after Ciara's body is found, Caporn throws a curve ball. The serial killer, he surmises, has picked up other young women. But for his own perverse reasons, or to protect his identity, he has let them go instead of harming them. Played the Good Samaritan, done a good turn, instead of showing women his real face. There is a chilling historical precedent in Perth. David and Catherine Birnie seduced dozens of women into their vehicle during their murderous rampage, but let all but four of them go. Caporn wants to hear from any women who have accepted lifts in the Claremont area in the past two years.

The killer will be watching. He may have hidden the jewellery and clothing someplace safe where he can later take it out and admire it, or given it to his partner or wife to wear as a sinister trophy. This woman, usually unsuspecting, may have already been taken to the disposal site, not understanding why her partner suddenly develops an overwhelming desire for sex, nor understanding a body is nearby while he fantasises about the kill. They are his girls. Tossed away in the scrub, their disappearances force police into a grim game of hide and seek. Tossed away to wait, through the rains and a pitiless sun that scorches their bodies, for someone to find them, for the game to move up a notch. Now it has.

He will be watching the news, reading the papers; he will behave as FBI profiler Robert Ressler said serial killers do at critical times in investigations. 'The first or second murder, they're very paranoid, very frightened . . . But when they get away with it three or four times, they develop this omnipotence . . . "I am God, because I've gotten away with murder."' He will be alternately apprehensive and gloating;

fear that he may soon be caught will mingle with exhilaration. He's given the cops three chances to get him for these murders and they've failed. He's tied them up in knots, had them running all over Perth. And he is prepared to break patterns if he has to, to leave a trail behind like a jagged jigsaw that they can't put together. He can't be too careful. A pattern can get him trapped.

He is reading the papers to see if the story has made page one, quietly celebrating when it does, channel-surfing, changing radio stations. Obsessed. He hears that they're exhausting leads. He's out the door again, on the prowl, watching and waiting for his next victim.

He is cleverer than they are, all-powerful. This is his handi-work; he has caused this chaos and grief. The entrapment, the abduction, the kill; all part of his warped brilliance. Sitting back, watching, seeing how long it will take until the next stage begins, when they start finding the bodies. It is such fun, playing hide and seek with the coppers. They have found two of his three hidden treasures. Now their challenge is to find *him*.

27

In the first winter after Ciara's murder, two doves nest in the alcove outside Denis and Una's bedroom window, huddling from the wind and rain. They have never been there before and they never return, leaving in the spring. The signs continue to come, intensely personal visions that slowly, slowly thaw the icy cold detachment that Una feels from the world around her. She incessantly reads her favourite poem, 'Requiescat' by Oscar Wilde.

> Tread lightly, she is near under the snow.
> Speak gently, she can hear the daisies grow.
> All her bright golden hair tarnished with rust,
> She that was young and fair fallen to dust.
> Lily white, white as snow, she hardly knew
> She was woman, so sweetly she grew.
> Coffin board, heavy stone, lie on her breast,
> I vex my heart alone, she is at rest
> Peace, peace she cannot hear lyre or sonnet,
> All my life's buried here, heap earth upon it.

It will take years for Una to find the answers, to regain her faith, to reconcile a loving God in a cataclysmic world, but she does so, eventually. Ciara is safe. Denis, broken with grief, burrows deeper into his faith. They find a reluctant acceptance of Ciara's death, but no closure. There will never be closure. They will never get over the loss of their daughter. 'I will only be fully healed,' he later tells journalist Tony Barass, 'when I am reunited with Ciara. That is not this day. Our family is not only for this life.' In his articulate and poetic way he explains the pain of grief: a pain you cannot physically isolate, a feeling of terrible emptiness. And it is worse, much worse that he knows how Ciara died. Her last minutes or hours, he knows, would have been utterly terrifying.

And again, there are numerous psychics and clairvoyants who wish to share their visions of these last hours with him.

28

A long-time sceptic, Bret Christian, who grew up in Claremont believes that clairvoyants have proven to be one of
the biggest problems in the Macro case. Either well-meaning
or malicious, they add, he says, nothing more than further
heartache to those already deep in grief. 'The saddest thing
about their "visions" is that they are not only usually wrong
but that they are foisted on people when they are at their most
vulnerable.' Overseas, neither US nor UK police services use
the findings of psychics; officially, Australian police do not,
either. Writing in the 2004 Autumn edition of *The Skeptics*,
Christian quotes a story told by leading US sceptic James
Randi. 'A man claiming to be a psychic attracted the interest
of police when he predicted a serious industrial fire. The
accuracy of the detail after the event could only have been
provided by the psychic's special powers. But police discovered that he had no need of paranormal powers to produce
his visions – he himself was the arsonist.'

Former police officer Jeffrey Noye – whose name is greeted
with sly smirks by serving officers because of Noyse's
protracted and determined resolve to clear his name from the
Argyle Diamond smear – says police take clairvoyants' calls
with a grain of salt. 'They ring and the protocol is they're
afforded the same civilities as anyone else with information.
But it doesn't work like that. In reality, the person shares their
vision and the cop rolls his eyes. It goes something like this. "I
see. Yes. Uh huh, uh huh. And when did you have this vision?
Last night, during the commercial break while you were
watching television? Uh huh, uh huh. And was there anyone
else with you? No? No one else saw this vision? No? Uh huh,
uh huh.'

I have first-hand dealings with a psychic who saw 'visions'

of a seaside unit that she passed on to police. After several emails, telephone calls and broken agreements to pass on information to me, this 'intuitive medium', as she prefers to be called and who boasts she works nationally and internationally, agrees to meet with me in Perth at which time, she promises, she will outline her dealings with WA police. But when we finally meet, she has forgotten to bring her notes and can't conjure any memories of her experiences with police except that Dave Caporn treated her as a 'crackpot' and refused to take her seriously. That, and the vague notion that she thinks she warned Paul Ferguson that 'someone is going to go tonight'. After further promises to email me her 'feelings' regarding the profile of the killer, she forwards a text message I can't decipher. The email, too, never materialises.

Paul Ferguson takes a broad view of psychics. 'It was accepted that if we're asking people for information, then we couldn't just pick and choose. But it was appropriate to prioritise information. Caporn was always blunt about them: he regards them as fruit-loops and advised us to piss 'em off. But from a corporate point of view, this message could not go out to the public.' Ferguson recalls the 'intuitive medium' that I met in Perth. 'I sent a policewoman out; she read her tea-leaves and indicated she had specific information to share. I went along after that and checked out every possible angle.' He pauses, struggling not to laugh. 'Let's just say nothing came of it.'

Just weeks after Ciara is found murdered, Denis Glennon suffers a public roasting by Claremont Mayor Peter Weygers. Glennon, he rages, has blamed him for not expediting security in Claremont and has demanded he retire from the position he has held for many years. 'Mr Glennon has virtually told me he holds me responsible for the death of his daughter,' Weygers fumes. 'I can understand that Mr Glennon is confused and upset, but I am totally confident that this council has acted properly . . .' In a letter addressed to the council, Glennon had earlier raised queries about the slow response to the installation of security cameras, telephone boxes and street lighting in the Claremont night strip. The unseemly verbal stoush, played out in the press, is greeted with incredulity. Denis Glennon's daughter was found just over three weeks before. It is not the time.

The security debate is about to become critical. When Weygers calls on the Continental Hotel and Club Bayview to up the ante and improve security for patrons, co-owner Jon Sainken responds promptly – with a writ for defamation. Though he later drops the writ, the acidic relationship between the two men spills over into the courts when the Claremont council spends a massive $100,000 to oppose expansion of the nightclub through the courts. Sainken again responds, this time with a full-page advertisement in *The West Australian* denouncing 'fascist over-regulation' and victimisation. While the community watches the public stoush with some bemusement, it wears thin very quickly. There are missing and murdered girls out there. That is far more important.

In 1997, Weygers's mayoral role comes to an end when he is toppled by young local voters for vehemently opposing the expansion of Club Bayview. To his supporters, there is no doubt that he has been made a political scapegoat.

Other issues also come to the fore, picked up by the press. The police Freedom of Information unit is embarrassed by a media report that they mistakenly sent a man seeking information under FOI a letter intended for the lawyer of a person interviewed by the Macro taskforce. The letter, acknowledging the man requested information regarding a polygraph test he had taken, named the person and the police officers who had interviewed him. The bewildered recipient of the letter contacted *The West Australian* about the gaffe. 'I haven't received a reply to my own request for information, so I don't know who might have that information,' he said.

The officer in charge of the FOI unit acknowledged the blunder, citing administrative issues and said the problem was now rectified. He asked that nothing be written about the mistake.

***

Psychiatrist Dr Tim Watson-Munro describes the Claremont killer as a psychopath who could survive high stress levels. 'He is not psychotic, which rules out paranoid schizophrenia and manic depression,' he tells the press. 'People like that would not be able to plan and kill so efficiently.' He appeals to the Western Australian police to be less limited in their thinking and to allow him to look at the case investigation. He does not mince words. 'You have a major problem,' he warns. 'This person is going to strike again.' He is not in the same mould, he says, as the backpacker serial killer, Ivan Milat, who killed his victims on site in the Belanglo State Forest and left them there. 'Broaden the scope of your resources. Sooner rather than later there may be a fourth abduction.'

29

Police don't take kindly to advice from outsiders. Shortly after Ciara's body is found, Assistant Commissioner Bob Ibbotson makes a direct plea to the media not to report the comments and opinions of criminal profilers or criminologists not designated by WA police. They are not, he says, armed with the facts and their comments can only serve to unnerve and distract the public. Captain David Caldwell, special agent in charge of forensic science services, South Carolina law enforcement division, has been summonsed to Perth to help advise police and is there when Ciara's body is found. Claude Minisini is also in Perth. These men, Ibbotson says emphatically, are advising police. They are the best in their fields.

But Paul Ferguson has grave concerns. 'Minisini was injected directly into the investigation at the say-so of the commissioner. He would brief me and I'd brief the media. But I often felt that we were being too narrow, and so did the media. There was a lot of sniggering that car washing was a national pastime, and not necessarily the tell-tale signs of a serial killer. It didn't always help what we were trying to do.'

Best known for his handling of the Susan Smith case in 1994 – the American mother who strapped her two children into their car seats and drowned them by sending the car into water – David Caldwell has no doubt about what the Claremont killer will do next. Slow talking with a distinct southern drawl, his assessments are delivered as though he has just ridden into town on a horse and is chewing a plug of tobacco. 'This guy's gonna be *really* nervous,' he says, staring straight down the camera lens. 'He's probably watching this now.' Caldwell has seen 'a lot of bodies', he boasts, and he figures the WA police need all the help they can get. This person is a cunning, intelligent and adaptable predator who is undoubtedly acting alone.

'These three abductions took place near popular nightspots, but there's no guarantee that future ones will be in the same location. The method of operation can be altered to fit their program. Unless he's caught or incapacitated in some way, he still wants to do this. He likes it. He likes it a lot. There'd have to be an awfully good reason for him not to do it again.' And that, Caldwell warns, could be as early as in a couple of days. He faces the lens again. When this bloke is caught, he says grimly, people will be absolutely astounded at who it is. 'They're gonna say, "I worked with this guy! He's my next-door neighbour! It can't be!" '

He recounts some chilling tales that speak of the banality of a serial killer's psyche. US killer Leeroy Martin, who terrorised his community and murdered five women in a short time, regularly gave his next-door neighbour a lift to work. 'It was kinda neat,' Martin told Caldwell when he was arrested. 'Here she was thanking me for the lift because she was scared to death that this killer was on the loose.' Another killed only in December and June. Asked why in those specific months, he shrugged. 'My wife goes to see her folks twice a year. December and June. That's when I've got the house to myself.'

Caldwell throws out a warning to the Claremont killer. 'I think he's a bright man – but everyone makes mistakes. Everyone makes mistakes.'

The use of outside assessors so infuriates the WA Police Service's head of the Criminal Behaviour Analysis Unit, Mark Devenish-Meares, that two days before Caldwell delivers his assessment, he resigns in high dudgeon from the position he has held for 18 years. Recently returned from studying at the University of Liverpool's Investigative Psychology Unit, under the tutelage of Professor David Canter, a foremost expert in criminal behaviour, Devenish-Meares is incensed that his credentials are overlooked in favour of US-flavoured profiles. He snorts at what he regards as the wrong approach to the problem. Police should stick to the *facts*, such as crime-scene analysis, he says, instead of trying to read the mind of someone they haven't met. 'Police can't arrest a type, they can only arrest an individual. Trying to get into the mind of the killer is like scriptwriting for *The X-Files*. The media loves it to death, but it's wide open to confirmation bias.'

Caporn bristles at the criticism. 'Ninety-eight per cent of the investigation is traditional, but we're doing things we've never done because we're not prepared to get up to double figures of victims without trying to force a breakthrough.'

Driven to get results, the taskforce officers work a 24/7 rotating roster, racking up so much overtime they see little of their families. After the initial high hopes that the case could quickly be solved and despite a grim determination to find the offender, the fear of crippling despondency and sense of failure becomes an occupational health issue and one that gets worse as the months drag on. To keep the troops motivated, senior staff organise runs together in the local park, 6 am volleyball matches and the occasional barbecue. They know this predator will always pick off the least able from the edge of the flock, will follow, chase and fell the person least able to get away. There is an all-pervading sense, born of a sickening knowledge of the serial killer's modus operandi, that his clock is ticking toward the end of his cooling-off period. With every passing week, the situation becomes more urgent. They need to try to get to him, first.

A 7 am start and 7 pm finish is regarded as a good day. More often, officers are calling wives and partners with news they are going to be home late for dinner, again. While the non-commissioned officers can claim overtime, no one ever claims their full entitlement. 'There is no way we can underestimate what was going on after Ciara's disappearance,' Paul Coombes says. 'We knew by her victimology that she just would not go missing for no reason. The entire community was in shock, and people were genuinely petrified. The stress on everyone – the families, the public, the police – was enormous.'

Police are also battling another unseen enemy: public perception. They are only too aware that the Macro taskforce is regarded as a disembodied, faceless entity. Security considerations have prevented the media filming footage of the taskforce squad room and there is now a pressing need to show the public that Macro consists of a large number of real people working on solving these murders. Police video technicians and photographers are directed to take specific footage and still photos, which are released to the media. The rationale is simple: it is harder to knock real people than a faceless, large bureaucracy.

30

The police PR machine rolls on, trying to placate the public. 'We do have a lot of clues, we have a lot of indicators of exactly where to go with this person,' Detective-Sergeant Tony Potts, the Macro taskforce's dedicated media spokesman, tells the media. 'But invariably and historically offenders of this nature have taken some time to track down and apprehend.' They are words that will prove chillingly accurate.

The media are proving problematic, a huge juggernaut that police liaison needs to get on top of, quickly. Incorrect media reports and the uncontrolled flow of information allow no room for guarantees that the information is true, unlikely to jeopardise the investigation, is worthy of comment or serves any real purpose other than to feed the public's appetite for a fresh news angle on a salacious story.

'There were so many incidences where the media got it wrong,' Potts recalls, 'that we really needed to rein them in.' He cites examples. 'It was reported that Macro officers had asked witnesses to identify a blond man who was captured on the Continental Hotel security video. The inference was that we had a strong suspect who was a blond male.' The reality was very different. 'The officers were tasked with identifying every person who appeared on the security video. One of the people interviewed contacted the television station and told them of parts of the interview he could remember. He had blond hair. But a person with a suspicion about someone with dark hair discounts that suspicion and does not contact police because they think we know that the offender is a blond man.'

Sometimes the reports threaten to seriously derail the investigation. Days after Ciara is found, the taskforce calls for the anonymous persons who had contacted them with information several days before to re-contact Macro investigators.

'Their information was believed crucial, hinging on movements around Pipidinny Road just after Ciara disappeared,' Potts recalls. 'The media supported our call for additional contact and called for those persons to once again come forward. But one of the television stations ran with the story that these people were two girls in the area late at night with their boyfriends. Needless to say, we didn't hear from them again. They were hardly likely to come forward after that.'

Desperate to work out how to get over the problem of persons contacting the media after being spoken to by Macro, they hit on a simple solution: giving them 'thank you' cards and asking they maintain confidentiality. The solution was in the problem.

With the discovery of Ciara's body, John Turner, whose daughter Kerry was murdered in 1991, publicly links the crimes. 'Kerry was dumped, like the other girls, on the edge of the city and had been to a nightclub,' he tells a British newspaper. 'There can't be that many people going around this city killing young girls in this way. The circumstances are almost identical.' Paul Coombes doesn't believe that Turner's murder is connected to Claremont. There is more than a hint of exasperation in his voice. 'We are constantly having people double-guess us, but they forget police know the facts. The crime scene and methodology for this murder are in no way similar to the Claremont girls. Everything is possible, of course, but we have to deal in "probable", "most likely" and "known facts". Anything else is just conjecture.'

Bret Christian scours old records of past abductions, rapes or assaults in the Claremont area. Some incidents had already been reported, but he is alarmed at what is not.

In the early hours of New Year's Day, 1994 – two years before Sarah Spiers disappeared – a young woman was dragged from her car after she left Club Bayview. The attempted rape failed only when the woman fought off her attacker, who ran into the shadows and vanished. The man was never found. It was not the first sinister incident in Clare-mont. Three months earlier, a woman had hailed a taxi in Bayview Terrace. She sat next to the taxi driver in the front seat and, within seconds, was attacked by a man who was crouched down, hiding in the back. Using remarkable presence of mind, she jumped from the moving vehicle onto Bayview Terrace, sustaining a broken ankle. By the time she managed to stand up, the vehicle was out of sight.

The most chilling incident was in February 1995, 11 months before Sarah vanished. A tall, pretty 17-year-old girl who had been partying at Club Bayview was abducted around 2 am as she was walking alone, back to her house in Clare-mont on the road that runs parallel to the railway line. At a park on the edge of a reserve, a man jumped out, put a bag over her head, tied her hands with telephone cable and threw her in the back of his van. The attack happened so fast, she neither saw the man nor heard his voice. The van turned into nearby Karrakatta cemetery, which is open all night. In a deserted section of the cemetery, he turned off the van's motor and violently raped her, driving off with her clothes and leaving her on the ground when he had finished. Terri-fied, the teenager ran naked toward the first light she could see, at the nearby Hollywood Private Hospital. Like the other attacks, the case was never solved. The area from which she was taken, the swiftness of the abduction and the obvious possibility that her attacker knew Claremont could not rule out that this was the Claremont serial killer's handiwork. A dress rehearsal for murder. He was never found.

In the same year, a young woman got into a taxi at Clare-mont and the driver drove her over the railway line to the golf course. Forcibly stripped of her clothes, she managed to escape, banging on the door of a nearby house and screaming for the couple who lived there to let her in. Completely trau-matised, it took an hour for her to finally splutter out what had happened. Bret Christian, whose suburban newspaper incorporates news in the Claremont area, took a call from the couple on Monday morning. 'They asked what had happened to the girl as they had seen nothing in the media about it; nothing on television, radio or in *The West Australian* newspaper. We rang the police to ask about it and they told us that local police had attended,' Bret recalls. 'They fobbed us off, putting us onto the cop who was on duty. The truth was, it was never properly investigated and was never linked to the other abductions. We didn't find the name, the police report or the cop who attended. We didn't realise the significance of it at the time but when Jane Rimmer went missing, it obviously became vitally important.'

31

Paul Ferguson, now at Major Crime, is at police headquarters when a call comes through from Casuarina Prison. 'Prisoner David Birnie would like a word with you,' the prison officer tells him. Ferguson knows intuitively that if Birnie is offering information, he will want something in return. He can apply for parole in 2007 and will use anything he can as a lever to gain it. The parole board could be very impressed with the fact that he helped the Macro taskforce in their hunt for Perth's serial killer.

Ferguson eyes Birnie at the maximum security section of the prison in south Perth. It has been a long time since this gaunt sexual deviant so casually confessed to murdering his four victims: eleven years and still no sign of remorse. Birnie has followed the Claremont case through the media and wants to share his expertise with his old adversary.

'You can read all the books you like,' he tells Ferguson in his familiar cocky tone, 'but you've got to use a serial killer to catch a serial killer.' They speak candidly, referencing where and why the Claremont killer has chosen his dump sites. *Think*, Birnie tells Ferguson. 'If you reverse the map – turn it up the other way – the disposal sites are identical. It is a pointer to the killer's thoughts. He has turned *right* on the Stirling Highway with Jane Rimmer, zigzagged and dropped her at Wellard. Turned *left* on the highway with Ciara Glennon, zigzagged in reverse direction and dropped her at Eglinton. *Think*. What does that say about where he has disposed of Sarah?' Birnie stretches out his skinny legs, leans back in the plastic chair. 'He felt comfortable when he dumped Jane, because Sarah hasn't been found. She will be down there in the Wellard area. For sure.' But, he cautions, be careful about profiles. 'You can't afford to be complacent. If that last girl hadn't got away, no one would ever have picked that it was me. No one.'

David Birnie is a living resource that Macro cannot afford to lose. Dave Caporn will also travel to Casuarina to talk to this prisoner, trying to elicit information about the Claremont killer. Using a serial killer to catch a serial killer.

32

The first review of the Macro investigation, a month after Jane Rimmer disappeared – July 1996 – was chaired by Inspector Dick Lane, providing input regarding the future direction of the investigation and commenting on practices and media issues.

It is the start of many internal police reviews to monitor the investigation's progress, reviews that are not open to public scrutiny. With intense external pressure from the media and government, four months later, in early November, the second review, chaired by Acting Detective-Superintendent Gregson, addressed issues such as status of the inquiry, resources, public perceptions and accountability of the investigation. By mid-January 1997 another WA police review, chaired by Acting Superintendent Lavender, looked at resources and direction. Three reviews. All internally chaired. Any criticism of the amount of reviews was met with the same response; that they are standard practice. 'You wouldn't bring in an international or even national review panel in '96 or '97,' the commissioner's media adviser Neil Poh said, 'when it was all still so fresh and the investigators were ploughing through a truckload of information.' What it says, he adds, is that the senior officers who conducted those reviews – including officers senior to Dave Caporn – were tracking the course of the investigation.

But by August 1997 – four months after Ciara Glennon's body was found – a police officer from outside Western Australia is called in for the first time to chair the most extensive review to date. Now retired, then Detective-Superintendent Mike Hagan of NSW police boasted 40 years of policing experience, including 26 years in Major Crime and ten years in homicide investigations. Hagan had headed the taskforce into the so-called 'Granny Killer', the vicious psychopath who over a 12-month period bludgeoned six women to death – all but one over the age of 80 – in Sydney's North Shore between 1989 and 1990. The Granny Killer had also assaulted many more women. The murders occurred on weekdays between 3 pm and 6 pm when the frail elderly victims were walking to their homes after shopping. They were all variously attacked with a hammer and fists or strangled with their own pantyhose. Some were left in obscene, staged poses.

Psychiatric assessments of the killer, John Glover, showed the murders were ritualistic attacks, the symbolic killing of his own mother, whom he had once witnessed lying in the sexually explicit pose in which he staged his victims. Of equal importance for the Macro taskforce was that they were all carried out in the same area. Sentenced to life imprisonment, his file marked 'Never to be Released', in jail Glover copies the style of his old adversary, Hagan, sporting the same mutton-chop sideburns.

Hagan's panel reviewed nine terms of reference, including an examination of the direction and primary focuses of the taskforce and resource allocation. No bad practices were identified; the operation, the panel concluded, had utilised best practice and Caporn and his management team were totally open and honest. 'No request from the panel was refused,' Hagan wrote. 'In fact, the enthusiasm, honesty and accountability exhibited by the management team is a credit, not only to themselves but to their senior officers and the Western Australia Police Service.' Hagan's analysis of their work is constantly shown to me as proof of what Macro had done.

'I draw your attention to the following extract,' Neil Poh wrote me. '[He said that] the review conducted is without doubt the most comprehensive ever undertaken since the inception of the Macro Taskforce . . .'

Macro examines the Granny Killer's modus operandi. He acted out his fantasies in a specific area. *The North Shore.* So does their offender. *Claremont.* This doesn't mean he won't move to another metro area, but there is something in Claremont, something intrinsic to and part of his psyche; something that relates to his life, past, present or both. Something that seduces him, time and again to return to his own killing field. *Something*. But what?

33

Three times a year, the Federal Police run an intensive four-week course on the management of serious crime, using investigators from Australia and New Zealand to speak. For seven years, former Macro team leader Paul Coombes was invited back to lecture on the unique aspects of the Macro investigation. 'For all the critics of this taskforce,' he says with more than a hint of chagrin, 'there are those who continue to recognise the immense work that was done. It's not over yet.'

In 1997, internal police advertisements go out for contenders for the rank of inspector. Working on the assumption that he has runs on the board as commander of both homicide and the Macro investigation, Paul Ferguson puts his application together in between working a 13-hour shift. Other officers – including Dave Caporn – take time off work to research for the interview. That isn't an option Ferguson takes.

A short while later, in a highly unusual move, Ferguson is summoned to Deputy Commissioner Bruce Brennan's office, who discloses the results of the interview. The news is not good. Dave Caporn, then Acting Senior-Sergeant who still headed up Macro, had gained the inspector's position and was going to catapult over the top of Ferguson in rank. 'This put us in a precarious position,' Ferguson recalls. 'I was leading an investigation, but one of my officers was going to outrank me.' Brennan's solution is cut-throat. He wants a seamless transition, he tells Ferguson. He must take leave.

Devastated at losing out on the promotion and with the system's decision not to acknowledge his hard work, Ferguson refused. 'I didn't have any animosity toward Caporn,' he says. 'The feedback was that I was too specialised in the crime area. But I wasn't about to take leave when there was so much work to be done.' Others are less charitable about the reasons for Ferguson's lack of promotion. He was, they say, thrown over in the desperate bid for the West Australian Police Service – acutely embarrassed by the lack of resolution to what is now becoming a long-running and closely watched murder inquiry – to be seen to be making changes in the Macro investigation by elevating a new face on the parapet to keep the public satisfied. Ferguson, they say, is proof of the old adage that no matter what a man does in public life, in political life he is just collateral damage.

Ferguson reaches a compromise with the commissioner. He will go to Broome and overview the Sara-Lee Davey case: yet another girl who is missing, presumed murdered. Last seen driving a 4WD vehicle in Broome on 14 January 1997 around 5 pm – 13 days before Sarah Spiers vanished from Claremont – police intelligence shows that further alleged sightings of 21-year-old Davey in Darwin are incorrect. She has not touched her bank account since she disappeared.

The shifting of personnel like pieces on a chess board and the feverish, secretive activity behind Macro barricades are of no interest to the general public. They only want answers to two questions: who is the Claremont serial killer and when is Macro going to make an arrest?

And if Ferguson is disappointed at missing out on the promotion, he will be gutted at what follows, later.

Part Two:
The Dark Harvest

Tread lightly, she is near under the snow,

Speak gently, she can hear the daisies grow . . .

'Requiescat', Oscar Wilde

34

October 1997. Warm spring nights. He is trawling along Claremont's Bayview Terrace in his white Hyundai sedan. Curb crawling. Circling, trawling again. Past the Claremont Hotel, opposite the railway station. Doing a U-turn. Driving back down the street, slowly, deliberately. Following a woman, visually locking on to her, accelerating and driving past. She doesn't know she is being watched. He swings back around side streets, starts all over again. Watching. Trawling. Parking off a side street, discreetly. Pulling the car back into traffic. Watching. Up and down the street, sometimes up to 30 times a night. Watching all the beautiful young girls. These young things out so late.

Ciara Glennon's murder has turned the axis of the investigation yet again. The taskforce decide to 'walk the girls' – police-speak for turning out decoys as human bait in a controlled environment. Decoys trained to walk, talk and dress like the victims, to look like potential targets.

They had noticed him in the last week of September, when he bumbled into the police net and they started covert surveillance immediately. His ability to stalk women without being noticed is highly skilled, learned behaviour: it is obvious he has done this many times before. And he is always out and about around the same key times and days that the victims went missing; on weekends between midnight and 2 am. The same time when the offences always occurred. If he is not the offender, they reason then he is at least a chance of being a witness.

Police run a licence test on the curb crawler. Name: Lance Kenneth Williams. Forty years of age. Owns a beachside unit at Cottesloe although he more often lives with his parents in

119

the same area. Public servant with the Department of Main Roads. Lance has lost his licence twice, though regained it two days after Sarah Spiers disappeared. No licence at the time of Spiers's disappearance, but he had a car at the time.

There is the beginning of a cool nip in the night air. Williams is amazed. The chill doesn't seem to stop them. All these girls out so late at night. Young things with midriffs showing and wearing low-cut tops. Exposing way too much cleavage. Very intoxicated, some of them, weaving around the streets as though they haven't heard there is a killer out here. As if there is no danger. Perhaps they think the security cameras will save them. Ciara Glennon also disappeared just two blocks from this area only 13 months ago. Don't they read the newspapers, watch television? Still they wander along in groups, in pairs. Or on their own.

Lance Williams is always on his own. Always has been. Even through North Cottesloe Primary and Swanbourne High he was a loner. At 14, he fell off the ropes at a Scout meeting and hit his head hard on the floor. Taken to the doctor, he was treated for concussion. Very bright, particularly at maths, but that doesn't help him socialise. He joins a bank as a teller at 17, stays there until he is 28. The work suits him: separated from the public by a security grille, he doesn't have to make eye contact or even speak, beyond a perfunctory hello, to customers. He works in the bank for 11 years, and no one gives him a second glance. At 23, he suffers his first nervous breakdown. It won't be his last.

He appears nondescript, ordinary. So ordinary. Brown hair with a wavy kink cut into a severe short back and sides. Slightly protruding, doe-like eyes. Healthy pink fingernails, perfectly trimmed. Soft hands, testament to a working life spent in an office. Average height. Medium build. Mr Average.

The oldest of five children, Williams is very close to his second brother, although his relationships with his other siblings are amicable. But they don't have a lot in common. They are all married, with their own lives and have all left home. His few other friends are now married, too and they have drifted apart.

Macro uses the expertise of consultant psychiatrist Aaron Groves to assist the negotiator's unit to build up a profile of Williams. He also has another crucial role: to counsel, advise and debrief officers before they succumb to the stresses of this high-profile case.

It is now April 1998 as he cruises up and down the Claremont street as he has done for months. Lance is 41 years old. He had a crack at living on his own from late 1995, but it didn't work out. Loneliness eats at him, drives him out to the casino at all hours of the night where he wanders around and watches people gamble. It is an instant crowd. There is no point him trying to go to pubs or clubs to meet people; he is so nondescript, no one ever notices him.

Police tail him through the casino, covertly at first and later, overtly, watching him move soundlessly amongst the slot machines. He used to gamble heavily but gave it up cold turkey. No self-help groups. No Gamblers Anonymous. Cold turkey. Now if he has the itch to take a punt, he no longer indulges it. It is, police will later claim, a measure of his self-control. If he sets his mind to do something, he does it. Lance Williams, they say, possesses a remarkable degree of self-possession, self-control.

'This is the same man,' a Macro insider confides, 'who gave up smoking and alcohol as well. He used to be an extremely heavy drinker but just gave it up, cold. Same with the smokes. No crime in any of this. But what we wanted to know was, does he have a deep resentment of women and particularly women who drink because in his eyes it renders them lower-class, worthless? Who knows? But we certainly wanted to find out more about him.'

Once, following a bout of depressive self-doubt, he tried to hang himself with an occy strap. Another time, he made a feeble attempt to slash his wrists before walking down to the beach and into the cool waters of Cottesloe beach. But self-preservation kicked in; unable to go through with the suicide attempt, he returned home. His father drove him to hospital.

Police monitor his every movement. They follow him so closely. It is like living in a high-tech prison, without the gates.

Lance battles the bottle through the 1980s and halfway into the 90s, an addiction that costs him dearly. His first two drink-driving convictions – two before he is 20 – warrant small convictions, but when he racks up his third in 1984 he is not eligible to drive again until 1994. He won't bother even trying to get it back then. His drinking exacerbates the maudlin, clinical depression that hangs around him, cloying and stale. In mid-1995, one of Williams's few friends died, a traumatic event that triggered him to stop drinking and smoking. Was this, Macro insiders ask, the emotional lever that tipped him over the edge into a killing spree? Living in his own seaside unit from mid-December 1995, by June 1996 he is plagued with the black dog – depression – and admitted to a psychiatric hospital in July.

His mother, Norma, recalls that time. 'He had more pressure at work, a lot of pressure with added responsibilities, and he was on a lot of tablets, for depression and the like. He was just not very well at all, and spent most of this time sleeping in the room down the back. He had to go to hospital.' By 26 September he moves back home with his parents, where he will stay until June 1997 when he again attempts to live on his own. But this time will prove as hopeless as the last. By June 2002 he is home again, where he will stay, although he still owns the unit.

Williams's parents managed a service station in Mosman Park, six kilometres from Claremont, when he was a young boy. He worked there for a time when he was old enough, helping out at the bowsers, taking customers' money. Well-to-do customers, mostly in flash cars, and young people dressed up on their way out to party. Williams is never invited to party, but he knows the streets in the area better than any postie.

Once, at high school, he took a girl out to the movies and held her hand, but it didn't go beyond the first date. She wasn't interested, she told him and she meant it, meeting another bloke soon after. He hasn't tried to take a woman out since. His mother claims he is acutely shy, that he wouldn't know how to approach someone and strike up a conversation even if he wanted to. It is an assessment directly contradicted by police. His voice, too, is as bland as his appearance. No highs or lows, just the same dreary monotone in a river of words. He avoids eye contact when he speaks and wears a melancholy air like a cloak. He is innocuous, non-threatening.

35

With a view to building a brief, the taskforce chooses a codename for their operation: *Damocles*. The tale of a sycophantic attendant in the royal court of the Greek tyrant Dionysius, Damocles is so in awe of Dionysius's excessive wealth and happiness that the tyrant decides to teach Damocles a lesson. At a sumptuous banquet, Dionysius invites Damocles to sit in his place of honour. Entranced with the riches surrounding him, Damocles looks to the ceiling and is horrified to see that a sword, suspended by a single horse hair, is hanging over his head. Dionysius has made his point: those with position and power also face constant danger; tragedy is forestalled only by chance and can strike at any moment. For the police, the legend is a perfect symbol. The stakes are incredibly high. Two girls are dead. One is still missing. All it takes is one mistake; just one mistake. But the sword isn't hanging over Lance Williams. It is hanging over them.

Police aircraft tracks the decoys, who walk up to 15 pre-arranged routes a night, from Thursday to Sunday. The air-wing is up so frequently over the western suburbs, there are concerns that the plane's incessant drone will alert residents that something is going on. The constant use of the plane four nights a week also causes rumblings of discontent within other sections of the police. When an explosive device is found at Geraldton Hospital, Perth investigators have to find alternative transport to get them there.

The police have had him under covert surveillance for months. Tracking him as he stalks women in his car, not taking his eyes from them. Up to 30 times a night. Police know his every move, sitting off the street to his unit, waiting until he steps into his car. 'Here he goes,' they say, starting the engine and slipping in behind him.

From Thursday to Sunday night, every week, he leaves his unit at Cottesloe at precisely 11.50 pm. It is the busy time, weekends, when people are out partying. Occasionally, rarely, he is later – exactly 12.30 am – but there is never any variation in these times. They can set their watch by him. He slips into the driver's seat, straps on his seatbelt, cruises a few laps through Claremont before making his regular drive-through at Hungry Jack's takeaway. Picks up a chocolate milk, sips it slowly through a straw as he drives on to North-bridge. He always takes the same route. Curb crawling, circling, watching, throwing the empty milk container in the same roadside bin every night, every week and then return-ing to Claremont. Over and over again, up to 30 times a night. Slowly, slowly driving his car through the red-light district.

Five hostage negotiators, part of the Tactical Response Group (TRG), are placed on the team from the moment surveillance on Williams starts. Each of them detectives, their role – though not full-time – is front-line and vital. Every time the TRG slips in behind him, they sit off about a kilometre behind, primed to action if they get an encrypted radio call regarding his movements. If a suspect takes a decoy and holds her hostage – a knife to her throat, an arm around her neck – they will need to start urgent though delicate negotiations geared toward achieving a non-violent outcome and not an armed conflict. 'In any situation like this, you have to also be aware of the potential for suicide,' a former Macro negotiator says. 'If people feel trapped, they can behave in very bizarre ways. But our over-riding concern was for the decoys, to ensure they were safe at all times.'

On any given night when Williams is under surveillance, there are approximately 50 police officers working. Surveil-lance, negotiators, TRG officers, aircraft personnel. It is a massive operation.

Not everyone on the hostage team is supportive of Caporn's methods. 'The reality was that about five detectives would track other leads, but the major resources went into this hounding of Williams. No doubt his behaviour was odd and, sure, Caporn was under enormous pressure to deliver a result. But the feeling was that that pressure led him into making decisions that weren't necessarily always right. Tunnel vision geared to getting a result.'

He believes that a better tactic with Williams would have been to go undercover at his workplace to find out if he had overtly violent or sexual tendencies that spilled over with his colleagues, to befriend him and get closer to finding out what made him tick. 'That wasn't an option for Caporn,' he recalls. 'A lot of people on Macro were textbook detectives, and they wouldn't step outside that. But there were opportunities there that in my opinion most definitely should have been taken.'

Williams is driving with the window down and has spotted a young woman at the T-junction of Gugeri Street, on the corner of Bayview Terrace. She slides over to the car, flashes him an apprehensive smile as she leans slightly into the car window. 'Hi. Can you tell me where the nearest bus stop is?'

He hesitates for a fraction of a moment. When he speaks, his voice is strong but there is a hint of a stammer, an awkward shyness. 'There aren't any buses this time of night. Where are you going to?'

'Mosman Park.' Mosman Park, a ritzy suburb heading toward Fremantle, a six-minute drive from Claremont.

'Get in,' he says. 'I'll give you a lift there if you like.' She takes a sharp, surreptitious breath as she climbs into Williams's car. The air-wing is up, monitoring their movements and unmarked surveillance cars slip in behind them. She is hot-wired for any conversation but still, it's always a risk.

Williams cruises quietly out of the street and back onto the darkened Stirling Highway and steals a sideways glance at the woman sitting next to him. She is attractive. Stupid. So stupid, to get into a stranger's car while a serial killer is lurking around. She says little on the drive, listening as he makes small talk, staring ahead and crossing and uncrossing her legs. He steals another sideways glance. There's something wrong. He senses it. She is incredibly nervous.

The street where she has asked to be dropped off is just ahead. 'Just here will do, thanks,' she says, her fingers already on the door handle. It is deserted and dark; not a soul in sight. He looks at her again. She is so stupid.

'Look, I don't want to drop you off here. It's not safe.' She doesn't listen, smiles at him as she quietly gets out of his car.

'Thanks, I'll be fine,' she says again, and disappears into the shadows.

The decoy police officer flown in from interstate has done her job well. 'Shit,' she says when she gets back into the squad car parked around the corner. 'There's something very weird about him. He wasn't concerned that I was walking alone out late while there was a serial killer around. He was so detached. All he did was talk about himself the whole trip.'

They decide to take Williams out.

36

He is curb crawling again. It is two months after the decoy, 3 am in the quiet hush between midnight and dawn. Sunday morning, 5 April 1998. Williams is following a woman walking south from the Stirling Highway – the same route Ciara Glennon had taken; following her as she strides into the southern part of the Claremont suburbs, deeper into the darkened streets. He has driven past her numerous times, not braking or slowing down but accelerating out of her line of sight, doubling up around the back streets and approaching her again from the rear.

The Tactical Response Group officers watch him, their radar primed. Something is about to give.

They pounce, pointing loaded Heckler and Koch submachine guns at Williams's head. 'Stop the car! Don't move! You are under arrest!' Terror grips Williams and a warm rush of urine is soaking through his underpants, seeping through to stain his trousers.

'What have I done?' he stammers.

Officer Nello Iopolo orders him out of the car. 'Stand still. Don't move.'

Williams feels the cold nuzzle of a submachine gun at his neck as he steps from his vehicle, eight armed officers pointing guns at his head. Spread-eagled against the car bonnet, he is ashamed that the wet stain is noticeable. His face is bleached of colour. Too frightened to articulate proper sentences, he can barely stammer out a question. 'What's this about?' Surrounded by officers, saliva samples are taken from his mouth before Williams is escorted into the Beaufort Street police headquarters.

He walks past Macro team leader Stephen Brown, sitting in his office. Struck by what he will later describe as Williams's nonchalant demeanour, Brown doesn't notice that Williams has wet himself. Police would have cleaned him up, he says, if that had happened. It is part of their duty of care and not in the best interests of police for a person of interest to be uncomfortable throughout an interview.

Williams does not remember this consideration.

Detective Senior-Sergeant Paul Greenshaw and Detective Senior-Constable Peter Norrish, the liaison officer for the Rimmer family, are waiting for him in the interview room. Refusing a request to videotape the interview, for 13 hours Williams answers questions that are hammered at him. He does not have a lawyer present, even when hair samples are taken from his head.

He does not ask for one.

While Williams is at police headquarters, police execute a simultaneous rollout of their forensic teams at his beach-side unit, his parents' home and his workplace. His car is impounded. The relentless questioning continues. Known by lawyers as the 'squeeze him until he pops' method, there is one problem: he doesn't pop. Even as he is forced to rigidly sit with his hands on his knees and to look at photos of the victims that police place on his body, he doesn't pop.

The questions are relentless. What were you doing at Claremont? Why are you cruising around the streets late at night? Are you married? Have a girlfriend? Any kids? Heard of Sarah Spiers? Jane Rimmer? Ciara Glennon? Tell us again what you are doing cruising around Claremont? Relentless, on and on as dawn gives way to daytime and morning fades to afternoon. The good-cop, bad-cop routine. Cajoling him, friendly, gentle. 'Come on, Lance, why don't you just tell us where Sarah is? Get it over and done with?' He can't, he shrugs. Because he doesn't know. He didn't even have a licence when Sarah went missing. That doesn't wash, either. 'You wouldn't be the first person driving around without a licence. Try again. Did you pick up Sarah Spiers?' *No, I did not.*

The bad-cop routine, yelling at him if he is too slow answering questions, yanking his elbow if he appears to be nodding off. 'Wake up! Answer the question!' Forcing him to look at pictures of the girls. 'Don't turn your head away! Take a good, hard look!' Why is his car, a white Hyundai, in such immaculate condition inside? Why is it washed and polished outside?

Williams answers in his monotonous, dreary tone underscored with a pout. 'I like to keep my vehicle clean. I wasn't doing anything wrong last night. I was just concerned for the safety of these women who wander about at night in that area and that's why I followed them.' Why did he pick up the woman he dropped at Mosman Park? 'I didn't think there were any buses. I was simply being a good Samaritan.'

They think it's bullshit, and tell him so. 'Give us a break, Lance. We know your routines. You may as well tell us.'

Stephen Brown admits they do not trifle with suspects. 'Williams digested everything we asked him, make no mistake. He thinks of everything before he answers, and has long, long pauses before he does so. We're never fooled by stuttering or awkwardness, but we were surprised that he didn't request legal representation. If we suspect someone of murder, we'll ask the hard questions and shove it right up them until we get the answers.' But they do it, he says, within the law. He defends his former boss, Dave Caporn. 'Caporn was holding the strings for this operation and he's of the highest integrity, genteel and approachable. He takes the gentler approach, putting his hand on someone's forearm, saying "I know you did it, you can tell me," and more often than not he'll get a confession. He didn't run the Williams interview but listened to the audio and watched through the one-way mirror. There was no "bash and crash" going on behind the scenes, no offering of deals. It was straight down the line.'

Not everyone agrees. 'They should never have run that interview the way they did,' the former hostage negotiator says. 'It required the skills of a negotiator to get the best out of him, not a police officer ping-ponging questions back and forth. In the end it got them precisely nowhere. But there was no point ever trying to get Caporn to look at other alternatives. This was a huge case and he was going to run it his way. There were a lot of senior police watching for the outcome.'

Williams did not flinch throughout the interview. 'The media reckon that he would have been scared stiff, but he wasn't,' Brown says. 'He was nonchalant, cool and detached as if it was happening to someone else. Everytime we brought him in, his demeanour was cool.'

Former Sergeant Con Bayens, who would later head up 'Operation Bounty' to clear prostitutes from the nearby Northbridge area, recalls what he heard of the Williams takeout. 'Caporn was back at the ranch – police headquarters – directing the troops by mobile phone and waiting for Williams to be brought in. He was so shit-scared, apparently he just about melted into his car seat, and he promptly wet himself. Who wouldn't? Faced with that amount of police pressure and with loaded guns in your face, you'd confess to being on the grassy knoll, wouldn't you? But he didn't. He didn't confess to a bloody thing.'

The police can't win. Fighting allegations that they were under pressure to charge a person of interest because of escalating costs, the service is adamant that this is not the case. But they also have to battle sniggers from within their ranks at their choice of decoy. 'Here's this woman in her mid-30s, a brunette about 172 cm tall and with a buxom build. Well, straight up it's bloody obvious she doesn't look anything like the Claremont victims,' one snorts. 'She's too tall and too old. To quote comedian Rowan Atkinson, putting on decoys seemed like a "cunning plan". But in reality, it was more like fly fishing for trout with a brick on the end of the line.'

The Claremont investigation, Bayens says, became known outside the taskforce as the best documented and best serialised failure the Western Australian police force has ever had. 'There just seemed,' he says, 'to be a ready list of excuses for every failure.'

The police keep going, holding Williams until late afternoon before releasing him without charge. It is only the beginning. Norma recalls the last words an officer said to Lance as he left the station. 'We'll hound you, Williams. We'll hound you.'

37

Lance is late for lunch, and Norma and Jim have no idea where he is. They ring his unit but there is no answer; by 1 pm they decide to go over to see him. He isn't home. 'That's strange,' she comments to Jim, in the whining tone she uses when confronted with things outside her control. 'Where do you suppose he is?'

On her return, Norma answers her front door, squinting through the flywire at the two police officers, Detective Senior-Sergeant John Brandham and Sergeant Julie Hansley, standing on her doorstep. 'Hello, Mrs Williams. We'd like to have a talk to you about your son, Lance.' Brandham is in control; it is a demand, not a request. Norma takes up her customary stance, moving an arm across her waist and holding onto her right elbow.

'He isn't here. What's this all about?'

'He's helping with our inquiries.'

'Inquiries? What sort of inquiries? Has he been a witness to an accident or something?' Her voice is thin, plaintive and she doesn't move to open the flywire door.

'No,' Brandham replies, holding her stare. 'We believe your son to be the Claremont serial killer.'

They return that night with search warrants, six police officers with torches raking through drawers and cupboards. Norma stands back and watches in horror as their personal belongings are ransacked. 'There was nothing we could do,' she recalls. 'They had a warrant to search.' They cart away clothes and other possessions for testing, but find nothing. They also scour the now-vacant beachfront unit that had been owned by Williams. Again, nothing.

Norma, who had never had any dealings with police, is still

shaken by the turn of events. 'We were living a normal life one day and suddenly it's all turned upside down. The trouble was, Lance didn't have an alibi for the two nights that Sarah Spiers and Jane Rimmer went missing. The night Jane was murdered – 9 June 1996 – we had been out for dinner with him and he dropped us home around 9.30 pm. He was perfectly normal. Just acted perfectly normal.' Her voice has taken on its wheedling tone, etched with bewilderment. 'It was the same with the night Sarah disappeared – no alibi. But with Ciara Glennon, that was different. He was home with us all night. Most definitely home with us, all night.' Their bathroom, she says, is right next to Lance's bedroom. 'We can hear every creak. And if he had gone out in the middle of the night, we'd have heard the car start up, wouldn't we? I mean, even if he rolled it out, quietly, like the police seem to think he did, well, we'd have heard it, wouldn't we? It's right outside our bedroom window.'

Not everyone in Macro buys Norma's argument. 'I don't think anyone believes for a moment that she knows her son to be the Claremont killer and is covering for him,' Stephen Brown says. 'But don't Mums always have a sixth sense about things?'

Luke Morfesse broke the story of Williams's takeout and the fact that a 'knife' was found in his vehicle. He also detailed that the only significant item discovered during a search of his flat was a receipt, dated only days after Ciara Glennon disappeared, for detailing a car. He recalls the story not just because it was an exclusive, a great 'get' in reporting terms, but also for the way in which a Perth television news director betrayed his trust by breaking the story ahead of an agreed time. 'I made an agreement with the approval of my editor, that they could run a brief in their late news at 10.30 or 11 pm,' he says. 'The agreed proviso was that they would not run the story until after our first, country edition – which goes out at 9.30 pm – had hit the streets. But instead of waiting, they started promoting the story through the evening and ran a 15- or 20-minute special report around 9.30.' The breach caused a huge fracas. 'My wife, who was four months pregnant at the time and one of their newsreaders, was so upset she threatened to quit.'

The story ran in *The West Australian*. 'Senior police denied last night that the decision to pounce at the weekend came because of mounting pressure about the ever-increasing cost of what has become WA's biggest murder hunt,' Morfesse wrote. 'The Taskforce was told several months ago by experts that the offender may be of such a nature that he might never kill again.'

But not all of the story rang true. 'The suspect has obsessive compulsive disorder which requires medication,' Morfesse continues. 'Because of the disorder police have been unable to bug his flat. They fear he may notice the slightest change in surroundings.' Listening devices were placed inside Williams's parents' home. Given the secretive nature of the investigation and knowing Williams would read the newspaper, had police fed the media a line to throw Williams off the scent? Given deliberate misinformation?

With gritty determination, taskforce officers elucidate their opinion. The circumstantial evidence against Williams for the Claremont killings, Tony Potts says, is compelling. 'Not everyone agrees, for sure. But my personal opinion is that I can't rule him out. And I won't unless I am given good cause.'

38

Williams went to school with Julie Cutler, whose car was mysteriously found off Cottesloe Beach in 1988. Twenty-two-year-old Cutler was last seen at 12.30 am on 20 June 1988 when she left the Parmelia Hilton Hotel in Perth's CBD after a staff function. Her car was found floating two days later in the sea off Cottesloe beach. *Cottesloe*. The next suburb to Claremont. Despite extensive inquiries by police and family and comprehensive media coverage, there has been no information regarding Cutler's whereabouts since the night she disappeared. Wearing a black evening dress with a high collar and gold buttons on the shoulder, Julie was 162 cm tall, with dark brown hair and green eyes. Media reports consistently claim that police told Cutler's parents she may be the first victim of the Claremont killer, but in Macro's management meetings investigators failed to reach a conclusion on this either way. 'It's known she had two boyfriends of European extraction, and word from police is they are implicated in her disappearance,' a journalist tells me. 'Julie is definitely dead, no question. The location of her car, in the sea off Cottesloe beach – close to where Lance Williams lives with his parents – certainly went part of the way toward them building a circumstantial case against him.'

For months I try but fail to locate Cutler's parents, drawing blanks at every turn. Eventually, I call a unit in WAPS that I think may be of some assistance. The police media officer yawns and asks me to repeat the name. 'Cutler. Julie Leanne Cutler. Car found in the water off Cottesloe beach, 1988. Her body has never been found.'

He yawns again. 'Long time ago. Never heard of her.'

'The woman,' I venture, 'who police claim may have been the first victim of the Claremont serial killer.' Now I've got his attention.

'We've got heaps of missing high-profile girls on our books,' he snaps. 'Why the hell should one name stand out to me above the rest? And it's not my job to find phone numbers for journalists.'

'No, I understand. Could you just try to see whether you have a contact for them and ask them to call me?' He assures me he will look into it and call me back, either way. I never hear from him.

Lance Williams, according to police, has also driven past Pipidinny Road, where Ciara Glennon's body was found. That raises a dour laugh from Luke Morfesse. 'Look, to get to Yanchep where Williams apparently went to with his parents in 1996 for a leisurely Sunday afternoon drive, you *have* to drive past Pipidinny Road. There's no other way to get there.' Police won't confirm whether Williams has been to Wellard, but there is a protracted, pregnant silence after I ask the question.

Dave Caporn's concerns about media interference reach critical levels in April 1998 when he criticises *The West Australian* for publishing details of Macro's covert operations. It is not a criticism that sits well with then-editor Paul Murray; he had emerged from an earlier meeting with Deputy Commissioner Bruce Brennan satisfied with the manner in which the story will run, but he was equally concerned that the paper will be fitted up as a 'scapegoat' if Lance Williams slips through police nets.

How did journalists know about the Williams takeout in the first place? The leak about him being taken in for questioning, according to a longstanding police reporter, came from a copper at a suburban station. In a scribbled note to his editor, the reporter wrote, 'Taskforce chief Dave Caporn is angry about what he describes as a beat-up out of all proportion by *The West Australian* newspaper. That's HIS problem . . . we actually interviewed a suspect some time back who was pulled in by the taskforce several times, grilled for six hours, DNA swabs taken etc . . . this apparently is no different.'

Not everyone inside the police force agrees that the case against Williams is overwhelming, either. For God's sake, they mutter. Are they trying to drive this bloke to suicide? It is a fact that offenders with an organised bent follow the progress of investigations through the media. In turn, police use the media to entice suspects to react in one way or another, to make a mistake or show their hand. And the best way to get them to do that is to leak information to the press.

Fear in Perth that the killer could be a cabbie has reached hysteria levels. Drivers are randomly abused and accused of being murderers – many are spat at or assaulted. From the time Ciara disappears, there is a 40 per cent drop in the taxi trade, despondent drivers waiting outside Claremont hotels and clubs for non-existent fares. The streets are virtually deserted. With the taxi industry under intense scrutiny, the pressure is on to install video cameras in cabs. The first tender to install them is cancelled by the government, with doubts raised about the reliability of any video taken while a vehicle is in motion. After fierce debate between the taxi industry and government, digital cameras are eventually installed. But it will take a lot longer for the public to regain confidence in cab drivers. Police crank up the pressure. For the first time in an Australian criminal investigation, they augment mass testing of DNA. Their target: taxi drivers.

By Easter 1997, the city's cabbies – around 2500 drivers – are asked to voluntarily provide mouth swab samples so their DNA can be obtained. Carried out at the taxis' licensing centres, most drivers are happy to oblige, to exonerate themselves from the investigation. Some grumble that they are under suspicion simply because of the job they do, and a handful refuse to provide samples. The highly public and voluntary testing of DNA did not stop police pulling over taxi drivers who had passengers in their cabs. It caused an uproar, with female passengers rigid with fear in the back seat while police searched taxis and took the taxi drivers' samples.

The genesis for the mass testing came from within the taxi

industry itself, which established an organisation called Cabbies Against Crime. Liaising closely with the police in setting up the testing, there were agreements made before they started. The DNA extracted from the mouth swabs would be used only for the Claremont investigation, and if a suspect was found from the pool of drivers who had volunteered their DNA, the remainder of the samples would immediately be destroyed. They are still waiting for that to happen.

It worked both ways, a former officer comments. 'If they refused to cooperate, then they were immediately under suspicion for not doing so. By virtue of their occupation they need to have police checks and clearances, but it wouldn't have looked too good against their name if there was a small note, "didn't provide DNA sample in Claremont investigation".' While police do not divulge whether any DNA was found on either Jane Rimmer's or Ciara Glennon's body, how do the taxi drivers know what they have to test against – if there is anything? Dave Caporn will neither confirm nor deny the existence of DNA evidence, so it is left to forensic scientists to deduce the possibilities.

Heavy rain had fallen at both Wellard and Eglinton before the discoveries of the two bodies. Almost eight weeks of hard rain over Jane Rimmer's body, almost three weeks over Ciara Glennon's; both too long in the elements for Macro forensic investigators to lift fresh, uncontaminated crime scene samples. Retired Tasmanian forensic pathologist John Presser worked on hundreds of cases in his long career, peering down a microscope to find the slightest trace of tell-tale evidence from a dead body, clothing or hair. Any blood traces the killer left behind on either girl's body would have been washed away, he believes. 'DNA is very fragile. Blood only lasts about a day if it is exposed to the elements, either rain or sun. The only way to stop rapid deterioration is if the DNA samples are frozen or dried. Semen will deteriorate quickly as well if it is on the body, but in the vagina – the body's natural cavity – it will last longer. The UV rays in sunlight destroy DNA, as do bacteria, so the chances of the girls having anything left on their bodies when they have been exposed to both heat and water is fairly remote.'

Civil libertarian Terry O'Gorman calls the mass taking of DNA from the Perth taxi drivers nothing more than an exercise in hype. 'On the information that's been publicly revealed, there's a very strong suspicion that there is no scene DNA; that is, there's no DNA left at the scene of the crime against which samples that are collected from the target, or from various cabbies, can be tested. Now if that's the case, then the whole DNA-gathering exercise has no criminal investigation value and is simply an exercise in hype whose end result again causes significant difficulties, either for the particular target who has been the subject of extraordinary police dubious practices or for some other person who's eventually charged.'

Using the dark humour for which journalists are well known, reporters knee-deep in the Claremont story let off steam in the sanctity of their newsrooms. 'After the cabbies gave DNA, we wanted to run a tongue-in-cheek piece,' Rex Haw remembers. 'We would have started it, in ponderous, dramatic tone like they start current affairs programs: "But first tonight – a public apology to all those hard-working, decent taxi drivers out there who keep being spat at, kicked and generally abused just for doing their job . . ."'

On another occasion, at a tense press conference, unbeknown to a senior officer, a bird flying overhead left a dropping on his coat shoulder, near his other pips. Haw kept a straight face. 'I understand you've been decorated today, Sir?' he quipped.

39

The use of DNA testing of taxi drivers is not the only means that Macro employs to try to track the killer. But if DNA was regarded as potentially of no value in the investigation because science most probably had nothing to compare the victims with the killer, the decision to use a polygraph (lie-detector) test for the first time in an Australian criminal case was seen by many as completely unorthodox and outrageous.

The polygraph test examiner police use – twice – is Ron Homer from Polygraph and Investigation Service, California. Flown to Australia for the first time in late August 1997, using money provided by the Secure Community Foundation, Homer tests 50 people. Six pass. Six fail. The rest give uncertain results. Four refuse outright to undertake the test.

Ron Homer does not respond to an email I send him to answer some questions about the test. I want to ask him if it was true, as told to me by various sources, that he told Macro officers it was his opinion that of the men who failed, one or more of those six was definitely responsible for the Claremont killings?

The methodology if a person passes or fails the test in Australia is vastly different from that in the United States. There, if a suspect fails the test, pressure is applied in the hope a confession is forthcoming. In Australia, once someone is tested, the result is handed to the police. 'In Australia,' a polygrapher said, 'it's like doing bits of the job with your hands tied behind your back.'

The average test takes about three hours to conduct and questions are divided into three main categories. First, the irrelevant questions with obvious answers: Is today Monday? Do you live in Victoria? The second set of questions are relevant – the questions which get to the crux of the issue. Did you shoot John? Did you take that money? These questions have to be succinct, unambiguous and carefully phrased. The examiner cannot ask, did you *murder* John? Because the person being tested will then think the tester has already made up his mind as to his innocence or guilt which can, in turn, affect the test result. The third type of question is the comparison, the one which gives the examiner a baseline to work from. Gavin Wilson, examiner for Australian Polygraph Services, says they don't give examples of what sort of questions these are. 'I imagine the type of questions that Ron Homer would have asked the suspects would be something like, "Did you have any involvement in the disappearance of . . . ?" or "Did you cause the death of . . . ?" He wouldn't have asked them if he had murdered the girls or if he knew where their bodies were. There are reasons for that: If he had an accomplice, that person may have disposed of the bodies in a place unknown to the suspect.'

Examining blood pressure, perspiration and respiration, critics claim that it is all too easy for people who should fail the test to pass it instead. Highly confident individuals, unmitigated liars and those with a psychopathic bent are particularly adept at beating the test; devoid of any feelings of guilt, psychopaths can fool the machine. Low responses to anxiety coupled with a lack of moral normalcy can ensure their physical responses are not an accurate representation of their guilt or innocence. And of much more importance, unlike many states in the US, polygraph evidence is not admissible in any Australian court of law.

Homer made his opinion public. It is a myth, he says, that psychopaths can't be tested. If someone cares about lying, they will get caught. Regardless of how adept they are in concealing their lies, the machine, based on the fear of telling a lie, will detect it.

In August 1998 Homer returns to Australia for one specific purpose: to test Lance Williams, who volunteers to take the polygraph. He fails the test, resoundingly. Somehow, the results are leaked to the press.

On Friday 31 August 1998, the ABC carries a story that police have a suspect in the Claremont killings under surveillance – and that he has failed a lie-detector test. Suddenly, the unwritten rules for the press to tread carefully are discarded. All bets in the media are off.

There is a not-so-subtle shift in Williams's rating following the results of the polygraph test becoming public knowledge. With media interest at fever pitch, journalists are summoned to a media conference at the police headquarters conference room. Dave Caporn is clearly not happy, peering through his glasses at reporters and berating them for the loose and irresponsible manner in which they are reporting Macro operations. A journalist queries whether Williams had failed the polygraph. Caporn glowers, responding he does not intend to release that information. But what he does give them is dynamite. For the first time since the inception of the Macro taskforce, he elevates Williams's status from a 'person of interest' to a 'suspect' – a shift that is immediately pounced on by the voracious press. Schooled by Macro over the years to use the term 'person of interest' instead of 'suspect', the change is startling. Deliberate or intentional? Caporn will not say.

Williams stumbles into a sea of reporters as he leaves work, squinting as the cameras' flashlights go off in his face. Network Ten's news manager, Chris Hunt, putting his five o'clock news bulletin to air, takes a call about which he needs to make split-second decisions. The prime suspect for the Claremont serial killing is in a media throng and talking. Hunt pounces on his lawyers, who advise him what to do. Identify him, they say. He hasn't been charged, so it's not sub judice, no one has warned that he is about to be charged and he is innocent until proven guilty. Identify him.

Leading the charge is Channel 9 reporter Judy Allen, who barks out the questions. 'Are you the serial killer?'

'No.'

'Are you innocent?'

'Yes.'

'How has this surveillance affected you?'

'It's been very distressing to me and my family.'

Williams avoids making eye contact with the reporters, casting an occasional sideways glance when the questions are persistent.

Hammering out the questions. How does this attention make you feel? How long have you been aware that you've been followed? And the question of the lie-detector test. 'Lance, it appears now that you've failed the polygraph test, can you tell us why?'

He is surrounded by reporters, can't avoid answering. His voice is low. 'Well, that was a very disturbing thing to me, because I'm the one that suggested I take that test initially, because I'd heard that other people they were investigating had taken it last year, and you know, I had no reason not to take it.'

They won't let up. 'Lance, I'll ask you again, because it's what everyone will want to know: are you the serial killer?'

'No, I'm not. No. I mean I went in voluntarily to do a test at the police station. I mean I was under no obligation to. I just wanted to, because the police were parked over across from my parents' house on weekends and, you know, sort of waiting for me at work and that, I just thought, "Well I'll just go in there, do the test", because I had nothing to hide, you know.'

The story leads all the news bulletins in Perth that night. All but Channel Ten – with more than 200,000 viewers – choose to hide his face with pixellation and to not specifically identify him. It is a decision that Chris Hunt long remembers. Lawyers scream that Williams has been hung by both police and press; callers bombard the Channel Ten switchboard with messages of outrage that he should be identified and his possible guilt prejudged. Hunt stands his ground. It is the other media outlets, he says, who have presumed his guilt by hiding his face. 'Look, the man voluntarily approached the cameras,' he told the *Bulletin*. 'We didn't pursue him down an alleyway, point the cameras and say "He's your man." That would have been scurrilous . . . It was put to him several times that he'd be identified, and it was not an issue. If he had asked for his identity to be suppressed, we would have done it.'

Lance Williams has failed a lie-detector test and Dave Caporn has promoted him from a 'person of interest' to prime suspect. And now all Perth knows it.

40

Police point out to me that since Williams has been under surveillance, there has not been another victim taken by the serial killer. 'This supports an undeniable inference,' Tony Potts says. 'Because he knows there has been such a high level of police scrutiny, his sense of self-preservation may have overridden any other desire or urge. The bottom line is that the circumstantial evidence gathered against him is so compelling that it would be virtually impossible for police to turn away and disregard him.'

Asked by Gerald Tooth on the ABC's *Background Briefing* about how the results found their way into the media's hands, Dave Caporn is defensive, vehemently denying the police had deliberately leaked the results. 'It was certainly not in our interests, either for tactic or judicially sound, or ethically sound, for us to do that, and there was no win in it for us,' he said. 'I mean I think when you put the facts on the table, no one could legitimately make a case as to why we would do that . . .' To other media, Caporn was equally as adamant. Police have never released this person's name, he said. It is the media that have broadcast it and Williams who has played to them. It appears, one officer remarks, to be a case of the 'four Ps'. Police Playing Pontius Pilate. Washing their hands of any dirt.

So the question remains: How, if police did not leak the information, did it find its way into the public domain? Why that one particular piece of information, when so much else has been kept secret? And why hasn't the leak been investigated?

Gerald Tooth was told by the program's researcher, Sue Short, that police sources from outside the Macro task-force had led her to the lie-detector test scoop. 'When she approached Macro to confirm the details, she was not discouraged from broadcasting them,' he said. 'The story was engendering its own head of steam.' Tooth recalls that Caporn was supremely confident when he went in to do the interview for the story. 'He perceived that it would be beneficial for the police. But when the interview tack changed, when it was perhaps obvious that it wasn't all positive, so did his attitude. He became very defensive.'

Luke Morfesse at *The West Australian* next picked up the story about Lance Williams failing the polygraph test. His source? The WA police. 'It may have suited the taskforce, or some people in it, that ABCTV had broadcast that the suspect had failed a lie-detector test,' he recalls. 'But I know we were contacted and told about the story, alerted that it could be in our interest to pursue it. We are the local newspaper with a big audience.'

Tooth heard that Sue Short was unhappy with the story, but that no one understood why. I call her to ask about that and to confirm with her the details about how she came to the story in the first place. She is brisk in her response. 'I don't want to discuss it with you.'

'Oh?' Her brusqueness has caught me off guard. 'Is there a reason for that, Sue?'

'Yes, there is,' she replies. 'But I don't want to discuss that with you, either. Goodbye.' She hangs up immediately and I stare at the phone in my hand, speechless. Are Perth journalists, operating in a small city, too scared to speak out unless their police sources dry up? What *is* it about this Claremont story? Tooth, based in the ABC's Queensland office, is preparing to leave the broadcaster for a stint at another job when I call him again. Can he shed some light on why Sue Short may have been so, well . . . short?

'Journalists too, now, eh?' Tooth says. 'It doesn't really surprise me. A lot of people are on edge about this whole case. Take the police. If you're even slightly challenging of anything police have done, you're on the outer. The trouble is, a lot of money has been spent and a lot of people have made a lot of proclamations, but there have been no results. And that's not good for business.'

Williams is unequivocal about why he failed the test. 'I was asked a direct question, about whether I'd ever deliberately hurt someone, and I thought about my answer, about the fights I had with my brother when I was younger,' he tells me later when I contact him by phone. 'That went against me.'

I think of another story, in which a prime murder suspect in another Australian murder case dismally failed a polygraph test. I wanted to run the results on a documentary television program and checked with the investigator at Major Crime. 'You can do what you like,' he advised me. 'But I would ask that you don't. If we get this case to trial, we don't need it falling over because the program has tainted the jurors' minds. The defence would have a field day with that.' I chose not to use it.

But what about the Claremont case? With Williams's name in the public arena, what sort of fair trial would *he* receive in Perth if he was ever to be charged? According to civil libertarians and lawyers, not much of a one. 'Good luck finding a juror who was living in Perth during this time to forget all the publicity against this suspect,' Terry O'Gorman snorts. 'The whole thing is an outrage. Despite what you see on television, lie-detector tests are not infallible. It should be an offence for any media outlet anywhere to publicly identify someone unless and until they are charged. It's a cynical exercise in police planting information with compliant reporters who run their story.'

Director of Public Prosecutions Robert Cock says he can't imagine a situation in which the results of a test – not admissible in court proceedings – could ever be justified. Stung by the criticism, Caporn sticks to his guns. Police have never released that result, he repeats. And police never *would* release that result. If the media put two and two together, he adds, they can't do anything about that. So the question remains inadequately answered. If police didn't release the test results, who did?

Tony Potts insists that it was Williams, playing to the press, who brought the publicity on himself. 'Make no mistake,' he tells me. 'If we had found one piece of physical evidence linking him to the murders – a hair, the girls' jewellery, anything – he'd have been charged.' He is defiant. 'You may think the Claremont case is unsolved. In my opinion – and the opinion of many other people on that taskforce – it's not. We are simply lacking that one piece of evidence that would allow a charge to stack up in court. That one precious piece of evidence.'

Cock says he would be 'extremely nervous' about his capacity as a public prosecutor to bring Lance Williams to trial if police charged him. He is aghast at the way Williams has been publicly outed. 'A judge could simply pull a trial up because of the intense pre-trial publicity he has endured. It's a fundamental principle that judges do direct juries properly, but no direction, however clear, would allow a jury, for example, to disregard the knowledge that Williams failed that lie-detector test.' But while a result is lacking in the Claremont investigation, Cock doesn't subscribe to the view that hard-nosed detectives are necessarily biased. 'The reality is, without men of Caporn's enthusiasm and intelligence, it would be a lesser investigation. It simply requires, like all investigations, decent checks and balances.'

41

The Williams's Californian bungalow house in the ritzy bayside area of Cottesloe is shielded from the street by a tall fence and greenery. The house is now a ghoulish tourist attraction, people slowing down as they drive past and pointing. I have decided that, instead of taking my chances with another telephone interview, I will go to the house on the off-chance of finding someone home. The gate is closed but not locked and I warily open it and walk through. A leaf flies past me, airborne on the slight breeze and I jump in fright, dropping my notebook. Berating myself for being ridiculous, I realise I am nervous. The gate has clicked shut behind me and I am alone in the courtyard. My fight-or-flight adrenaline has kicked in and I need to make a fast decision whether to continue or turn back. I take a long, deep breath and stride to the front door.

Norma Williams answers my knock and peers at me through the locked flywire screen. Her face, denuded of makeup, has the exhausted, washed-out look of the hunted. She shakes her head when I tell her what I want. No, she will not talk to me, she says. No, her son won't either. I think she will close the door in my face.

Petite with light grey hair, Norma is dressed neatly in a denim skirt and a muted coloured shirt in geometric patterns. Her voice has a martyred air, her words cushioned in a sigh. Her soft voice rises and falls with the hint of a mewl and frequently trails off, leaving sentences unfinished. 'Oh well . . . You know . . .' The dark, wide passageway behind her shoulder is spotlessly clean, but a faint, musky smell wafts toward me, as though the home needs to be aired. It strikes me as a fortress, in which the family hole up against the world, Norma the guard of the palace. I shuffle in the intense February heat, silently willing her to invite me inside. She doesn't. Instead, she holds court from behind the door while I am condemned to stand in the 35-degree furnace for more than an hour.

There is someone else inside the house, though I neither see nor hear him. Norma's husband, Jim, sequestered from prying eyes, is watching television in the room off the hallway. I recall a story a Perth journalist told me of the day he attempted an interview with Norma. 'Her husband is significantly taller than she is – a giant in comparison – and after I spoke to her for a minute or so, Jim appeared at the doorway. "He is known to be a nice bloke, and he was simply trying to defend his family. I don't want you coming 'round here upsetting us anymore," he said. The reporter thought Norma would close the door on him, but the opposite happened. "Go away, Jim," she ordered her husband. "Go back in the lounge room." So this big man slunk off, just as he was told to do.'

Norma and Jim have long since celebrated their 50th wedding anniversary, and she smiles when she mentions his name. 'He's a gentle, gentle man,' she says. Jim had a stroke some years back and doesn't deal with the media. He is the invisible partner. I peer back at this 74-year-old woman and reflect on what a police officer said to me. 'Met the mother yet, have you? Don't be fooled by appearances. She is a real control freak.'

'Mrs Williams,' I start. 'People say you are very controlling of your family. Is that true?' She looks startled, as though I have verbally slapped her.

'No, it is not!' she replies, more hurt than indignant. 'I have never tried to run my children's lives. People who know me well say I've always been too soft with them. Lance comes and goes as he pleases. Who said this? The police?' She sighs. 'They just think they can say anything they like.'

Fed up with the constant carping from the media questioning why Williams became – and remains – their prime suspect, a former senior Macro insider decides to disclose to me previously unknown, intimate features regarding Williams's behaviour. 'We had him under constant surveillance, so much that we knew his every move, day and night. What we saw often wasn't pretty, but everything is documented in the police files. Everything.' He pauses, weighing up whether to continue. 'We didn't just target him because we could,' he says. 'It's all fact, and if and when there is an inquest it will be revealed.' According to psychiatrists and profilers, he says, Williams was a 'square peg in a square hole' for the murders. 'The fact is, he wasn't nominated by an outsider. It was his behaviour that put him on a collision course with us. It is quite possible that he has murdered these girls. He may not have, but we cannot eliminate him.'

He has, he discloses, been involved in 'very serious and extreme acts of violence' in the past. 'I can't tell you what it is and he wasn't charged for it, but we saw everything in his background to support our suspicions about him and the benefit of the world's leading psychiatric minds back up our beliefs.'

They know his routines. The incessant driving and watching, the odd behaviour. They follow him as he goes to prostitutes, spending up to $300 a time, sometimes three times a day, and they talk to the girls in the brothels. They always remember this client. He jokes with them, they say. He's childlike, boyish, with an insatiable sexual appetite.

'This is not the single, naïve boy the press presents him as,' the insider tells me. 'He is absolutely and utterly preoccupied with sex and with following women.' He takes the prostitutes presents, wrapping them in hand towels when he has finished his mandatory shower, laughing, joking, daring them to find the small gifts. Never intercourse, only hand relief, sometimes satisfactory, sometimes not. He returns, often to the same prostitute, forming a bizarre bond with them. He tracks one, with the pseudonym 'Angel', down at home where she lives with her parents, who have no idea what line of work she is in. He knocks on her door and she demands to know how he got her address, tells him to piss off and leave her alone before she slams the door in his face.

The police don't know how he found her, either. 'Maybe he tracked her through her number plates, or perhaps he followed her home one night. Who knows? The point is, she didn't welcome his advances.' My next questions are obvious, and he pre-empts them before I ask. 'Yes, the girls did look similar to the Claremont victims, and, yes, they did know who he was after we started overt surveillance. They saw him on television.'

But what if police have got it wrong? *What if they have got it wrong?* Police have heard this question before. 'All the indicators are, from our surveillance, that we were right to keep on his wheel. All the indicators.'

They track down the former girlfriend that Lance took to the movies when he was 16 years old. She is in her 40s now, and is startled that police are interested in talking to her. 'Tell us about your relationship with him,' they ask and she laughs, outright.

'Relationship? What relationship! We went to the movies once and held hands, that's all. I met someone else straight afterwards.' The police look at each other. This is a far cry from the story Lance has given them, of being in love with his teenage sweetheart, the love of his life who dumped him and broke his heart. 'We took the story to world-renowned psychiatrists who said it's the classic case of unrequited love, with fantasy and rejection. There hasn't been a girlfriend since.'

An electronic bug placed inside the Williams's home picked up the subtle nuances in the house. 'Issues were shoved under the carpet,' he says. 'After we went overt in our surveillance, and would knock on their door asking more questions, the family would act as if nothing had happened after we left. Saathoff, a leading criminal psychiatrist, analysed what we picked up in that house. He commented that the relationship between Mum, Dad and Lance is like a three-legged stool. Take a leg away, the unit falls over. They are so symbiotic, they start and finish each other's sentences.'

Lance is treated like a 14-year-old in the household. On one occasion the bug picks up an argument between Lance and his mother. It is a trifling matter over what to have for dinner: beef or lamb? Lance loses the argument and is sent to bed.

Norma sighs again when I ask her if the story is true, if Lance is female emasculated. 'Oh, there are so many stories. So many.' She appears bewildered by the whole situation, as though nothing will ever surprise her again. 'When Lance was recuperating from a depressive bout, he took some cooking lessons at rehab. I may have suggested he try things a different way and he may not have liked that. He can be moody, difficult nowadays since this whole business started. He gets into arguments easily. But I wouldn't have sent him to bed. He would have just gone, himself, maybe in a temper.'

His temper. It peppers Norma's conversation, the sudden explosive flashes of anger that ignite without warning. She admits that Lance's mood swings can be hard to live with. 'Most people would tell him to get out, I suppose,' she sighs. 'But, oh well, you know. He's our son.' There is an edgy weariness in her voice, as though she is tired of tiptoeing around her own home for fear of triggering an explosion from his temper.

'You know,' she adds, almost as an afterthought, 'Lance wasn't like this before. It's only since they've been hounding him. The police have got a lot to answer for.'

Many psychologists believe that serial killers have often suffered a trauma to the head in their childhood. I ask Norma about the severity of the blow to the head when he was 14. She thinks about it for a second. 'It was nothing major. Not serious. But yes, he hit his head.' She shifts on to another foot. 'I'd better go, now,' she says, but makes no attempt to move. Virtually imprisoned in their own home, perhaps talking to a stranger – even a stranger who is a journalist – can break the endless monotony.

It wasn't just Lance who was under surveillance. When

Norma or Jim had to leave the house, they were recognised by the public. 'It was just terrible,' she says, her eyes panning past me to the gate as though someone might suddenly walk through, uninvited. 'Terrible. The police were getting around here of a night-time, sort of sneaky. I think they've probably gone now, but how would we know? They still could be around the place. They could be anywhere.'

They were. In the ceiling cavity above Williams's desk at work, police secreted covert surveillance equipment. But it wasn't as secretive as they planned. Without warning, the monitoring equipment, the size of a mobile phone, fell out of the ceiling, hanging by a thread above his desk. His work-mates watched in alarm as it fell out, but Williams didn't. 'He didn't bat an eyelid,' Stephen Brown says. 'He looked up, looked down and then went back to his work.' The camera also picked up something else: Williams working at his L-shaped desk, turning every so often to re-stack a pile of A4 papers. He counts and stacks, then counts and re-stacks, over and over again. Moulds them to shape so they are perfectly square, and then does it again. An obsessive-compulsive ritual.

Macro officers also talk covertly to some of Williams's female workmates. 'This was prior to him being named as a suspect,' Brown says. 'They told us that he can fly off the handle so fast that they have no warning it is coming. They have been known to ask supervisors not to be left alone with him to lock up the office or to be left alone in the room with him. He has the most mundane processing job in the Western Australian government: stamping permits. No stress – yet he explodes to anger for no reason.'

42

Using funds partly provided by the Secure Community Foundation, in mid-1998, Dave Caporn and Detective-Sergeant Paul Zanetti travel to the United States to meet with Park Dietz, recognised as the world's foremost forensic psychiatrist. Following a two-day review of Macro, Dietz tells Caporn he could not come up with a strategy that hasn't already been tried, apart from a polygraph test. But he does offer one possible, but very unpalatable, solution. 'To solve Claremont,' he says, 'you need another offence.' With already intense pressure from the media, internal police and politicians, that is the last thing they want. Dietz, unable to travel to Australia because of a back problem, recommends Macro consult with criminal psychiatrist Dr Gregory Saathoff, who comes to Perth for the first time in 1999. Impressed with the Macro taskforce's strategies, Saathoff leaves them with an enigmatic message. Referring to the suspects and investigation, he says, 'When this case is solved, it will be the case study of all case studies.'

Following separate reviews in the US by Dr Park Dietz, and then Dr Janet Warren, Associate Professor of Psychiatric Medicine at the University of Virginia and liaison to the Behavioral Sciences Unit of the FBI, FBI criminal profiler Greg McCrary and retired Lieutenant Eddie Grant undertook yet another paper-based review. McCrary had forged a reputation as the profiler who spoke directly on television in 1992 to the unknown person who had abducted, raped and murdered 15-year-old student Kristen French. 'If you are watching,' he said, 'I want to tell you that you are going to be apprehended.' The killer's family, he warned, were in danger and particularly his accomplice and wife. McCrary's strategy worked. Seven months later the killer's wife – who *was* his accomplice – went to police with details of two murders and a series of rapes for which her husband was subsequently convicted. These reviews were a part of the process of casting a critical and independent eye over different areas of the investigation, but important as they were they did not achieve results. Robin Napper, a former high-ranking officer in the British police now living in Perth, was not surprised. 'What a waste of time giving bits and pieces of the case to different people. By 1998, it was already cold. They needed to push it along.'

The reviews continue. In 1999, Macro calls on the expertise of Detective-Inspector Chuck Burton – the Derbyshire designer of the 'CATCHEM' Database in the UK, used to assist with the investigation of child murders. This is now the eighth review. With the definition of 'child' as a female victim under the age of 22 years at the time of death, the database analyses common elements relating to modus operandi of offenders and compares the psychological traits of the people who have been arrested. It also uses an index to predict matching ages of offender and victim. This review, concluded in consultation with other forensic experts, provided advice to the taskforce on aspects of offender profile and likely behaviour that may be exhibited by the killer. This is the first time that Macro has utilised the combined resources of a scientific database and experienced police officers. Still, the results are negative.

MP and former police counsel John Quigley rues that coppers who worked in the 'old-fashioned' way are no longer able to use those skills. 'By "old-fashioned" I mean they didn't have computer profiling; all they had to rely on was intuition and nous. In the practice of criminal law, you can be a great technician but unless you've got the intuition and nous, you're not going anywhere. It's the same with police. Everyone needs a mentor, and where are they today for these young detectives? Where are all the experienced murder investigators?' Falconer, he says, was known to have little time for the CIB. 'They were strange days, indeed. Falconer himself ended up on a criminal charge of breaking secrecy provisions of the police force. He was charged and committed for trial but the DPP stepped in and stopped it.' At one stage, Quigley says that he spent so much time in court defending cops from their own that he hardly ever saw daylight. 'All this litigation was happening in a blaze of publicity, but the damage to morale was incalculable.'

What investigations like Claremont need, according to Quigley, is the old-style detective work. 'Take a former copper like Peter Coombes, for example. He had been involved in that many investigations, including tracking around Australia to find a bloke that no other cop had been able to locate: the Fox, otherwise known as Bruno Romeo. The Fox had leased up to a dozen cattle stations around Australia where he was growing marijuana crops. Romeo had dug out an underground camouflage area and covered it with netting so it couldn't be seen from the air. His wife was in the caravan preparing a Sunday roast when Romeo felt the barrel of cold steel under his left ear and heard Coombes's dulcet tones. "Bruno Romeo – my name is Peter Coombes. You're mine."' Quigley chuckles. 'Not bad, eh? In my opinion he's one of the best investigators in Australia, but he was driven out of the police force during this mad time that resembled the Salem witch hunts and was reduced to laying limestone blocks in landscape gardening, wasting his talents.'

Another investigator who was driven out of the force by Falconer started off an international security company, doing corporate investigations for overseas corporations operating in areas where there is an insufficient police force. 'A South African mining company thought they were being massively ripped off by their executives and called his company. Coombes did the whole presentation in the boardroom, just as he would have for the Western Australian police and they got the blokes. So he's not good enough for the Western Australian force, but he's good enough internationally. This is the calibre of people that Falconer got rid of. But I tell you: if

I wanted anyone to look at Macro, I'd go straight to blokes like Peter Coombes. No risk.'

Quigley ribbed Falconer in the press, particularly after he had successfully defended police officers in court. After one monumental battle – which Quigley won – and a celebratory bottle of wine, he banged out an email to the editor of *The West Australian*. 'I must have pressed the send button,' he grins, 'for the next day there was a picture in the paper with a cartoon attached of the police commissioner with a ten-gallon hat over his head. It read something like, "Methinks the midget sheriff has got a hat too big for his head and it's falling over his eyes and ears, he's lost sight of the posse and the bandits have ridden into town and taken over." Detectives blew the cartoon up and stuck it all over the lifts and walls in the police building.'

Falconer admitted, just before he left the job, that he was disquieted about the fact that the Claremont murders remained unsolved. And they would stay that way, he warned, without fresh new evidence.

In June 1999, there is a change of policing leadership, with New Zealander Barry Matthews becoming the state's first commissioner appointed from overseas since 1867. The deputy commissioner in his native country, Matthews stayed with the police force after being admitted as a barrister and solicitor. But despite his academic qualifications, his appointment to the highest police position in WA was not welcomed in all quarters. Bringing to the office what his supporters called a spirit of reform and his critics called the 'cut and slash years', his time in the chair would be marked by controversy and battle royales with government which were gleefully related by the press.

Beleaguered by claims that he had a combative and turbulent professional relationship with Police Minister Michelle Roberts, under his stewardship taskforces came to replace the specialist squads that had dealt with homicides and missing people. Commissioned staff were offered early retirement, a salve for the problem identified as a pyramid top-heavy with management. More than 90 police above the rank of inspector left the force, but detective numbers were not boosted. This, according to its many critics, left a dearth of experience and saw the meteoric rise of inexperienced, younger officers.

But the most important event on Matthews's watch was the Royal Commission into police corruption that delivered its findings in early 2004. They were explosive, and less than flattering. Then came the Argyle Diamond investigation.

'Police looked at allegations that millions of dollars had been stolen out of Argyle,' Quigley says. 'Matthews is in the chair and who do they appoint to do the review of Argyle? Bob Falconer's private investigative firm in Melbourne that he started after he retired: FBIS. Argyle had happened while he had been commissioner, and now he's got the job of reviewing it all! During this process, all the dinkum, highly experienced investigators are thinking, this police force is going to mud; soon they won't be able to find their own shoelaces! They started leaving in droves, and they left behind no mentors in place for the younger coppers.'

In 1999 a police stake-out of Williams's home goes embarrassingly awry. A scout hall opposite his parents' home was the base for the surveillance team, who used the premises 24-hours a day to keep Williams under tight watch. But the squad used something else, as well. The toilet. At a regular council meeting an incensed ratepayer, unaware of the supposedly covert operation, rose to complain that police were refusing to foot the water bill at the scout hall. The complaint was picked up by a reporter from the *Post*, who dutifully ran the piece. Now exposed, the police shed their covert approach and became overt in their around-the-clock surveillance. Regardless of where Williams goes, plain-clothed police in unmarked vehicles tail him.

'He had to catch a bus one day and they jumped on that to follow him,' Bret Christian recalls. 'They were chasing Williams, and the media were chasing the police. It was like

something out of Keystone Cops, but with a marked difference. At its heart, this story is about murdered young women.
And there is nothing funny about that.'

Shortly after, the taskforce is again the butt of jibes when
Williams's parents' home is burgled in broad daylight. The
burglar, disturbed by an elderly neighbour, does not steal
anything, but police are forced to defend themselves against
biting criticism.

'You'd have to ask,' a reporter laughs, 'that if they can't
manage to keep a burglar out while Williams is under surveillance, how are they supposed to find the Claremont killer?'
Williams, police respond, was not in the house when the
break-in occurred.

43

Norma Williams has given me Lance's direct work phone number but cautions me about how he may receive the call. 'He's so sick of this whole thing,' she sighs.

He certainly is. He answers the phone immediately in a curt, no-nonsense tone. 'Lance Williams.' It is a strong voice, much stronger than the one used in his doorstop with journalists, and underpinned with more than a hint of irritation. I introduce myself, but sense that getting him to talk is going to be a challenge. Surrounded by a few loyal workmates, they advise him to hang up from the moment he takes my call. I have to speak fast, before he heeds their advice. The press has not exactly been kind to him; a headline in *The West Australian* pointedly asked in July 1999 whether he was 'Public Servant or Public Enemy?' So beleaguered was he by the constant police presence following him day and night, that he would call police himself if he was going anywhere out of the ordinary.

'Lance, why didn't you have a lawyer present the night you were taken into the police station?' I had been told he is acutely shy but instantly I sense abrasiveness in his tone. Not just the wariness of a hunted man dealing with an unsolicited call from a journalist, but an aggression, a tacit warning to me to back off, a warning that he could explode at any moment. He repeats the question, threading his way through his sentences with intricate caution. 'Why didn't I have a lawyer present? I don't remember them even offering me a lawyer.'

'And have you had legal advice since?'

'I saw a solicitor once, but the cost is prohibitive. Look, I am not going to see a solicitor – ever – and I don't talk to the press.'

I plug on, quickly. 'What about your alibi for the night all three girls went missing? Do you have one?' There is a deep sigh on the end of the line. 'I was home the night Ciara Glennon went missing and when the other two girls disappeared.' That is not exactly what Norma told me. No alibi, she said. Lance had no alibi for those two nights.

'How come your car is in such perfect condition?'

'Oh, the police reckon I cleaned it because I needed to, that I had had something in there, but that's not right. Detailing the car was part of my warranty offer. I could have opted for tinted windows, whatever, but I took detailing instead.'

'And the rumour that before you got your licence back – the timing of which would have made it impossible to abduct Sarah Spiers – you hired a car? Did you?'

'Not true. The only time I've ever hired a car is in Penang with my parents in 1980. And as if I'd suddenly start driving again after all those years and then murder somebody.'

I can hear the incessant whispers of his workmates. 'Hang up, Lance. Hang up.' He is clearly becoming agitated.

'Look, I'm at work and there are people wandering around. I'm tired of all this.' His voice has risen, as though he will suddenly start shouting. 'All this nonsense. Like, they reckon there was a knife in my car; it was a fingernail cleaner on my key ring. I want to try and put it behind me. How would you feel if it was you? How would you feel if you had eight guns shoved in your face?'

'I would be terrified,' I admit to him. 'I wouldn't like it at all.'

I want to ask him a very sensitive, personal question and have little time in which to do it. As much as anything, I want to check the veracity of the police report. 'Lance, sorry to ask you this, but I have a reason. I am told you wet yourself when police pulled you over. Is that right?'

Now he is clearly aggravated, a mercurial swing from the relatively calm person who had answered the phone. 'What do you think! How would you react? I was terrified!' His exit from the call is swift. 'I'm hanging up. Right now.'

The line goes dead.

***

Williams sounds so aggrieved I am reminded of the cele-brated case of Richard Jewell, the former security guard finally exonerated of involvement in the July 1996 bombing at an Atlanta park during the Olympics, in which 100 people were injured and two killed. Hailed first as a hero for noticing a backpack in a city park and clearing the area before a pipe bomb exploded, within days Jewell's status had changed. Hounded as a suspect after his name was leaked to the media, he was under overt surveillance for 88 days but never charged. Jewell, who lived with his mother, endured house raids, inces-sant media interest and FBI profilers 'matching' him to fit the characteristics of a bomber. But there was one problem: despite their best efforts, the FBI could not produce one skerrick of evidence to prove he was guilty. His reputation in tatters, an often tearful Jewell made a televised criticism of how his case was handled after the US District Attorney's office cleared him of all involvement. The FBI 'latched onto me,' he said, 'in its rush to show the world it could get its man. I am a citizen with rights. I am a human being with feelings, just like everybody else.' He saved his biggest salve for the media for distorting his background to show he fitted the profile of a bomber. 'Let the headline be based on the facts,' he told them. 'Don't shape the facts to fit the headline.' And then he sued them, reaching out-of-court settlements with all outlets who had inferred – incorrectly – he was the Atlanta bomber.

Liam Bartlett, who covered numerous stories on the Clare-mont case for Perth ABC, originally thought the Macro task-force was a good idea. 'It seemed to focus and crystallise all the leads in an efficient manner.' His attitude, however, changed. 'They just seemed to become incredibly preoccupied with Lance Williams, as if all roads led to Rome. But no charges were laid, and neither was he cleared. It seemed to the media that it was a Mexican stand-off.' Bartlett, whose brother-in-law is press secretary to the commissioner, sees what he regards as fundamental problems in the way WA police do business. 'They're never wrong, they're never going to apologise and they don't see that they need to change. The Claremont story is a subliminal powder keg. All they need is just one more body.'

Following the initial taking of Williams into police custody, over the next 18 months he is taken in for questioning another six times. He never complains, never asks for a lawyer, never refuses to go to the station.

'We knocked on his door at around 9 pm one night,' Stephen Brown says, 'and explained that a psychiatrist that Macro had brought in from overseas, Saathoff, would like to spend some time talking to him. I said we'd be back the next morning at 7 am to pick him up. "Okay," he said and he was there, waiting. This man can be unpredictable, but make no mistake: he has the patience of Job. He sat through almost three days of conversations and psychological assessments with Saathoff and never raised an eyebrow.'

Lance Williams's living arrangements attract incredulity at best, and outright scorn at worst. The general consensus from the public is that police have got their man, but that they don't have enough evidence to charge him. If challenged to explain why they are so sure, the reply is often a simple repeat of the bland assessments they have read about him in the press and no more educated than that he seems 'odd'.

'What do you mean, "odd"?' I ask.

'You know. *Strange.*'

'In what way?'

'Still living at home at his age.'

'But that's not a crime.'

'No, it's not a crime. But it's *strange.*'

Williams is not the only subject of conversation or news reports in Perth. Women, paricularly, are alarmed at the number of sexual predators in the city. A woman wrote to the *Post* expressing her alarm that a man of European descent was pouncing on women in or near the Claremont area, jumping out in front of them and aggressively coercing them to do his bidding. Police, she said, discounted this person as being of any interest in the Claremont investigation. 'Maybe no one associated him with the western suburb social scene, but he was definitely around, definitely a sexual predator and a person who disappeared around the time Ciara Glennon was murdered,' she wrote. 'A mild-mannered 46-year-old public servant is a far easier target than a street-wise drifter who can vanish without trace until he leaves his bloody mark somewhere else.'

44

Between 1982 and 1985, Paul Ferguson worked as a detective team leader on the-then drug squad with Bob Ibbotson. By early 1998, amidst consistent agitation for a Royal Commission into police corruption from journalists and the opposition, Ferguson himself became a target for corruption slurs. A drug dealer, convicted during Ferguson's time at the drug squad, alleged that police had stolen some drugs from him. 'Everyone knows that corruption festers from the top down,' Ferguson says. 'The real scalp they were after was Ibbotson, by then the assistant commissioner. They thought they could somehow get to him through me.' Wanting to avoid the potential fallout from a Royal Commission into policing on their watch – a slur no serving government has ever survived – Richard Court's government created the Anti-Corruption Commission. A fierce and aggressive agency, the ACC was seen by many as a political puppet with an agenda to get quick scalps. Enter Ferguson. Pulled in to answer questions about a person with alleged links to Ibbotson, he did not give the ACC the answers they wanted to hear. 'They needed to shake the tree a bit harder, so they accelerated the pressure by arresting me. In normal circumstances I would have been summonsed, but they wanted to make a big deal of this and threw me straight in the bin on 27 March 1998.' Charged with giving false testimony to the ACC, Ferguson was released on bail. Warned that the fight ahead would be long and dirty if he elected to go to trial, Ferguson crossed sides, preparing the mother of all defence battles with the help of Malcolm McCusker QC. Ferguson, the 'copper's copper', would be out of the force for four years, waiting for the trial.

The politics of policing are of little interest to the Spiers and Rimmer families who attempt – often fruitlessly – some semblance of normality. The Glennons try, too, leaning hard on their faith to get them through. At a memorial service for Ciara in 1998, Denis articulates the family's continuing grief. 'To date Ciara's murder is our life's worst pain,' he says. 'The burden of sorrow can never be fully lifted, but we are learning to carry it. Alongside the pain of the loss of Ciara, the torment of the way she died and frustration associated with an apprehension of the person or persons responsible, there was another more debilitating source of anguish, namely the mysterious dark side of death, the silence of the grave, the absence of evidence of where Ciara is.'

The politics of policing would seep into other areas, as well. In October 1998, 63-year-old great-grandmother Dolores Chadwick died in hospital after a car driven by Dave Caporn's 73-year-old father, Roy, careered through a hairdressing salon in suburban Perth and pinned her to a workbench. The police explanation for why Roy Caporn was never charged was that the accident occurred in a car park and not on the road, and that charges of either unlawful killing or dangerous driving causing death were difficult to prove without evidence.

Amongst other evidence, Chadwick's inquest heard that the day after the crash Dave Caporn – then Detective-Superintendent – had put a call through to junior crash investigator Senior-Constable Trevor Howard, advising him that his father was seeking legal advice and would not be answering police questions. It was a low-key start to the case that would seriously reverberate with police and the public.

Coroner Alistair Hope criticised police actions following the crash as unsatisfactory, including their failure to either photograph or seize Roy Caporn's shoes. He found Dave Caporn had not interfered with the investigation, but that his call to Howard was 'inappropriate' and had led to a perception of impropriety in the investigation. Hope recorded an open verdict, finding that the accident was not a result of Caporn's slippery shoes but of the mental and physical effects of ageing and that Dave Caporn had called in the capacity of a concerned son and not as a senior police officer.

The Royal Commission reviewed the case. 'There is no evidence,' it found, 'that the decision not to charge was affected by considerations in favour of Superintendent Caporn or was otherwise improperly reached.' After examining the documents, the commission decided that further investigation was unwarranted and it was satisfied with both the Coroner's findings and the internal review undertaken by the West Australian Police Service.

There was incredulity in Perth at the outcome of the incident. 'People were saying that they should have been called "Teflon" because nothing sticks,' a former officer recalls. 'Bottom line is, if the average person in the street jaywalks, their arse is grass. People did not understand this at all.' And they still don't.

45

If the public are alarmed at the lack of resolution to the Claremont case, officers outside Macro are also feeling the pinch. The CIB overtime budget, they grizzle, is constantly being plundered to renew the coffers of the Claremont investigation. It's an expensive business and one that is consistently justified by the Macro hierarchy. With young women falling victim to an active serial killer, resources are found. Nothing is ever refused. It is a justification that is vehemently defended. 'Gary Ridgway, the so-called "Green River Killer" who murdered at least 48 women around the Washington area in the United States, killed about six women before a taskforce was put on that case,' Tony Potts says. 'In comparison, we got straight onto it. And we put our money where our mouth is.'

The Green River Killer's confession gives a chilling insight into the warped mind of a serial killer and, apart from his victims being mostly prostitutes, bears uncanny resemblances to the Claremont case. Gary Ridgway admitted the women he targeted were strangers. 'I killed them the first time I met them and I do not have a good memory for their faces. I killed so many women I have a hard time keeping them straight . . . I picked prostitutes because I thought I could kill as many of them as I wanted without getting caught. Another part of my plan was where I put the bodies of these women. Most of the time I took the women's jewellery and their clothes to get rid of any evidence and make them harder to identify. I placed most of the bodies in groups, which I call "clusters". I did this because I wanted to keep track of all the women I killed. I liked to drive by the "clusters" around the county and think about the women I placed there. I usually used a landmark to remember a "cluster". Sometimes I killed and dumped a woman, intending to start a new "cluster", and never returned because I thought I might get caught putting more women there.'

The largest unsolved murder investigation in US history, Ridgway stalked and murdered women for 20 years and eluded police for a decade. The Green River killings created acute fear in the community, and the taskforce was openly criticised by the public and from other investigators. Many of his victims did not make the police list because their disposal sites were not inside the parameters where the killer was known to dump women. Ridgway used six dumping grounds and all except one victim were found partially buried or covered with garbage or foliage. Officers working the Green River Taskforce believed the killer either worked or lived close to the disposal sites; when plotted, those sites formed a rough triangular shape. It was this that led profilers to correctly believe that this audacious killer would live within that triangle.

But the most disconcerting element was the apparent manner in which Greenway stopped and started. 'There is something a bit fishy here: we are led to believe that Ridgway went into a killing frenzy in the 1982–84 period and then stopped completely, until he murdered once more in 1990 and then once again in 1998,' a journalist wrote in *Crime-Library*. 'Unfortunately, that is not usually what happens in the world of a serial killer. They can slow down, especially when there is a great deal of police activity, but not really stop. Are we to believe that he really went so long without killing after 1984 when he killed some 46 women in just a few years? . . . Our expectation is that there are many more victims buried within and outside of King County . . . It may take many years to find the rest of them. It's not really over yet.'

The spectre of the Ridgway killings looms over the Claremont case. Is it really possible that the Claremont killer had suddenly swung into high gear with the Sarah Spiers disappearance? That he had started his operations in a high-risk area? There is a disquieting sense that there *had* to be victims before Sarah, that the killer's self-preservation would ensure that he would practise his craft in lead-up offences before he made his first murderous strike. It is not in the best interests of police or politicians to highlight this as a distinct possibility. There is enough panic in the community already and pointed questions as to why this killer is still at large.

46

The Dodd family emigrated to Western Australia from England in 1990. It was shortly after that they heard news that Margaret Dodd's niece had been savagely beaten to death by her husband, the murder weapon a piece of wood stuck with nails. The young woman's father, a paramedic, attended at the scene, unaware that the call-out was to his own daughter, who died in his arms. The murder was so violent that Margaret struggled for months to comprehend it. 'We didn't know at the time,' she says, 'that a few years later, we would be facing our own shocking situation.'

On 29 July 1999 Hayley Dodd, a shy, good-natured 17-year-old, was en route to a new farm job at Badji, 200 kilometres north of Perth. Last seen by a motorist walking toward the farm at 11.35 am on the same day, she didn't turn up. The following morning, Margaret called 000. The situation, she was told, was not an emergency. It was Margaret's first dealings with authority, the start of the nightmare that would continue for years. They treated Hayley as just another runaway. Margaret pleaded with the police to understand that her daughter would not do that to the family.

'We were very close. I wish she were a runaway. I wish she were. But I knew straightaway she were not.' It was to get worse. 'When we complained that nothing was being done, we were told that we were lucky it was being investigated at all.' Determined to keep her daughter's name in front of the police, Margaret embarked on an obsessive campaign, never letting up with phone calls and letters. It got their attention – and their backs up. Margaret shudders when she recalls the insensitive way she was informed that Hayley was most likely dead. On 24 August 1999 she rang a divisional inspector, begging that sniffer dogs be put in the area where Hayley was last seen. She was in tears, but he was adamant. 'There will be no dogs,' he told her. 'That is just not going to happen.' But this time the inspector went further, his voice dripping with uncontained exasperation. 'Look, Margaret, let's be frank. You don't seriously think that Hayley is walking around, do you? The fact is, Hayley may never be found.'

In shock at the blunt way in which the news had been delivered to her, Margaret gasped, cupping her hand over her mouth to stop the heaving sobs.

'Yes, I had wanted to hold onto the hope that she is still walking around,' she said, before hanging up the phone.

Margaret talks so quickly, and with so few pauses it is hard to keep pace with the conversation. Slightly built, her physical appearance belies her feisty Yorkshire spirit. She once appraised a police officer, whom she believed was not taking Hayley's case seriously, with a critical eye and a dash of her caustic wit. 'I can see a promotion coming your way very soon,' she told him. The officer, pleased with the compliment, grinned and asked her why. 'Because,' she replied, 'they only promote the incompetent.'

He was promoted within a week.

A week after Hayley disappeared, detectives walked into the Dodds' home, uninvited. Brandishing a search warrant, they brusquely demanded that Ray and Margaret declare who they were. Margaret felt the blood rush from her face and steadied herself lest she faint. 'Is this about Hayley?' she asked. 'Have you found her? Is she dead?' Confused, the police looked at each other. 'I rang a liaison officer we were dealing with, who had a quiet word with one of them,' Margaret recalls. 'They nearly fell over themselves backing out of our door. The idiots were there for a drug bust! They had the wrong house!'

Margaret also vented her spleen on Dave Caporn, then Detective-Superintendent of the Major Crime Division, when he rang her. 'We had heard nothing from him – absolutely nothing – and so I was none too pleased when he finally called. He was trying to pacify us after an avalanche of bad publicity.' It didn't work.

Caporn introduced himself. 'Hello, Margaret, you don't know me,' he started in smooth voice.

'Oh, yes I do,' she told him. 'I know exactly who you are. Round face, round glasses, balding. I know exactly who you are.' When Caporn visited with another officer, she deliberately sat them outside in the blazing sun. 'They just about melted. We'd been to hell and back: police not believing that Hayley wasn't a runaway, the whole way the investigation had been handled. I didn't think a bit of sun and my dog jumping on them would do them any harm at all.'

Caporn, she said, would go to great pains to address inaccuracies in media reports and to write her lengthy letters in which he outlined what the police had done. All had the line: 'I ask that you support the investigation by keeping the details contained within the confines of your family members.'

'I wasn't about to do that,' Margaret grimaces. 'We've had so many official assurances that resources have been poured into Hayley's disappearance, but these seem to be just empty words. They didn't like me going to the media but no one had a clue where our Hayley is.' At the end of a visit from Dave Caporn, Margaret quoted an old saying to him. 'You know what they say, Mr Caporn?' she said, suppressing a grin. 'The further up the ladder the monkey climbs, the more he shows his arse.'

In mid-February 1999 Dave Caporn, 38, becomes the youngest officer in the history of Western Australian police to attain the rank of Superintendent. Now in a managerial role in tactical intelligence at the Bureau of Criminal Intelligence, his experience is cited. Detective-Sergeant and then Inspector at Macro, where he was chief for four years from 1993. Involved in other high-profile investigations, including the Wayne Tibbs murder. Officer in charge of the Major Fraud Squad. Joining him in the promotion are 22 other officers, including Mal Shervill, who will later figure prominently in the Andrew Mallard inquiry.

By November 1999, as the city starts to gear up for another sweltering Christmas and the holiday season that brings young people out in droves to party, police stop the overt surveillance of Williams. But they do not resile from their resolve. He is, they say with pointed chin, still a suspect. Like other 'persons of interest' targeted by the team, Williams is neither charged nor cleared. Instead, he is doomed to a purgatory of suspicion.

Soon after, an exhausted and drawn Denis Glennon appeared on Perth television confirming his belief in the police force and assuring viewers that an arrest is expected very soon. The police operation, he said, had been a success because no other girls had gone missing from Claremont.

Sarah McMahon's family would not agree.

47

The last time Trish McMahon saw her 20-year-old daughter, Sarah, she reminded her to say goodbye to her father. 'He's going away on business, Sarah. Don't forget.' Sarah never would have forgotten once but had become troubled and intense, she needed reminding. Deferring her university studies for one year, she had worked that day – 8 November 2000 – at the job she had started two weeks before, as a receptionist at a gardening supply shop in Claremont. In the late afternoon, she took a phone call from a friend who was suicidal and asked a co-worker the fastest route to get to his home. Sarah walked out of the shop into the late afternoon sunshine and vanished.

By the next afternoon, when Trish had not heard from Sarah, she was panicking. Sarah had failed to pick up her sister as arranged the night before and her bed had not been slept in. Trish rang the police and her husband, Danny, begging him to return home. 'Come back. Sarah's missing.' He drives the 1500-kilometre return journey at breakneck speed.

The second youngest of four, Sarah, a perfectionist, was gifted at classical piano and dreamed of becoming a journalist. Blessed with beauty and an arresting personality, she was also plagued with low self-esteem and demanded the most attention in the family. 'It is the squeakiest hinge that gets the most oil,' Trish smiles, ruefully. A loving, outgoing girl, Trish accepts that of all her children, Sarah is the only one capable of leaving home and not making contact with her family. But she wouldn't have done that, she knows. She obsessively goes over in her mind events leading up to Sarah's disappearance. She had been troubled before she disappeared, losing herself in dark classical music and mixing in bad company. Moody and rebellious, relationships with her siblings had become erratic, but the family was close and strong. Danny adored all his children and Trish never doubted Sarah would revert to the loving young woman she had once been.

The police, acutely aware that Sarah had gone missing from Claremont, were on the McMahons' doorstep every day when she first disappeared. After a couple of weeks, that attention tapered off. Terrified of the answer, Trish asked them if her daughter could have been abducted by the Claremont serial killer.

'They said no, definitely not,' she recalls. 'But I couldn't work out how they would know that? How *could* they know that? Until they find the Claremont killer, nobody has a clue.' Police ask the family whether Sarah could have committed suicide. Trish shakes her head. 'I can't imagine her doing that. And if she had taken her own life, I'm sure she would have been found by now.' She also clings to hope, born from a strong belief in God and a mother's prayer, that Sarah is still alive. 'There is as much chance of Sarah being alive as there is of her being dead,' she says emphatically. It has become a mantra, but the passing years tinge her hope with hollowness. 'Why must she be dead? How can anyone say with certainty that she is? That's the point: no one knows anything with certainty.' Her voice trails off and she lowers her head in a vain attempt to hide her tears.

Days after Sarah disappears, the family receive a call from a school friend saying she had seen Sarah driving up the hill toward the house. The family is plagued by questions they can't answer. 'Was it her? And if it was, she would have driven into the garage and spotted her father's car there. She thought he had gone away and she would have freaked out. She'd have thought she was in trouble. So did she just drive away again?'

Some nights, it is only Trish's faith in God that keeps her going. 'God hasn't stopped listening,' she says, 'even though I've stopped talking.'

Without warning, the family become the recipients of letters and phone calls from crazed people, clairvoyants and psychics. Always with different information. Sarah is the victim of a cult, they claim. On and on, never any thought for the rollercoaster ride the family endures every time they listen to yet another hypothesis.

Shortly after Sarah's disappearance makes the news, Trish goes to a health shop. The man who serves her gives her some free advice. 'Think of it like this,' he says, his opinion uninvited. 'If she's been held captive, victims are usually only held and tortured for a few days before they are killed, and she'll be dead by now and out of her misery.' Trish stares at him, dumbfounded, before stumbling out of the shop.

The family travels all over Australia looking for her, putting up posters, beseeching police to study Sarah's face. 'Have you seen her? Have you seen her?'

The McMahons cope differently with their emotions in the first few years after Sarah disappears. Trish loses herself in books; Danny shrinks from the world, working obsessively in the garden. It is, Trish says, as though their heart has been ripped out, and she cries when she discusses how grief has broken her husband's spirit. Gardening is the only way he copes, what he does to try to ease the pain of missing a daughter he adores. In an attempt to find some reason in the inexplicable, he sought counselling from Dr Andrew Dunn, whose house they had bought and who knew Sarah, once treating her hand after a horse-riding fall. Trish did not have counselling but panic attacks overwhelm her when she sees mothers and daughters together, and she scans crowds to find Sarah's face. She has become expert at 'silent screaming' – being with people and breaking down without them knowing. They live in a world of 'maybe' and 'if'. When a female body is found, Trish's knees buckle until the person is identified and she berates herself for losing faith. 'Of course it's not Sarah,' she tells herself. 'Sarah is not dead.' There is never any warning from the police that the news program is going to air, never any warning to be prepared.

The reality – that it is very possible that Sarah is yet another victim of the Claremont serial killer – is too hard for Trish to embrace. The mantra 'Sarah is not dead' is the only thing that keeps her sane.

Trish is completely dissatisfied with the police investigation into Sarah's disappearance. 'I don't think they've done enough.

I don't begrudge one penny of the money that's been poured into the Claremont investigation – millions of dollars – but I think a lot more could be put into the other missing girls. A lot more effort, a lot more time. They say the police are understaffed and overworked, but I'm not interested in that. My only concern is Sarah.'

In comparison to the saturation media coverage the Claremont girls received, she says, the other missing girls have been virtually ignored. 'There is nothing for them at all. No one remembers them but their families. The Bali bomb victims, for example, have a memorial to them, and it's right that they should have. But they are no more victims than the mothers and fathers and siblings of all the children here who have just vanished into thin air. John Howard said the Bali bombings were an outrage – well, so is this. So is this! These are our children who have been forgotten.'

Trish's eyes, set in a gentle face, are bright with indignation when she recalls that it was the family, not police, who found Sarah's car when she had been missing for ten days. 'We had gone to Swan District Hospital to visit our grandson who was in hospital with a broken arm. We couldn't find a park, went round and round until we eventually did. And there was Sarah's car, right behind us! We were overjoyed, thought she was in hospital and that is why she hadn't contacted us. We ran screaming through the corridors, joyful, calling out her name. But she wasn't there.' The driver's side door to Sarah's car was closed, but not locked and the window behind the driver's seat slightly open. Her handbag was on the floor, tipped over. But there was no sign of Sarah.

Trish recalls a police constable who said, when they found the car, 'I didn't used to believe in God, but I do now.' The family's hopes were raised in the first critical days after the discovery. 'The police came and cordoned off the car, turned it into a crime scene. It was in a real mess when they brought it back to us, but they hadn't found anything of any value to them. They found some fingerprints of people who could be accounted for, they said. That was all.' Unbeknown to police, Trish's son had deliberately placed his fingerprint on the vehicle, to ensure police were thorough in their testing. They missed it.

Sarah's mobile phone was also missing, and the family believed that it could provide real clues as to where she was. 'Police had found it 18 months before they told us they had,' Trish says. 'When I asked why they failed to mention it, I was told it was because it was an ongoing inquiry.' All three McMahon girls had special rings, a filigree with an antique coin. Given the fact that jewellery had been taken from Ciara Glennon and Jane Rimmer, they asked Trish about jewellery that Sarah had worn. 'They wanted to look at my other daughter Amanda's ring. When they left the house, they left the search warrant behind. They came back for that and left their street index behind. When they returned to pick up the index, they left a briefcase behind them. This was Major Crime, the people who were leading the search for our precious daughter. It didn't inspire much confidence in us. Not much confidence at all.'

Police, Trish says, now have nothing to do with the family, apart from the phone call that came in the day after 'He Who Waits' – a telling examination of the Claremont case – aired on *Australian Story* in February 2004. 'I took a phone call from a police officer who announced that he was our new liaison officer. I was speechless and angry. What utter incompetence! "I didn't realise we had an old one," I told him.'

Trish keeps Sarah's memory alive, regularly freshening her bedroom and, on the nights she is most distressed, sleeping in Sarah's bed. She looks out her window and up to the sky, talking to her daughter. 'Your sky is my sky, your stars are my stars. Where are you, Sarah? Where are you?'

Bret Christian is not convinced that Sarah is not another Claremont victim. 'Without a body', he says, 'how can anyone know?' But another Perth journalist, who requests anonymity, is in regular contact with police sources. He tells me police know Sarah is dead and also know who is responsible, but they are unable to find her body. 'A relatively senior police officer gave me the information about Sarah,' he says. 'There was all this scuttlebutt about her possibly being a Claremont victim but he told me, categorically, that that is not right. A female police informant told him she had helped a man clean up the crime scene where Sarah was murdered. It was a real mess, but she didn't help dispose of Sarah's body. This man, a nasty character who is well known to police for attempting to murder a prostitute and has an extensive criminal record for drugs and violence, had some drug involvement with Sarah.' The journalist is convinced police are right. 'You're wasting your time if you're going down any other path about Sarah. This information is definitely correct.'

So what happened to Sarah McMahon? How could a young woman simply vanish into the ether without anyone noticing anything? Is it too much of a coincidence to think that she just happened to disappear from Claremont? Certainly she was troubled, but not enough by all accounts to take her own life, and not enough to stay away from her family for years without contact. It is not in the police's best interests to admit that she may well be a victim of the Claremont serial killer. That would put the number of victims that they now categorically acknowledge to four. Where would it end?

Sarah was a young, bright, intelligent woman. Who did she know outside her immediate circle of friends? Who would she trust enough to get into their vehicle? An older person she has met before? An acquaintance or friend of her family? There were no sightings of her once she left her workplace, suggesting the chances that she actually disappeared from the Claremont area are high. Why would her car end up in the hospital grounds? What was she doing there? Or had someone else driven it and dumped it in that area, a place known to that person. What happened to Sarah McMahon?

Police have named the person they believe responsible for Sarah's disappearance to Trish and Danny, but Trish does not believe he is responsible. 'They clutch at straws,' she says. 'Anything but admit they don't have a clue. And they *don't* have a clue. It does not placate us.'

***

I talk to Luke Morfesse about some other missing girls, starting with Julie Cutler. Three weeks before Cutler disappeared, another woman had been abducted and bound after leaving Perth's Sheraton Hotel, and later dumped near a bridge. Could it be the same offender? We move on to other names. Lisa Brown? Nineteen years old, 175 cm tall with dirty, dark-blonde hair, brown eyes and a slim build. Brown, a junkie, mother of two, and street worker, has been missing since 12.30 am on 10 November 1998 from a Perth city street when she was touting for business. Her approximation in appearance to the Claremont girls – hair colour, height and build, but certainly not her profession – drew immediate comparisons with their disappearance.

'The year in which Brown went missing raised fears that she may have been another Claremont victim,' Morfesse says. 'But police are certain that she was murdered by a pimp.'

A pimp. If anyone knows about them it's Con Bayens, 26 years in the force – who headed up Operation Bounty to clear prostitutes out of Perth's Northbridge and Highgate areas. Home to nightclubs, restaurants and brothels, these areas crawl with street workers and their clients, the flotsam and jetsam that cruise at night.

Bayens has a clear interpretation of what happened. 'When the three girls went missing from Claremont, it attracted a lot of media attention. As a consequence of all this activity, no further girls went missing in Claremont. However Lisa Brown and Darylyn Ugle – both known street prostitutes and both murdered – worked the nearby Highgate and Northbridge areas. Did the murderer change suburbs because of the police activity in Claremont? Who knows?' But, he says, he knows one thing for certain. 'Street prostitutes don't have pimps. They perform sexual services, normally fellatio, for $50 a time. The money is immediately spent on a drug hit. All street prostitutes have terrible drug habits and there simply would be no money for a pimp in it. If the police reckon that Brown was killed by her pimp, it goes to show how far off base they are, and how little chance they have of catching the person responsible.'

48

Established in August 2000, Operation Bounty was given eight undercover officers with the unofficial brief to go for the trifecta: to lock up prostitutes, punters and pimps. By night, the plain-clothed officers trawled the Northbridge streets, watching as up to 200 men a night solicited the services of street prostitutes. Often, the prostitutes waylaid a prospective client on his way to a massage parlour, offering their services for a greatly reduced rate. Over a two-year period, Operation Bounty put away 938 people. Its intelligence revealed that at any one time there were around 370 active prostitutes, aged between 14 and 41, working the area. All had a substance abuse addiction.

'Operation Bounty,' Bayens recalls, 'was an important attempt to clean up the streets. We got so many sickos in our net during that time. Coppers who showed their badges and got a freebie from the girls; lawyers, doctors, a high school principal, politicians. All out for what they could get, all out there hustling. We got a priest who told a prostitute, "Suck on my staff and your life will be saved." I don't know if she believed him or not.' Another night, they netted a police security officer who had made it known to a prostitute he was a police employee. 'He had asked a girl for fellatio and under normal circumstances he'd have been charged with soliciting and let go. But because of his position, we had to lock him up in case he went back to headquarters and shut down all the computers.'

With the Claremont killings fresh in their memories, Bayens told his blokes to be mindful of that case and to take particular notice of any crimes that were sexually motivated. 'When the taskforce was in its planning stages, I ran into Dave Caporn at police headquarters. We knew each other really well, having gone to recruit school together.' Bayens told Caporn what he was doing. 'I offered him the taskforce as a resource and told him that if he gave us some direction, we may be able to help him with Claremont. We were going to be out amongst these people every night, blokes who trawled the streets for women. It seemed natural to work together if we could.' But Caporn, according to Bayens, had other ideas.

'Thanks anyway,' he told him. 'But we don't need any help. We've got our man.'

Stunned at the lack of interest, Bayens could only assume that that 'man' was Lance Williams. 'If he's that good for it, why isn't he locked up then?' he asked Caporn. The question was ignored. 'That was the end of that,' he says. 'They didn't need our help. I really believed that they were on the verge of arresting someone, as it appeared they were confident they had all the evidence. But as time was to tell, they had sweet fuck all.'

Driving around Northbridge late one night, Bayens notices a Holden Commodore parked in a dark side street. He uses the police sign to call communications on his radio. 'VKI, this is GC 450. Can I talk to the unmarked car currently in Smith Street, Highgate?' Fitted with all the options that Holden add to police cars, but accessible by anyone – pursuit rims and tyres, lowered suspension – it was the same model that was being used at that time by the police. When a prostitute got into the vehicle, Bayens pulled the car up.

'I thought it was perhaps a drug bust and wanted to somehow warn the bloke to get out, that he could jeopardise our operation by being there,' he recalls. 'He was very tall and exuded confidence. If he approached you, and wanted something from you – information or whatever – you would accept him without question as a police officer. Even in the plain clothes that he was wearing, you wouldn't hesitate. I'd been in the force a long time but I didn't recognise him.' The radio room didn't either, coming back with a negative. He wasn't a cop after all.

With his mental antennae up, Bayens told the couple they would have to come down to police headquarters. 'Hand over your keys,' he told him. 'We have to secure your vehicle.' There was, he explains, a simple explanation for taking him in. 'It got my attention because there was a lot of talk around that whoever had done Claremont either was, or pretended to be, a person in authority. Like a cop or a cab driver.' In the boot of the car, Con's team found an arsenal of abduction weapons: zip ties, a balaclava, gaffer tape and scissors. 'The boot was fully lined with plastic, top and bottom. I put together a report on the bloke and did a running check on him. He'd completed a taxi driving course and done one shift. He was so hot as a possible Claremont suspect that the Bureau of Criminal Investigation wanted to put their dogs on him. But, as I'd been told, they "had their man".'

Furious and disgusted at the lack of action taken, Bayens points to the difference between Macro officers moving in on Lance Williams when the decoy officer was in his car and the information he wanted to pass on. 'The sort of thing that happened to the decoy with Williams was happening every night in Northbridge. But they just didn't want to know.' He pauses. 'Because of the Prostitution Act, it is illegal to release the personal details of any person who has been arrested. But in saying that, I can assure you that what I have told you will stand up to any scrutiny. The best we could do was try and charge the bloke with soliciting a prostitute, which we couldn't do because there had been no financial transaction. We had to let him go.'

Bayens was only too aware of how tight the Macro taskforce was. 'A cop mistakenly got out on the wrong floor at Curtin House headquarters because it used to be his office. The Macro guys grabbed him, frogmarched him into the supervisor's office and made him sign something akin to the Official Secrets Act. He kept trying to tell them he'd made a simple mistake, but they weren't really interested in listening, apparently. They didn't muck about there in terms of security.'

49

On Hayley Dodd's 18th birthday, the family erect a wooden wishing well with three wishes on it. 'We wish she was home safe and well. We wish it never happens to anyone else. We wish the person who is responsible is brought to justice.' They are still waiting.

In May 2001, Margaret penned yet another letter to Police Minister Michelle Roberts. She quotes some of the responses she received when she dared to ask questions of the investigating officers. 'I can't comment, it's more than my job's worth'; 'If I've got time'; 'I don't know nothing about your case'; 'We don't want a media circus'; 'That won't happen'; 'We are understaffed'.

By June 2002 Roberts openly criticised the investigation in the media, claiming that there were 'clear deficiencies in the way the investigation into Hayley's disappearance was handled'. Margaret concedes that because of the distance from Perth, and the place from which Hayley disappeared – halfway between Perth and Geraldton – it is highly unlikely that she is the victim of the Claremont serial killer. But doubts niggle. 'She vanished into smoke. No clues left behind. That's not the work of a killer who has simply seized an opportunity, is it? If that had been the case, her body would probably have been found by now. That's the work of someone who is good at what he does. Practised.'

Almost five years to the day after Sarah Spiers disappeared, in late January 2001 Dave Caporn was awarded the Australian Police Medal. In his speech, he gave credit to the detectives who had put their careers aside to work on Macro and reflected on the legacy of the murders. 'Today is a day of mixed feelings for me. It is usually a day where I reflect on what Don and Carol Spiers are going through and certainly what the Glennons and Rimmers are going through. We may not have solved this case yet, but I get a sense that the team may have prevented others from becoming victims.'

The sentiments, though noble, are not shared throughout the community, least of all by the 'persons of interest' highlighted by the Macro taskforce. And certainly not by the Dodd family, who still wait for news of Hayley; by the McMahons, who mourn for Sarah; by Jane Rimmer's family, who have little faith in a resolution; or by all the other families of missing women or unsolved murders in WA.

Dave Caporn was appointed commander of Operation Zircon, a bold attempt to curb the violent excesses of Western Australia's bikie gangs, formed immediately following the murders of retired police officer Don Hancock and his bookmaker mate, Lou Lewis, on 1 September 2001. The colourful names of the gangs – the Coffin Cheaters, Club Deros, the Gypsy Jokers, God's Garbage – and their actions, invoke fear in Perth, used to the incessant media coverage of drive-by shootings and revenge killings. The police needed a way to get to the big fish. When Gypsy Joker member Sidney 'Snot' Reid did the unthinkable and implicated his bikie boss, Graeme 'Slim' Slater, in the murder of Hancock and Lewis, they had apparently found it.

Hancock had spent 35 years in the force before his retirement in 1994. The former commander in charge of the CIB, he was responsible for the arrest of the Mickleberg brothers – Raymond, Peter and Brian – who, despite proclaiming their innocence, had each served lengthy jail terms following their 1983 convictions for the audacious swindling of $650,000 worth of gold from the Perth Mint. But shortly before his death (and following Hancock's death in the car bombing) disgraced former detective Anthony Lewandowski confessed that he and Don Hancock had beaten up and verballed the Mickleberg brothers in order to secure their convictions. His confession marked a new low in the history of a force persistently dogged by rumour and allegations of questionable practices, of police protecting their own. Riddled with guilt and an urgent need to unburden his conscience before he died, Lewandowski's affidavit, signed 5 June 2002, was a damning indictment of corruption and evidence tampering. 'At the time when they [Mickleberg's brothers] were charged with the offences on 26 July 1982,' he wrote, 'I said to Don Hancock that I didn't believe he had enough evidence and he said to me, "Don't worry, it will get better."' While Brian – who later died in a helicopter crash – was released and his name cleared after nine months, Raymond and Peter, who respectively served eight- and six-year sentences, fought through four unsuccessful attempts to have their convictions overturned. The detectives, they claimed, had lied, fabricated confessions and planted damning evidence. In three of those appeals, Lewandowski and Hancock testified. Finally, 25 years after their first trial, the Western Australia Court of Criminal Appeal quashed the criminal convictions. But former WA Assistant Police Commissioner Mel Hay came out swinging. He and other police, he defiantly told a huge press contingent, still believed the Micklebergs were guilty.

In retirement, Don Hancock – regarded by many as the Roger Rogerson of the WA police – had incurred the wrath of some Gypsy Jokers when he demanded they leave his country tavern, near Kalgoorlie, after one swore at his daughter. An hour later, bikie Billy Grierson was shot dead as he sat next to Slater at the Gypsy Jokers camp site.

'The police officer at the tavern that day had left the bar after Grierson and his mates were abusing Hancock's daughter,' John Quigley recalls. 'Yet this same officer is now sent to investigate Hancock! He couldn't see anything wrong with that, he later told the coroner, because there was no other CIB available. Well, last time I checked, it's a 40-minute flight from Kalgoorlie to Perth by the police plane. They could and should have put fresh police investigators in there.'

Declaring they would take revenge on Hancock, whom they blamed for Grierson's death, Hancock made the decision to relocate to Perth with his family after his home and pub were destroyed by bombs and fire. But his close connections with police could not save him. In an act more akin to a terrorist attack, Hancock and Lewis were killed when a car bomb exploded in a suburban Perth street. A snitch by a gang insider was a gift for Caporn, who had long waited for someone to roll over. A court win was hotly anticipated.

That Reid had planted the ammonium nitrate bomb was never in question. Copping a life sentence at the 2004 trial after he pleaded guilty to his role in the murders, what was in contention was whether Slater, as Reid claimed, had handed him the parcel containing the bomb and later, in a scene reminiscent of a Bond movie, used a mobile phone to detonate that bomb. Already a marked man in bikie circles for turning on his own – for which he earned a 10-year reduction in his sentence – and for breaking the code of silence, he scored himself further ignominy when he took the stand against Slater at his trial. Slater's alibi – that he was 100 kilometres from Perth when the bomb went off – was backed by his mother and sister. Slater's defence lawyer told the jury that Reid was a liar and that police had showed him favour in return for his testimony. Police are not, he said, always the heroes anymore than bikies are always the villains. The jury believed him and Slater was acquitted of wilful murder. Four other bikie associates were found not guilty of plotting and then planting bombs at Hancock's property.

Stunned and disappointed by the verdict, police covered their faces with their hands and sat open-mouthed in silence. Later, a grim Caporn tried to put on a brave face. 'We considered that Slater was a dangerous criminal who committed violent crimes. We considered that he killed Don and Lou, but he's been found not guilty and we have to live with that decision.' But, he added, the investigation had brought many important results.

There were compensations. In 2004, Caporn won an international award for Most Outstanding Investigation on behalf of the WA Police Service. While Operation Zircon failed to net Slater, police did not hesitate in pointing out it had resulted in busting the Gypsy Jokers' WA state president, Lenn Kirby, for possession of amphetamines with intent to sell, and the conviction of Gypsy Jokers' associate Garry White for the 2001 wilful murder of Anthony Tapley.

While a beaming Caporn boasted that Zircon secured the rollover of key members of a bikie group and in doing so had broken new ground in the fight against outlaw gangs, his opponents in the force were aghast that a failed operation had netted him an award. Next, they grizzled, he would be rewarded with a knighthood for the Claremont serial killings when they are still unsolved.

50

With Macro officers constantly asking for help from the public, they have a battle sorting out facts from fiction. In the first flush after the three disappearances, more than 12 people are repeatedly nominated as serious suspects. Caporn is quick to point out that they have all been thoroughly investigated, but three men, aggrieved at what they claim is police inaction in investigating their claims, take matters into their own hands and call a press conference.

Calling their group Citizens for the Apprehension of the Real Killer, with the unfortunate acronym CARK, their spokesperson Frank Silas reveals his suspicions about a casual employee who had worked at a suburban factory while Silas was a supervisor. The man, he claimed, had worked until 10 pm the night Ciara vanished, missed work on Monday and then returned to the factory with deep scratches on his face that he passed off as having been inflicted by his pet dog. Silas didn't believe him; weeks before, around 2 am, he said he had seen the man and his girlfriend offer a lift to young women waiting for taxis near the Stirling Highway in Claremont. They also offered Silas a lift, which he accepted, but when the man started talking about going to a marijuana crop in the bush, he bailed out of the van at the first opportunity. Not long after, the man by chance started work at the factory.

Silas backed up his claims, flourishing sheaves of letters he had written in the past four years to people in power, including the police minister, police officers and the police commissioner. Eight months after he claimed he had made the first overture to Crime Stoppers about his suspicions – just days after Ciara's body was found – the man was formally interviewed about the matter. Bemused reporters scribbled furiously as Silas continued. He named the man and claimed that once at work the accused had pointed a small knife at Silas's ribs, saying this was how he dealt with street kids. More bizarre claims followed. The man, Silas said, had once boasted that he was 'more famous than Christopher Skase' after a newspaper carried a report on the Claremont killer on page one, and a report of Skase on page three. The circumstantial evidence mounted: he had been sacked – though later re-employed – for assaulting a female staff member and his girl-friend sported a claddagh ring, identical to the brooch Ciara had worn. They worked as a team, Silas surmised.

Proof that police had dealt with Silas's claims was contained in letters shown to the press. One, in which Silas refers to police as 'high-school dropouts', incurred the wrath of Police Commissioner Barry Matthews, who seized the opportunity to outline at length the educational qualifications required of detectives.

A defensive Caporn later told the media that despite the 'great lengths' that police had gone to placate Mr Silas, it was without success. He could barely disguise his sarcasm. He felt for Mr Silas, he said, because the issue 'was obviously taking up a large space in his life'. He added that another person had recently threatened to put the information about a suspect he had on the internet, 'because we wouldn't arrest this person for the Claremont murders'.

'This sort of thing really irked Caporn,' a Macro insider recalls. 'He was busy enough trying to put out fires that existed, let alone ones that arsonists had started just so they could watch them burn.'

Jane is no longer alive.
Sarah is still missing.

Can you help with some of the unanswered questions?

Jane Rimmer was at the Continental Hotel, Bay View Terrace, Claremont, on the evening of Saturday the 8th of June, 1996. She was last seen alive at the front of the hotel shortly after midnight. On Saturday, August 3rd, Jane's body was found in Wellard.

Sarah Spiers was at the Club Bay View Night Club, St. Quentins Avenue, Claremont, in the early hours of Saturday the 27th of January, 1996, the Australia Day weekend. Her last known location is 2.00am at the telephone booth near the corner of Stirling Road and Stirling Highway, Claremont.

Like Jane and Sarah's family and friends, you're agonising over the events because someone close to you may be involved in what has occurred to Jane and Sarah. You're concerned because you noticed a change in their routine or behaviour. Whatever it was, something just didn't appear right around those times.

Ease your mind, call Crimestoppers now. Alleviate your fears.

CRIME STOPPERS 1800 333 000

Crying out for help. This poster asked the public to unburden its conscience and pass along any information on Jane Rimmer or Sarah Spiers. Ciara Glennon's name would soon be added to the list.

Young, beautiful, brilliant. Ciara Glennon shortly before her murder.

(PHOTO: WESTERN AUSTRALIA POLICE)

Claremont's Continental Hotel, a cool hangout for young partygoers. Was it also a hunting ground for the killer? (PHOTO: NEWSPIX/NEWS LIMITED)

The phone box on Stirling Road where Sarah Spiers called a taxi at 2 am. By the time the driver arrived, she had disappeared.

(PHOTO: WESTERN AUSTRALIA POLICE)

Deserted and dangerous. Stirling Highway, where Ciara Glennon was last seen. The killer must have travelled this dark road. (PHOTO: WESTERN AUSTRALIA POLICE)

Woolcoot Road, Wellard,
where Jane Rimmer's body
lay hidden in a roadside
verge for 54 days.

(PHOTO: WESTERN AUSTRALIA POLICE)

Dumping ground. The desolate area at Pipidinny Road where Ciara Glennon's
body was found, as indicated by the arrow. (PHOTO: WESTERN AUSTRALIA POLICE)

High-profile suspect, former Claremont mayor Peter Weygers. Police have still not formally excluded him. (PHOTO: NEWSPIX/NEWS LIMITED)

Key suspect Lance Williams. Neither cleared nor charged, he has endured years of surveillance and suspicion. (PHOTO: NEWSPIX/NEWS LIMITED)

The heat is on. Former head of Macro Taskforce, Dave Caporn, outside the Continental Hotel, five months after Ciara Glennon was murdered.

(PHOTO: NEWSPIX/NEWS LIMITED)

Grim find. A popular police officer, Senior-Sergeant (now Inspector) Paul Ferguson fronts the press regarding the discovery of Ciara Glennon's body, 4 April 1997. (PHOTO: NEWSPIX/NEWS LIMITED)

Superintendent Paul Schramm and team at Jane Rimmer's disposal site, commencing an independent forensic review, 2004. (PHOTO: THE WEST AUSTRALIAN)

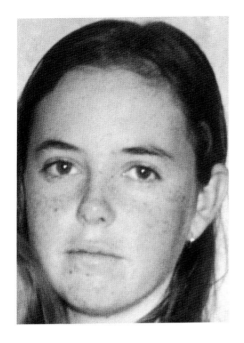

According to WA police, 17-year-old Hayley Dodd was a 'gift' to her killer when she innocently decided to walk along the roadside to her new farm job.

(PHOTO: WESTERN AUSTRALIA POLICE)

The first Claremont victim? Julie Cutler's car was found floating off a beach at Cottesloe. Her body has never been found.

(PHOTO: WESTERN AUSTRALIA POLICE)

'Gone but never forgotten.' Ciara Glennon's final resting place, Karrakatta Cemetery. Here at least she has dignity.

(AUTHOR'S PHOTO)

Jane Rimmer's plaque at Karrakatta Cemetery, where her family go to talk to her. The fun-loving woman's murder decimated this courageous family.

(AUTHOR'S PHOTO)

The face of grief. His life a torment, Don Spiers wonders what happened to their loving daughter Sarah. Without a body, they have no place to go to mourn their loss.

(PHOTO: *THE WEST AUSTRALIAN*)

Part Three
The Lonely Lilies

'Nothing is right and nothing is just;
We sow in ashes and reap in dust.'
Violet Fane

51

The West Australian Police Service is in spin control. At 10.55 am on Tuesday, 2 December 2003 this memo is broadcast to all members of the force.

Subject: Macro Investigation into the Claremont Serial Killings

Staff may have seen in recent editions of the *Sunday Times* a story, then a column, regarding the Macro investigation into the Claremont serial killings. It was a concern and disappointment to me and others that, despite repeated approaches, the newspaper chose not to publish the Police Service's point of view. In essence, journalists from the *Sunday Times* have claimed that the Macro case has not been the subject of satisfactory, independent reviews, and should be. This is wrong and needs to be corrected. It is important that staff be aware of the following information concerning Macro.

Contrary to what was reported, the University of Western Australia's Robin Napper was not approached by the Police to review Macro; instead he held discussions with senior police regarding cold-case review methodology generally.

Since 1996 there have been ten independent, major reviews of the Macro investigation, five of which have not involved a member of the WA Police Service. One review was conducted in the UK and four in the United States. 150 recommendations have emanated from those reviews and have been addressed. We were the first police service in Australia to invite an independent senior investigator to chair a review of a major investigation, by a Superintendent from NSW with extensive experience investigating homicide and serial-murders undertaking that review. Recently, an independent forensic review was initiated and this is continuing. Western Australia maintains one of the world's highest solvency rates for homicides which, over many years, has been comparable or better than the United Kingdom's own rate. While the suspect referred to in the media cannot be excluded from the investigation, this has not deterred investigators from conducting comprehensive investigations regarding many other persons of interest.

Authorised for Broadcast by the A/C, Crime Investigation & Intelligence Services.

The same month, Assistant Commissioner Mel Hay is invited to participate in a workshop comprised of members of the International Homicide Investigators Association at the University of Western Australia. The free policing workshop, where forensic advances are networked and shared to help solve difficult cases, attracts the interest of members throughout 15 countries. Hay's letter is polite, though firm. Due to 'competing priorities and other commitments', he writes, it is not possible for the police service – including officers from Major Crime and forensic areas – to participate.

John Quigley, 57, started his life as a truck driver before practising criminal law for 25 years, making a name for himself in the small legal fishbowl that is Perth as an eccentric and often brilliant firebrand, a man unafraid to speak his mind. He acted for the police, a lone voice defending them in court, obsessively taking up the cudgels on their behalf. A colourful character, Quigley often sported a Balinese t-shirt which read: 'Admit nothing. Deny everything. And then make counter allegations.' He often used the motto to help police clients. 'This is the way we'll proceed!' he told them. But defending police took its toll. Tired of what he regarded as the shambolic way the police force was being run, in 2001 he sold his lucrative legal practice and entered parliament, hoping to expose the disarray. When Premier Richard Court lost office, he instead found himself sitting on the backbench. It was from this position that Quigley, using parliamentary privilege, would raise the bar on what would become a high-profile, shocking miscarriage of justice story in Western Australia: the Andrew Mallard case.

Working pro bono for Andrew Mallard, who was wrongly imprisoned for the murder of Pamela Lawrence in 1994, in 2002 Quigley brought his incisive legal prowess to the case. By July, he had uncovered evidence that had been withheld from the original trial. The legal team fought hard for police documentation to be aired, but despite the findings proving to be legal dynamite, in December 2003 the Court of Criminal Appeal found the evidence that had been withheld would not in any way have changed the guilty verdict. By October 2004, when Mallard's legal team, headed by Malcolm McCusker QC, is given leave to appeal to the High Court – the stage for eminent judges to reconsider trial transcripts but hear no witnesses – Mallard had been incarcerated for nine years. Their findings were unanimous and damning: quashing his conviction, the High Court found a myriad of issues with which to argue, including withheld evidence and unreliable confessions. '. . . It also became apparent that a deal of [evidence] had been in the possession of investigating police before and during the trial, and had not then been disclosed to Mallard . . .'

The High Court was also scathing about aspects of the police interviews. Mallard complained that detectives set him up to sketch a plan of the shop in which Lawrence was murdered. Asked during a polygraph test why he did that, he replied, 'Because that's what the detectives told me to do. One of the detectives put a pistol in my face as well, in the car . . .' But it wasn't over yet. The High Court ordered a retrial at the discretion of the Director of Public Prosecutions, Robert Cock. With no new evidence, a retrial would always be difficult, but Cock did not rule out the possibility. He was supported in this by Commissioner Karl O'Callaghan, who stated in a media release from 2 December 2005, 'I strongly support the DPP decision to proceed with a retrial of Andrew Mark Mallard and I am unaware of any matters that could not be tested at the retrial . . . There is no information to hand that would warrant me to stand down or stand aside any of the concerned officers.'

Using parliamentary privilege, in December 2005 John Quigley raises the Andrew Mallard case in state parliament. He aims his missile with deadly precision: his speech, picked up by journalists, paves the way for the Crime and Corruption Commission to announce the following month that it will investigate the case.

Urging a presumption of innocence to all concerned pending further inquiries, Quigley says he believes the Mallard affair was an attempt to pervert the course of justice and that the Crime and Corruption Commission was the right avenue through which to investigate the matter. Quigley concludes: 'A man has been in jail for 11 years and the High Court has said it is because the police and prosecution suppressed evidence. This throws a great big question mark over the credibility of senior police in this town at a time when we as a community must place more and more trust in them because of the powers vested in them by the terrorism laws. The Assistant Commissioner [Caporn] in charge of the terrorism laws was one of the investigators involved in the Mallard case. Although there is a presumption of innocence, I am sure that all members share my concern about how people at the highest level in the police department have been conducting themselves.'

But if the police and the prosecution hoped the ripples from the story would quietly fade, they were not only wrong – they were about to be hit with a tidal wave. And if the Macro task-force had enjoyed a relative lack of criticism, able to take refuge in the police line that no information could be given because it is an 'ongoing investigation', the worm was about to turn. And two of those worms, according to many Macro insiders, have names.

Robin Napper and Rory Christie.

In mid-November 2001, Canadian Rory Christie's former wife, Susan Christie, a 42-year-old Australian, disappeared without a trace from her Perth apartment. The couple, who met in Canada in 1995, had moved to Perth after their wedding, where their son Fraser was born. But the marriage, strained by what the prosecution would later describe as mutual 'loathing and hatred', quickly eroded and the pair legally separated. The same year that Susan went missing, presumed murdered, Rory Christie gained full custody of Fraser, based on ugly family court documentation that showed Susan was a promiscuous alcoholic who mixed with equally hard-drinking friends. Despite her body not being found and his protestations of innocence, Rory was charged with Susan's murder several months after she disappeared. The celebrated 2003 trial was itself something of a mini-drama, titillating the public and avidly followed daily in the press. The real murderer, Christie's defence lawyer Belinda Lonsdale enigmatically told the court, could well be a witness for the prosecution. Rory Christie, she said, had neither motive nor opportunity to kill his former wife, but there was no shortage of other suspects who did. The police did not agree. They claimed Rory, then living in a de facto relationship, had lied about his whereabouts on the day Susan disappeared, had shown signs of panic when his car was to be forensically tested and had also tried to charter a yacht to leave Perth.

Found guilty, two years into his life sentence Christie's conviction was overturned and a retrial ordered. Canadian blood-splatter expert Constable Joe Slemko ('rent-an-expert' as the police call him) would testify for the second time that the blood found on Rory Christie's tie – the equivalent of the prosecution's 'smoking gun' – was not his former wife's but potentially watermelon juice, rust or horseradish. In a dramatic move, Judge John McKechnie ordered the charges be dropped and that Christie be released due to lack of evidence.

Christie, who bolted back to Canada with his son as soon as he was set free, told a Canadian newspaper that Western Australian police had used 'shoddy detective work' to build a case against him. 'If we held the case to Canadian standards, there wouldn't have been a trial,' he said. 'Everything they did was completely flawed and exaggerated. They didn't care if I was guilty or not. They wanted to get someone.'

Sergeant Brian Cowie, from WA police media, defended the original police investigation. 'It doesn't mean we didn't have the right person,' he said, defiantly, 'but we didn't have enough to convict that person.'

Two months after Rory Christie's acquittal, a government poll released its report that the satisfaction rating for WA police was an abysmal six per cent below the national average. The response from senior officers was that because there had been a delay in the opening of a call centre for the public, the dissatisfaction rating had risen. But journalists questioned this rationale. Eight weeks after Christie's acquittal, no police officer had been assigned to review the Susan Christie murder. Despite assurances that the case was open, it was gathering dust. It soon became obvious why: the case, according to many police, was already solved. There just wasn't enough evidence to keep Christie in prison.

One of the witnesses called in the Rory Christie trial, amongst a phalanx of people including Perth taxi drivers, that Susan Christie knew, was medical practitioner Dr Andrew Dunn. The name rings a bell and I rifle through papers to find my notes. He had started his testimony at Christie's trial by talking about his karate training at the University of Western Australia, later moving on to how he knew Susan Christie. Christie, Jenny Rimmer told me, had once had a drink at the local hotel, since razed, that she and Jane had favoured. I keep flicking through the pages. There it is. Sarah McMahon's family had bought Dr Dunn's house, and he had counselled Sarah's heartbroken father, Danny, after she went missing. Then I find Neil Fearis's notes. It was Dunn who had visited Fearis, sharing the information given to him by a patient that Ciara Glennon was to be offered up as a sacrifice over the Easter long weekend.

Perth seems to be getting smaller and smaller. Not six

degrees of separation, but far less. I add another note to the list. *Call Dunn.*

There is a pervading sense of parochialism in Perth, the sense that it is locked in a time warp, either unable or unwilling to shrug off vestiges of the past. A city where the adage 'six degrees of separation' converts to three, where the wealthy unashamedly rub shoulders with politicians and where judges attended the same private schools. Where interlopers with pretensions to wealth are snubbed on the cocktail circuit but the nouveau riche, their money built on booming real-estate or mining investments, are accepted in the city's most salubrious areas. A city of traditionalists, of bluebloods, where pedigree *does* matter. And that, according to one faction, is part of the problem. Perth, they claim, is crawling with Freemasons who protect themselves and each other. It is a city where half the judiciary are shaking hands with half the police.

In his inimitable, tongue-in-cheek fashion, Quigley describes in colourful language the taking of the Freemasons' oath. 'They put a bag over their head and a noose, and swear never to betray the brotherhood. They say they will hang and have their life snuffed out as this noose will snuff their life out; believe me, it is a serious business. Judges get up and swear to this, standing on one foot with a bag over their head and with their dinner suit on.' He takes a gulp of coffee. 'People say I draw a long bow, but I don't agree. To understand what is wrong with policing in the West, you need to go back in history.' The force, he says, was alternately run by two factions: the Catholics and the Freemasons.

Quigley's detractors – and he has many – point to what they regard as his, and others', obsession with Freemasonry in Western Australia. It is naïve and fanciful, they say, to claim that the city's power base is held by those who keep each other's secrets. 'The idea seems to be that if you are a Mason you can cover pretty much anything, including murder,' one tells me. 'Of course there is room for corruption always, but the system is open to so much more scrutiny than it used to be. Being a Mason cannot cover a multitude of sins. That's just a paranoid idea of the conspiracy theorists.'

It is the secrecy of the Masons that adds to its enigma. Threats of terrifying violence are levelled at every Mason candidate in case they transgress their codes of secrecy. For only the first three degrees of initiation, the oaths are a warning about the ordeal that awaits the Apprentice should he break that code. In the First degree, the Apprentice must agree to have his throat cut across, his tongue torn out by its roots, and his body buried in the rough sands of the seas, at low-water mark, where the tide ebbs and flows twice in 24 hours. Quigley recites the findings of the Standing Committee of the House of Lords in Britain which handed down its report on elements of Freemasonry in the UK in the 1990s. 'They said that the links between the police and judiciary at executive branches of government through Freemasonry were leading to miscarriages of justice because the judges weren't scrutinising their fellow lodge members. In Australia, after Queensland's Fitzgerald Inquiry, there was a parliamentary committee that looked at the impact of Freemasonry in that state's police force. They also reported that the close connections weren't right. Bottom line is that all police officers should be required to sign a register of their membership to secret societies.'

If Freemasons are relentless in promoting their brothers into high positions, how do I find out who is a Mason and who isn't? Unless they volunteer the information, it appears I can't. It is a secret society.

I could pose the question outright. 'Are you, or have you ever been, a Freemason?' They are hardly likely to tell me and this tactic will be problematic when so many police officers won't speak to me. And if it's right that Masons permeated the force in days gone by, what about now? I ask a colleague for advice.

'There's a register of names of Freemasons in Western Australia, though it's not public,' he tells me. 'Why do you want it?'

'Because if the inference is that some police may have been improperly protected because of links to Freemasonry, I'd like to know who is on that list. Can you check for me?' He says he'll see what he can do. I give him some names.

Two days later, he calls me back. Not one name I gave him, he says, is on that list.

52

In February 2002 – 38 years after he was found guilty of murder – WA appeal judges finally quashed John Button's conviction for the 1963 murder of his girlfriend, Rosemary Anderson. On the night of her death – Button's 19th birthday – Anderson had stormed out of his car after a petty tiff. It was an argument that, 40 years later, would continue to haunt those involved. And it would seal the reputation for Western Australia as a state renowned for shocking miscarriages of justice.

John Button came upon Anderson's body lying on the side of the road. On instinct he picked her up, put her in the car and drove to her family doctor, who took her to hospital. Interrogated for hours by police, a terrified Button begged to know of Rosemary's condition. Ignoring his pleas, he was finally answered. 'She's dead,' he was bluntly told. 'She died an hour ago.' Heartbroken and exhausted, in the early hours of the morning he signed the confession that police shoved in front of his face. Charged with wilful murder, what Button wasn't told was that earlier that evening, following an examination of his car, police officer Trevor Condren had given his opinion that Button's vehicle had not collided with a pedestrian. His advice was ignored. The driver, he was told, had confessed.

Convicted of manslaughter and sentenced to ten years with hard labour, Button would have hanged had the jury found him guilty of the original charge of murder. While he was released after five years and later married, his life was overshadowed by the stigma of his conviction. Dogged by depression and suicidal thoughts, over the next three decades Button crusaded for his innocence to be acknowledged and begged for his case to be reopened.

Bret Christian financed American car-crash expert Rusty Haight to test identical vehicles that both Button and serial killer Eric Cooke had driven on the night of Anderson's murder. His consensus – that it was Cooke's car that had hit Anderson, and not Button's – was overwhelming proof that the wrong man had been jailed for her murder. There was also Cooke's confession, that had not been believed. Chief Justice David Malcolm noted: '... Button's actions in taking Ms Anderson's still living body immediately to the nearby doctor, his persistent denials when questioned and his confession, only after several hours in police custody, all combine to lead me to the conclusion that the verdict must be regarded as unsafe and unsatisfactory on the grounds that there has been a miscarriage of justice ...'

I want to meet John Button, to talk to him about his perceptions of the police and the judicial system in Western Australia. Now 63, this gentle, reflective man, who has suffered numerous nervous breakdowns, only found peace when he finally found God. Bitterness and regret have gone; instead, he channels his energies into the Innocence Project he helped establish, which assists those he believes to be victims of miscarriages of justice in WA. It keeps him busy. 'All the people who have been put away for crimes they didn't commit – including me – constantly face the police, the DPP, judges and the silent jury members who will not come forward and admit they got it wrong,' he says. 'It is all so political. The Attorney General Jim McGinty once told me that there wasn't enough money in this state to pay me out what I should have got. What a shocking, shocking indictment on the system.'

In February 2002 Button's son Gregory, a doctor, sought an apology from the West Australian Police Service over the way they had handled his father's case. In June, Commissioner Barry Matthews replied. He had, he said, requested a full examination of the investigation by senior officers within the WAPS. After careful consideration – including a full review of the transcript of the decision by the Court of Criminal Appeal

– he was advised there had been no judicial criticism of police investigations or tactics at any stage of the trial, appeal and recent Court of Criminal Appeal proceedings.

'Accordingly,' he concluded, 'whilst it is regrettable that from time to time the best interests of parties associated with the justice system do not appear to be served, it is not appropriate in these particular circumstances that I apologise on behalf of the Police Service. I am conscious that you may not be satisfied with this decision and that over the years your family members have endured a significant amount of distress in this matter; however, I consider that it accords with the decisions of the respective courts.'

John blinks and looks to the ceiling, a nervous habit learned from years in prison. He hands me the letter to read. 'What it means is this: mistakes are made in this state but no one says sorry. So they've charged the wrong person? Bad luck. Jailed the wrong person? Bad luck. And, by extension, today in the Claremont case – if they target the wrong suspect, bad luck. Make mistakes? That's bad luck, too. They are never accountable.' He pauses at the door. 'But it isn't just bad luck, is it? It's tragic. Police say that my case happened years ago and that it could never happen today. But it does happen today. There are people in prison in this state that shouldn't be there, who are living proof of that. How are they going to solve the Claremont case if they continue to ignore the lessons of the past?'

53

In 1959, with no arrest after 12 months for the murder of chocolate heiress Jillian Brewster, and increasing pressure on the police to charge someone, the net closed on 19-year-old deaf-mute Darryl Beamish who, like Claremont suspect Lance Williams, lived at home with his parents. Profoundly deaf, his disability ensured he was no match for the relentless police questioning. For three days he protested his innocence; exhausted, terrified and sobbing, on the third day he finally confessed.

Convicted and condemned to death with the chilling words '*At a time and place to be fixed by the Governor, you be hanged by the neck until you are dead*', and with no interpreters to explain what was going on, Beamish was led down to the cells. Only after he had spent four months on death row was his sentence commuted to life imprisonment. When word filtered through the prison that Eric Cooke had confessed to Brewster's murder on the gallows, prisoners and wardens alike congratulated Beamish on his imminent freedom. Instead, he served 15 years. Even in the face of a government inquiry, born from disquiet at Cooke's last-minute guilty plea, that the Beamish case should perhaps be reviewed, the Supreme Court stood firm. Beamish would do his time. This case would go down in Australian crime annals as one with the longest time lag between sentence and its overturning on appeal. Finally, on 1 April 2005 – after six appeals – Beamish was exonerated. He was now 64 years old.

In his booklet *The Beamish Case*, which would later form part of the successful appeal's case, the late law professor Peter Brett warned that the story had all the hallmarks of a monstrous miscarriage of justice: shoddy police practices; a deaf-mute man who was ill-prepared to defend himself against the power of the state; a flawed prosecution and a system where the original judges were also the appeal judges on the case. Against this judicial tapestry, Beamish had no hope.

Like Button, Beamish was not aware that Eric Cooke had confessed to Brewster's murder and for the murder of seven others, six for which he was charged. Scotching Cooke's confession for Brewster's slaying as that of a man simply seeking notoriety, Beamish languished in prison while the police and judiciary avoided a public flogging for imprisoning the wrong man.

The closing sentence in Peter Brett's booklet leaves the reader in no doubt as to how he felt about this case. 'The judges, Crown law officers and police who participated in the sorry proceedings which I have described can be left to live with their own consciences.'

Following the granting of Beamish's appeal, Detective-Sergeant Owen Leitch – then the chief investigating officer on the case who would later become police commissioner – commented that he was 'deeply disappointed' by the court decision. So, too, Crown Prosecutor Ronald Wilson – later knighted and who would gain fame for penning the 'Stolen Children' report – who commented that he did not believe he was at fault for Beamish being convicted.

Beamish had some powerful supporters, among them his former lawyer. Sir Francis Burt would become Chief Justice and Governor of WA and openly admitted that this case shattered his belief that the judicial system would rectify its mistakes. When his conviction was finally quashed, Beamish famously stated that he did not want financial compensation. All he wanted was his good name back but even that, it seemed, was too hard. Despite the exoneration, Beamish remained under a cloud. In early January 1997 Macro taskforce officers stood on the front doorstep of his home, flashed their badges and told him they wished to speak to him about the Claremont serial killings. This time, Beamish was able to provide photographic evidence as an alibi, showing pictures of himself at a social function at the time one of the girls disappeared. As the police questions continued, the memory of his 1961 conviction, where he could not hear or understand anything that was said, must have returned to haunt him.

The Macro officers did not take an interpreter.

If policing has changed, John Quigley reflects, then so have the crooks. 'Gone are the old style who copped a fair whack and did their time; now, in the wicked grip of narcotics, the criminal world narks on each other and makes allegations about police officers, whether they are innocent or not. Paul Ferguson was the subject of one of those allegations. I defended him and the jury took about ten minutes to throw it out. It should never have got to court in the first place.'

Six months before Paul Ferguson's trial started in 2002, Commissioner Barry Matthews stood him back up on non-operational duties.

On 18 November 2000, *The West Australian* carried the frontpage story of Ferguson's return to the force under the headline 'Top Cop Back'.

> Senior-Sergeant Paul Ferguson walked back into Crime HQ at Curtin House yesterday after two and a half years on suspension on full pay and still facing trial next May for false testimony. Also, a review into Detective-Sergeant Peter Coombes is under way. After three years off the job with no charges having been laid, Commissioner Matthews said some officers would not be considered for reinstatement. Mr Ferguson is very popular. WA Union President Michael Dean said Mr Matthews had inherited a suspension policy from former commissioner Bob Falconer and had agreed to review the policy.

'That essentially meant I was standing in the box, in front of the jury as a serving police officer,' Ferguson says. Acquitted of all charges, he was promoted in 2003 to the rank of inspector. It was a moment he relished. 'It vindicated me, finally. I never blamed the police service for what happened to me, but I did blame the ACC. I was made a political scape-goat.'

Ferguson knew that serial killers don't start off with serial murder. 'All the old coppers knew that,' Quigley says. 'I once asked Jeffrey Noye – who was suspended over the Argyle Diamond investigation and is still fighting those allegations – what he would do if he had headed up Macro. He replied it would be hard work, but he would call every police station surrounding the Claremont area and coastal strip and tell them they had seven days to produce every offence report and any investigation into any act of perversion in their area. Someone who has jumped the back fence and been spotted sniffing a pair of G-strings on the line? He wants him. Someone who has put his hand on a girl's bum? He wants him. Throw the net wide, he said, and start aggressive inter-views with all those people. And if the bloke sitting in front of him who had jumped the back fence wasn't the murderer, he would know someone who knew someone who did know who the killer was. He'd shake the lemon tree as hard as he'd dare, this side of legality.' Instead, Quigley believes, 'One guy moved across the radar screen and they locked onto him at the risk of ignoring everything else. This is the new policing: putting a profile of suspects into a computer program and seeing what it spits out.'

54

In 1995, Britain led the world in its introduction of the first national DNA database, and the impact on policing was profound. Gone was the plodding, traditional means of cracking a case by relying heavily on the use of informants, or the obtaining of a confession. Now DNA, the 'unseen witness' at every crime scene, could also help investigators. From this point, the crime scene would belong to the scientist and the investigation to the police; both would work together in a symbiotic relationship, a fusion of forensic and intelligence-driven data. Within a short time, Europe and most areas of the United States followed the model set by the UK.

The concept of a National Crime Faculty, a 'one-stop shop' where investigators could access information and receive help or advice, was developed by Peter Ryan – who would later serve a sometimes controversial role as NSW police commissioner – and other police officers in Britain in the 1990s. Designed to target high-profile, low-volume crimes such as a complex murder or sexual offences, the information would be fed into the system and accessed by officers with limited experience in those crimes.

With a background as the national police adviser to the prison service for two years in which he did reviews of more than 40 jails, including the Sexual Offenders Unit, Detective-Superintendent Robin Napper had interviewed scores of serial killers and, he boasted, worked on more than 200 murder cases. Appointed Head of Operations for the National Crime Faculty, he was given the task of turning concept into reality. Over two years from 1996, the experience of police colleagues from all forces in Britain was collated into a database, with emphasis on those experienced in more obscure homicides. These were easily accessible under headings: 'Child Murder', 'Strangulation', 'Poisoning'. With this information at their fingertips, investigators could quickly find colleagues who had experience in specific areas and the forensic people with whom they had worked. The names and contacts of these specialists were recorded. In the event of a crime anywhere in Britain, no time would be wasted finding the appropriate specialist help. This would prove invaluable, particularly in the first, critical 48 hours after the commission of a crime. Regional liaison officers were appointed, working with the senior investigative officer to ensure the operation ran smoothly, and a 24-hour help desk was started to ensure immediate accessibility in the event of a crime.

Napper's faculty became particularly expert at looking at cold-case reviews. 'We were mandated in the UK to keep forensic exhibits – we couldn't get rid of them, even through the duration of a life sentence for a prisoner. So we could go back years after a crime and still have the evidence at hand.' In 1998, Napper was offered a position in Australia by Peter Ryan, then NSW police commissioner. Ryan needed people with forensic investigative skills – limited at that time in Australia – and there was no DNA legislation in place. Napper embarked on presentations about DNA in most Australian states, including information about its cost and impact on policing. In 2001 the University of Western Australia asked him if he would become involved in a forensic program they were offering to students; not a dry academic subject, but one that would be recognised in the wider community as a forensic force to be reckoned with. Napper agreed and was appointed marketing director.

'WA police were very friendly to me when I first arrived,' he recalls. 'I was invited for coffees and lunch. They saw the faculty as complementing what they do.' But that changed, he says, when he was approached by families asking if he would look at other cases, not just those in which the police had an interest. 'Science is neutral, it doesn't belong to anyone. But as soon as our view differed from the police standpoint, down came the shutters. I naïvely believed that Western Australian police would welcome knowledge of new techniques, but I quickly found that I would not be appreciated for introducing outsiders, or different methods of policing.' While the police see it differently – that Napper had his own agenda in getting bums on seats at the university course and his ego was dented by the apparent snub from police – the chasm grew wider.

Then came the Rory Christie case.

Napper made his opinion about the way the case had been handled abundantly clear to police. It was a shambles. Brought in by the defence halfway through the first trial, he came to the conclusion that there was a host of people who could have murdered Susan Christie. The trouble was, in Napper's opinion, one of those people was decidedly *not* her former husband, Rory. After Christie was convicted, Napper met with Commissioner Barry Matthews in December 2003 and aired his views that this was a shocking miscarriage of justice. 'I told him where I thought the police mistakes had been made and my opinion that the jury had been misin-formed. The police and prosecution's claim of blood on his tie, for example: it was never proved to be blood, only that it was Susan Christie's DNA. Police said also that when they did the presumptive test for blood, using Luminol, there was blood all over the unit. The problem is, Luminol reacts to other things as well. I don't disagree that Rory should have initially been a suspect, but there were others who were much stronger suspects – and particularly one man who for legal reasons I can't name. But no one else was regarded as a suspect. They just set their sights on Rory and never took them off him.' It is a story that I have heard about this police force, in different versions and different cases many times.

'Why would they do that?' I ask.

Napper shrugs. 'Don't know. Ask them.'

'I want to,' I remind him. 'But they won't talk to me. About anything.'

***

Napper's goal in meeting with Matthews and the assistant commissioner at the Forensic Centre was to suggest an independent investigator be assigned to the case to verify his suspicions about the man Napper believes is responsible for Susan Christie's murder.

'With my own police background, my review of the police investigation in the Christie case and the facts I had gained from interviewing people who had been scared to give evidence, I talked to them about what I regard as the link between other missing people in Western Australia and the person I suspect of Christie's murder. It was a two-hour meeting during which time I produced all my evidence.' Matthews's face, he says, grew longer and longer, and he left deep in thought. 'I asked whether he was prepared to bring in an investigator from out of state and three weeks later I got my reply. The answer was "No". Instead, he asked the Detective-Sergeant who was the office manager on the Christie case to come and see me. What an absolute waste of time that was! I never bothered because I knew nothing would come of it. Had Matthews got independent advice, Rory Christie could have been out of prison much earlier. He was eventually acquitted and released on 30 November 2005 – some two years later.'

Contemptuous of the information being handballed back to the original investigators who, Napper believes, already had tunnel vision, he says that the days that had passed before Major Crime took up the case from Missing Persons flawed the investigation from the beginning. 'Before Major Crime picked up the case, the crime scene was badly contaminated. No less than 14 people went through Susan Christie's flat during that time. *Fourteen* people.' Because of Christie's background as an alcoholic with a reputation for promiscuity, Napper asked to test the blood that was found on the couch and which was known to be hers. 'We reasoned it could have been menstrual blood, not blood from a murder scene. "Sorry, mate," the police told me. They had lost that piece of evidence! But the tragedy is, loss of evidence in the Christie case is not a one-off. It's still happening today in Perth. We've asked to look at a number of cases but when we go for the exhibits, we find they are either lost, destroyed or in one case, sold at public auction!'

The Christie case was a defining point in Napper's relationship with the police. From that moment, he says he was banned from every police station in Western Australia and from lecturing at the police academy. He was also barred from speaking to police officers when they came to the university. Napper shakes his head at the numerous times he has been approached by families to review prisoners' cases. 'I think there are so many wrongly convicted people, not only in Western Australia but right across this country, that governments are terrified that the truth will come out.'

In 2003, Napper was asked to write a paper on cold-case reviews by a family member of one of the Claremont victims. 'It was my understanding that this person then took the paper to the police commissioner and attorney general, and the thrust for the independent review came after that. I can't confirm that this is the case, because I was not there, but I believe this is so. I can't divulge the identity of the person who asked me to write the paper as I was sworn to secrecy and that person is still alive.'

55

Outlining the minutiae of how the National Crime Faculty operated, Napper stressed that officers learn as much from failure as success. 'With a combination of the rise of DNA, forensics and the NCF,' he wrote, 'senior officers increasingly saw an opportunity to have a completely fresh look at some older unsolved crimes. Prior to this, all unsolved crimes were retained by the police force that had primacy for the crime. The chief constables had absolute control, and were in some instances understandably reluctant to share with the outside world what they may have considered to be "failures".'

Napper moved to the problems initially encountered by the first cold-case reviews. In hindsight, he sighs, these problems would mirror the attitude he encountered in Western Australia after this paper was submitted. 'Many detectives felt affronted by the inclusion of an outside team,' he wrote. 'Some had strong suspects for their crimes and tried to steer the review team down a particular line of investigation . . .' In order to progress, four unbreakable rules were laid down. These rules would need to be addressed before the NCF would agree to conduct a cold-case review.

First, the chief constable would invite the NCF to conduct the review. Second, every skerrick of material held in connection with the investigation would be made available to the review team. Third, the forensic science laboratories handling exhibits for the case would be prepared to hand them over. Fourth, all costs would be carried by the chief constable's policing authority.

Admitting his knowledge of the Claremont case was limited to media speculation and general talk, under the heading 'Macro taskforce' he wrote, 'My strong belief is that a comprehensive "cold-case review" should now be considered.

With the improvements in forensic technology and the number of investigators and experts around the world skilled in these types of reviews, it would be possible to put together a formidable team to assist the West Australian Police Service. These forums have proven to be one of the most powerful investigative tools in the world. Clearly it is absolutely essential that the WA Police Service is supportive of such a review. This is not about criticising a police service who have had to cope with a very complex and difficult investigation. Rather it is about supporting the police service . . .'

Napper suggested other independent and highly experienced investigators who could be brought in to help, including criminal and geographic profilers, pathologists, general forensic experts and forensic archaeologists. The names forwarded included those who had worked on the macabre 'Cannibal' case in Germany, in which a man advertised – and found – another man willing to be killed and eaten, and the infamous OJ Simpson murder case. Napper noted that Dr David Barclay, a pre-eminent forensic expert with the National Crime Faculty in Britain, whom he holds in high esteem, had already advised on selected parts of the Macro investigation. For this reason, Napper opined that it may be beneficial to 'consult with someone else, fresh to the case'. This advice was ignored. Dr Barclay was used.

'From what I know of the Macro case,' Napper continued, 'it is highly probable the police are dealing with sexually motivated homicides involving a predatory offender. It will be essential to include other investigators skilled in this type of crime. The thinking, background and hunting pattern of these types of killers have been extensively studied elsewhere in the world.' Three criminal profilers' names were forwarded. None was used.

Napper spelled out his working knowledge of geographic profilers. 'Any case involving multiple crime scenes such as abduction and murder requires interpretation by a geographic profiler. The possible identification of "comfort zones" and "anchor points" has proved crucial in other investigations around the world. It enables investigators to focus their geographic attention onto suspects by their use of such things as the transport system and topography of the area.' Amongst the three names listed were men with years of experience in dealing with serial rapists. None was used.

Napper also stressed the importance of using the expertise of a forensic archaeologist. 'With one of the Claremont victims still missing, there is a possibility the body is buried in the bush. In addition, if a review turns up another suspect and the possibility of other concealed bodies, the advice of a forensic archaeologist will be invaluable. He/she would work in conjunction with the geographic profiler to narrow down a possible search area. Methods of searching, from cadaver dogs to ground-penetrating radar, are available. This method, together with triangulisation of mobile phone aerials, has proved very successful in the past.' The name of a forensic archaeologist who had worked on the Rose and Fred West case in Gloucester, England, with great success was put forward.

No archaeologist was used in the review.

Of the 12 names Napper nominated, only one – forensic expert Dr Malcolm Boots, whose role was to examine body fluids, hair fibres, DNA and interpretation of crime-scene evidence – was used.

Napper is now, according to WA police, persona non grata. 'I am dead in the water in Western Australia because I was prepared to listen to people who alleged they had been victims of miscarriages of justice. I was totally unaware at first of the "closed shop" mentality of the WA police. Even *talking* to people who claimed miscarriages had occurred barred me from the mythical police club. The attitude was: how dare I have a mind of my own and make my own decisions? In hindsight, I now realise they were terrified of the skeletons in the cupboards that modern DNA technology could expose. I was seen as the trailblazer of DNA in Australia, and if they couldn't control me, there was a danger that my new tactics could expose them. At least they got that bit right!'

Napper recognises that the culture in WA is very different to the UK. 'There, you are invited to help and be part of the team. Here, it's a "them" and "us" scenario. The attitude is, if they can't solve this, no one can.' Napper leans against his desk and peers intently at me. 'The saddest thing about all this is, they haven't solved the Claremont case. This is about power and ego blocking receptiveness to new techniques. And that's a tragedy.'

The whole point about crime investigation, he says, is being courageous enough to admit when you may have got it wrong. He recounts the story of a case he worked on in the UK 15 years ago. 'The police got a match through DNA and rang me. "Was I close?" I asked them, and they laughed. "Nah, you got nowhere near it! This guy was a serial rapist and traditional policing methods would never have got him." When we started working the DNA database, we discovered so many serial offenders travel around. But in Australia, the technology of DNA is still not linked up across the states. This, in a country that has such an itinerant population, where people think nothing of jumping in a ute and driving thousands of kilometres across the country.'

Napper counts the cases he has worked on that have highlighted miscarriages of justice in Western Australia, including Beamish, Christie and Mallard. 'All these cases exposed appallingly bad investigation techniques. As a result, some people in the WA police force would like to see me on a slow boat to China with no return ticket. Their lack of understanding of modern forensic and investigation methods puts them at least 20 years behind the culture I came from.'

He is amazed, too, at the lack of financial accountability in the WA police force. 'In Britain, we have a system called Midas where every cent spent on an investigation is accounted for. Rates of pay for officers, overtime, travel – every cent. Here, it's a financial bottomless pit. Ask how much the Claremont investigation has cost, down to the last dollar and cent, and see if someone can answer you. I bet they can't.'

Napper is right. When I ask Detective Senior-Sergeant

Anthony Lee the question, I am met with a general, vague answer. He doesn't know, he says, waving his hand in a figure-8 pattern through the air as he speaks. I would need to ask someone else that question. But who?

Napper remembers being astonished that the day Rory Christie gave evidence at the first trial, numerous detectives turned up at court. 'There was no reason for them to be there, other than the sheer weight of numbers to put pressure on Christie. It is doubtful they all had the day off work, so how much did it cost to have them there, off their shifts? Without being able to see the figures, the short answer to that is – a helluva lot of taxpayers' money.'

Napper says all the serial killers he has met have one thing in common. 'They can't switch on and off like a light switch. They've got what I call a disease: they can't stop. They can change modus operandi, they can change the way they operate, but they cannot *stop*. Whoever took Sarah Spiers, Jane Rimmer and Ciara Glennon was at the top of his form, operating at peak performance. Like an athlete in training for the Olympics. To actually have the nerve to go into an area, single the young women out, take them away and get away with it – he's not going to stop. He loves his work.'

'How long does it take to reach that peak performance?'

'How long does it take a sportsman to get there – five years, ten? And therein lies the clue. The answer to Claremont is in the precursor crimes that this person has committed. Instead of going to the day that the individuals disappeared, investigators should go back just before that. He – or they – wouldn't have just hit that area. He would have done his homework, he would have been down there before. It could be something as simple as a speeding ticket, a traffic accident, but he would have been there. He would know the way in and the way out. He could live there, be working there, just moved in there, socialising there. Look hard: he will be there somewhere, before that first girl went missing.'

56

Napper concedes it is not easy to catch a serial killer. 'Whoever did this is not going to worry about being caught. He'd make sure he had current rego papers, good tyres, a clean car and is sober. If he's pulled up on a random breath test, he's going to know he's okay even if the body is in the boot. His sense of self-preservation is incredibly high. Some of these people are so damn good at what they do, they are streets ahead of the police and the best the police can hope for is a lucky break. The trick is in recognising when they have got one.' The killer would work on the 'least effort' principle. 'Once he has killed, he will take the body to a comfort zone where he knows they won't be disturbed, and dump it not very far from the track or road. There is no need to take the body any further. Once the death has occurred, whatever thrills the killer got out of it, it's over. He will not spend a lot of time obsessing over a dead body; he will simply cover and dispose of it. That's not to say that some don't return to the scene to play with the body later.'

Serial killers exist for four things: they need to eat, drink, have shelter and sexual satisfaction. Nothing else matters to them. They have absolutely no feelings at all for another human being. 'The important part of geographic profiling is where the two bodies were dumped. Not only does this killer have a vast knowledge of Claremont, he also knows the areas where the bodies were tossed. He would not have taken the bodies somewhere unless he felt safe and comfortable at that disposal site. Even though one girl was dumped north and the other south, there will be a very strong link with where Jane Rimmer was found at Wellard, and Ciara Glennon at Eglinton. Investigators shouldn't be just looking at the Claremont area before the first girl went missing; the disposal sites are just as important. There will be a combination in the killer's background that will link all the areas. And that's not an easy job for the police. The parameters have to be set, information picked over. They should start with motive. Is it sexual? Who do the police know who has ever been convicted of a minor sexual crime in Claremont or any of the other dumping sites? Go through the local court registers, back a few years and look at who has been picked up for flashing, indecent assault, loitering with intent – offences of that nature. One of the biggest precursors to sexual crimes is house burglary: testing their mettle to see how good they are, to see if they can get away with it. So look in the background for domestic burglary, theft, violence, sexual crimes. Start getting a list of people together who may fit that list. It's hard work, bloody hard work. But there is no safe shortcut.'

Napper recounts the story of Fred and Rosemary West, the foul House of Horrors case. Then working at the National Crime Faculty, he sat through a two-day debrief on the case where all the main players, including pathologists and senior investigators, shared the information they had gathered with representatives of every force in the UK. 'It was about sharing the lessons. A major one that arose was medical confidentiality. One of the party tricks that Fred and Rose perfected was, when their girls were old enough, they took them down to the cellar and sexually abused them. They literally crucified them to the table, hammered holes in their hands to keep them still. These girls would eventually end up in hospitals around Gloucester to have all their injuries checked. They told doctors they had fallen over rusty nails, gave them any excuse at all but the truth. Rose had taken them in countless times, but because of medical confidentiality there was no back checking done. There was no sharing of information between hospitals. And so the Wests literally got away with murder, time and time again.

'The problem in Australia is lack of communication between police services. The DNA databases don't talk to each other. Timelines of individuals – where they have worked, where they have been, where they have lived – should be standard practice. Lay a template over a map of Australia and timeline the suspect's movements on the dates the offences occurred. Tie all the other information together and see what comes out. Chances are, when it is all sifted through, the identity of the Claremont serial killer could well become obvious.'

'But how,' I ask him, 'are we to know what police have and have not done?'

Napper frowns. 'With this highly furtive investigation and officers running around like secret squirrels, there is no way we, the public, can know anything with surety. And that's the problem. We have no comeback. We are told to sit back, let them do their work and to stop meddling in police business. But this attitude overlooks one bloody obvious point. They haven't got the Claremont serial killer. Whoever did it is still out there.'

And whoever is murdering prostitutes near Northbridge is, too. In April 2003 25-year-old street worker Darylyn Ugle's decomposing body was discovered by bushwalkers in a burnt-out tree trunk near a large weir north of Perth – some 60 kilometres south-east of Eglinton. An itinerant of Aboriginal descent, Ugle, though well known in the Northbridge area to other prostitutes and clients, was not reported missing. Hit with ferocious force by a blunt object, police admitted that while there was no real evidence to suggest the cases were linked, there could well be a connection between her murder and that of street worker Lisa Brown. And that connection was a serial killer who targeted the most vulnerable people in the community, next to children: prostitutes.

57

ABC television journalist and producer Wendy Page has been producing stories in WA since *Australian Story*'s inception in 1996. Although not her exclusive patch, her interest in justice issues in the West started with a story she produced in July 1998 about Tony Cooke, son of serial killer Eric Edgar Cooke. One story led to another; over the following years, her interest remained aroused with the number of overturned convictions and cases she believed were brought to trial on the flimsiest of circumstantial evidence and seriously flawed police investigations.

In February 2004 Page, who won the prestigious Walkley Award for her insightful and poignant programs on the Cooke story, aired a program on the Claremont killings. Entitled 'He Who Waits', it was a no-holds-barred exposé of the girls' families' grief, their opinion of how the investigation was handled and alternative ways of examining the evidence. If ever the WA Police Service was under the pump it was here, on national television, when opinions were aired that the investigation needed to be ramped up and that it was highly likely that more than three girls had fallen victim to the Claremont killer. While the program received extremely positive feedback from the public, the WA police were less than enthusiastic. Page and her team, they said, were afforded a lot of time but, despite that, a great deal of what they told Page ended up on the cutting-room floor.

'I had contacted *Australian Story* through their Brisbane office,' Paul Coombes says, 'and was put onto Wendy Page. My idea was to do a program on the Spiers family, to air their grief and to see if we could get some positive feedback about the Claremont girls from the public. But instead the program, to our disappointment, was used as a free kick against the police.

Almost none of the interviews I had organised for Wendy ended up on air. It was very disappointing.' It is not an argument with which Page agrees. The story, she says was poignant, sensitive and fair. The police were given an opportunity to speak and did so. In a half-hour show, she argues, the challenge is to fit in all points of view. Some just did not fit the Macro line. Others did, providing police with a prime opportunity to show what they were searching for.

'I think one of the very tangible ways that this crime could be solved is in the tracing of the particularly significant items of jewellery that are missing in relation to this case,' Caporn told the program. Anthony Lee showed replicas of the clothing worn by the girls the night they disappeared. 'Starting with Sarah's clothing, and in particular we'd like to locate a key ring, a sunflower key ring. Most notable with Jane's clothing and property is the small bag. And with Ciara's clothing, the most notable is a small brooch.'

Despite this, it is this program that police claim changed the parameters of their relationship with the media, a reason Page – who would later do an *Australian Story* segment on Andrew Mallard and a three-part special on the so-called Walsham Three, boys now serving time for a murder many believe they did not commit and which was, they claim, accidental death – also does not buy. But Robin Napper, who ventilated his opinion on the program that an independent review should be undertaken, finally got his wish. The day after 'He Who Waits' aired, police announced that just such a review would take place. Review number 11. Napper was not invited to join it.

'Look,' he says, 'I offered to help in the meeting I had with the assistant commissioner and the following year some members of the International Homicide and Investigators Association – of which I'm also a member – came over to Perth and also put their hand up to help, free of charge. That offer was also rejected. Why? Who knows? But I wasn't about to offer help again if all I got in return was a door slammed in my face.'

With no trace of embarrassment that the announcement of the review so quickly followed 'He Who Waits', Assistant Commissioner Ian Johnson made it clear to ABC radio that the investigation was about Sarah, Jane and Ciara. 'If these people can get together as a team and come up with some new lines of inquiry or validate what we've done, then that's what we're here about.' Johnson defended the officers who worked on the Macro taskforce as being dogged by the desire to bring a resolution to the case. 'We don't have a closed mind, we've never had a closed mind on Macro,' he said. 'All we want to do is solve the bloody thing.'

The fallout from the program was enormous. Napper's criticism of the way Western Australian police handled the Claremont investigation and his suggestions for how to improve their work are met with outright hostility from within the force. They fight fire with fire.

Police invite journalist Luke Morfesse to look up a report by the NSW Police Integrity Commission, known as Operation Malta. They also suggest Luke take a closer look at a review into the 1998 investigation of Wagga Wagga triple murderer, Matthew James Harris. Morfesse followed the suggestion and duly reported in the newspaper what he found. If police had hoped to publicly embarrass Napper from the story, it worked. It also soured Morfesse's previously cordial, professional relationship with Napper. 'The next time I saw him, at the university where a few journalists had gone for a story, he pulled me aside and said the article I had written was professionally damaging for him,' Morfesse recalls. 'Other journalists were pumping up his tyres but, as much as we sometimes like to, unfortunately we can't decide not to run a story just because it may offend someone. We constantly run the risk of losing contacts because of that, but we have to tell it like it is. So I ran the report.'

In 1998 Matthew Harris was charged with strangling to death three people in the space of 35 days. Napper was approached by NSW Police Comissioner Peter Ryan to take a fresh look at the triple killings. Ryan had raised concerns that some of the information surrounding the case was incorrect and approached Napper because of his experience with cold-case reviews in the United Kingdom. Putting his concerns in writing to Ryan, Napper suggested two of the murder charges against Harris be revised. This was despite Harris' own admissions, during a police record of interview, that to murder, keep murdering and to get away with it was an achievement. 'I'd still be going if I hadn't been caught,' he boasted. On the strength of Napper's recommendations a new investigation, codenamed Operation Novassa, was initiated. It drew blanks and the charges against Harris stood. Pleading guilty, he was imprisoned for life with no parole. 'When *The West Australian* asked Mr Napper if he had recommended that the charges be dropped,' Morfesse wrote, 'Napper said: "On the material that was made available to me, that's correct." Later, Mr Napper said that he had only suggested that the charges be referred back to the DPP. But a source close to Operation Novassa . . . claims he clearly sought to have the charges against Harris dropped.' Morfesse didn't stop there. Writing that Napper had denied that his work on the Harris case could be called a review, he added that 'the NSW Police Integrity Commission report on Operation Malta clearly states: "Ryan requested that Napper and (fellow seconded officer) Seddon review the investigation . . ."'

Why has Napper been overlooked by the West Australian police? His work was fundamental in solving the horrific rape case of a 91-year-old virgin in Wee Waa, NSW, on New Year's Day, 1999. Implementing mass DNA testing, the prime suspect cracked under the pressure while waiting for the results from his mouth swabs to come back from the lab. The result did not surprise Napper, but the DNA testing almost didn't take place. The plan was initially met with outright hostility and opposition by the NSW Assistant Commissioner Clive Small, who had commanded the Ivan Milat backpacker murders. Small told Napper that that type of technology 'would not work in the scrub'. The bad blood between Small and Napper was spectacularly aired at the Police Integrity

Commission (PIC) hearing, when Small described Napper as an 'outright liar' who appeared disconnected from the real world. His attack was savage. 'In my view, Mr Napper was a well-trained and highly polished second-hand car salesman and an operationally incompetent officer,' he continued. Small did, however, make one concession, acknowledging that Napper had done an 'excellent job' of selling DNA testing. In retaliation to Small's less than flattering assessment of his work, Napper sniped to *The West Australian* that Small was 'the most un-forensically directed head of a crime organisation' that he had ever come across.

Napper's critics also point to his boast that the UK DNA database has 'hundreds of hits per month' as being a little off the mark. In reality, they claim, many of these 'hits' are for crimes that have already been solved, such as a confession that had already been made. Napper also, they say, ignores the difficulties experienced by the UK program, including the huge numbers of UK police who point-blank refused to provide their own DNA for elimination purposes, lest it could be used in paternity suits, or the furore that evolved when it was found that the UK Forensic Science Service had illegally stored the DNA profiles of thousands of innocent people.

58

It was one of the more sensational scandals in Western Australian history, one that saw police pitted against police, with allegations of corruption, sexual abuse and preferential star treatment and, when it finished, it was a scandal that left more questions than answers. At its heart was Deputy Police Commissioner Bruce Brennan, who had overall operational command of the police force, Superintendent Dave Caporn and Inspector John Brandham. It also pivoted on a woman codenamed at the subsequent Kennedy Royal Commission as Q1 and a legendary sports star who would come to be known as Q2.

In 1998, months before a review of the Child Abuse Unit showcased serious deficiencies in the system, a woman in her 40s complained to the unit that for years, from the age of 13, she had been systematically sexually abused by the sporting hero. Taking the distressed woman's statement was Detective-Constable Cristina Italiano. In light of Brennan's perceived friendly association with Q2, in August, Detective Senior-Sergeant Mick Miller briefed Caporn and Brennan about the investigation.

By October 1998, Caporn was reviewing the file. The following month, he advised Brandham that there was insufficient corroborative evidence against the suspect to proceed. But this did not change Caporn's belief, proven in a document later tendered to the Royal Commission, that Q1 was telling the truth about her claim of sexual abuse.

In the explosive atmosphere that had been generated by Operation Cathedral, an inquiry into international paedophile rings which involved more than 100 search warrants being executed in no less than 13 countries, Caporn described it as a 'judgment call' as to whether this case was the Child Abuse Unit's most important one.

With the fallout from the allegations and counter-allegations becoming a lethal time bomb, Brennan steadfastly denied a friendship with the sporting legend. Despite this, over the next few months, Brennan met or telephoned the sports star five times.

On 10 November 1998, Caporn instructed Italiano that, regardless of whether the suspect confessed, he was to be released without charge so that Caporn could reassess the evidence. A week later, when Italiano and another officer surprised Q2 at his home early in the morning she was surprised when he invited them to come in. 'I've been expecting you,' she recalls him saying – a comment Q2 would later deny.

Taken down to the station, Q2 was not charged. The inference in Italiano's statement was undeniable. If the sports star had knowledge of their impending arrival, it was reasonable to believe he could have been tipped off about the visit. Shortly after the November interview, Brennan and Q2 went bike riding together around the Swan River. The investigation, they would later say, was not discussed. By December 1998, Brennan wrote a letter supporting Q2's application for a youth grant.

Distressed at what she regarded as senior police interference in the inquiry, Italiano had originally taken her complaint to Anti-Corruption Commission investigator Paul Lines, who warned her that she should 'watch her back'. Caporn, Italiano later told the ACC, had told her to terminate the interview and issued an order that even if the suspect had confessed, he must not be charged. This was, in her opinion, corrupt. ACC chairman Terry O'Connor QC did not agree, insisting that there was nothing improper in Caporn's instructions. Italiano's complaint, and that made by the woman at the centre of the allegations, were dismissed by the ACC, as was the allegation that Brennan was a friend of the sports hero. The officer in charge of the unit stopped the interview with the former footballer, he said, because the man's lawyer wished to be present.

When the matter reached the Kennedy Royal Commission in 2002, with a brief to investigate whether Brennan and Caporn had interfered in the case prior to the termination of Q2's interview, the former officer in charge of the abuse unit, Detective Senior-Sergeant Mick Miller, said he had never seen a case handled as this had been. It was, he said, tantamount to 'death by memo' from senior officers – 37 memos that just kept coming. Both Caporn and Brennan defended the allegations made by the four detectives originally involved in the case. Brennan, who described his friendship with Q2 as 'professional', denied any interference. Caporn – at the time of the allegations head of Macro as well as the Personal Crime Division, which included homicides and sexual abuse – suggested that the idea was nothing more than a conspiracy theory in the minds of the alleged female victim and Italiano and that suggestions of a corporate cover-up were baseless. His involvement came about because the case had not been handled at all well by the junior officers.

'I did nothing more than my job,' he declared resolutely. 'There is no whitewash here. I sit here with absolute confidence that any reasonable thinking person who examines all of the material on this could not come to this conclusion.' Brandham, who had been handed responsibility for the Child Abuse Unit in September 1998, said some junior detectives would not accept that there simply was insufficient evidence to charge the suspect and that he was in full support of the review undertaken by Caporn.

The outcomes left a rancid taste in Italiano's mouth. In a letter to the Royal Commission she said she requested and received a transfer. 'It got me out of Curtin House, which was where Mr Caporn was working from,' she wrote. She was, she added, still not satisfied that there was no interference in the investigation.

An editorial in *The West Australian* was also scathing. Why, it asked, was Q1 never interviewed by the ACC? Why did the Royal Commission not delve into claims that Caporn had told a child abuse detective that he would have lost his job if Q2's arrest had gone through? Why, of all the cases investigated by the child abuse unit, was this the only one that had the imprimatur of senior officers? '. . . Here is a case where four serving detectives have clearly stepped outside the so-called blue wall of silence to name their own and have been stopped in their tracks. It is safe to say that nowhere is the Australian tradition of not dobbing as strong as it is in the force. More importantly, why would they risk their careers and hard-won reputations by accusing Superintendent David Caporn and other senior police of improper conduct if there was nothing in it . . . ?'

The 'State of Excitement' as WA is called has another side, a darker side not mentioned in the postcards. As the gateway to Asia, its untamed, unwatched coastline is the perfect door through which to import hard drugs and its massive, remote cattle stations are ideal for growing marijuana crops. Where there is money in drugs, there are major organised crime syndicates. And where there are crime syndicates, there is corruption. It was the brief of the Kennedy Royal Commission to discover the extent of the police corruption in WA.

It opened in an explosive fashion, with the hearings of the so-called 'Kalgoorlie Six' detectives, alleged to be involved in morphine deals and high-level subterfuge. By the time the commission opened, two of the six had been sacked and two had resigned. It would continue over the next 18 months, dragging from one allegation of corruption to the next and cost a staggering $28 million. The inquiry would pit cop against cop and elicit this warning to corrupt police from John Quigley, their former saviour. 'They're not going to look after you, fellas! From here on it's every man for himself.'

Hot on the heels of the *Australian Story* exposé, on 2 March 2004 Royal Commissioner Geoffrey Kennedy delivered his much-anticipated findings into the West Australian Police Service. While some of former Commissioner Bob Falconer's Delta reforms, which saw the rationalisation or abolition of some branches within the service, were commended, overall the report was blistering in its criticisms. Spanning 1000 pages, Kennedy shone the spotlight on what he perceived as significant, sustained conduct by more than 50 past and present police officers that was both corrupt and criminal. Police culture and poor management, he found, had allowed the corruption to flourish. Officers had been involved in drug dealing, fabrication of evidence, assaults and burglaries. The force was insular and riven by different factions. In short, he found, this service was the most mediocre in the country. The final report of the Royal Commission concluded that, '... [The West Australian Police Service] has been ineffective in monitoring those events and modifying its procedures to deal with that conduct and to prevent its repetition ... The fact that there remain in WAPS a number of officers who participated in this conduct, and who not only refused to admit it but also uniformly denied it with vehemence, is a matter of concern.'

Kennedy, who did not make a ruling on whether an officer was innocent or guilty was circumspect, warning that the age of the allegations would ensure that they would be difficult to prove and that, as a result, many officers would not be prosecuted. That decision would be left to the Corruption and Crime Commission, the police commissioner and the DPP. Kennedy did not mince words. Recommended in the clean-up was the appointment of a new police commissioner, two deputies and an executive director who was not serving in the force.

Former Premier Geoff Gallop described the findings as revealing a totally unacceptable situation. 'We set this report up to tell us the truth ... the truth carries a very, very significant message and I think what we've got to do is respond to that message,' he told the media. But his views weren't shared by Falconer, who was cautious in his assessment of the report. 'The people who put this report together I think have underdone the achievements and the good work of a whole host of honest police who thank goodness are the majority,' he told Perth's

ABC Morning program. Outgoing Commissioner Barry Matthews was aggrieved. The Royal Commission, he griped, was a political decision. But the challenge now was to find a new broom to sweep the force clean. A new commissioner.

He was in their own backyard – Karl O'Callaghan, then acting deputy commissioner. This time the government would ensure the top job went to an officer from within Western Australia's own police ranks.

Forty-seven years old, O'Callaghan – the first WA police commissioner to boast a PhD and the youngest ever appointed to the position – joined the service in Western Australia at 17. One of his first priorities is to put in place the recommendations of the royal commission – and to choose an executive team. In line with addressing the findings of the Kennedy commission, O'Callaghan looks to driving the police forward with a new philosophy: sending the right person to the right place at the right time to do the right thing. He introduces the 'Front Line First' policy and an organisational name change. From now on, the force will be known as Western Australia Police. O'Callaghan is also not adverse to courting the press. Journalists speak of enjoying curry nights with the commissioner, who is a known raconteur with a broad range of interests, from playing guitar to enjoying his home indoor theatre.

Margaret Dodd is not interested in his extracurricular activities. Within a short time of his taking office, O'Callaghan becomes the recipient of her letter-writing campaign.

Firstly please except [sic] my congratulations on the appointment of your new position; I look forward to the possible changes to improve our police . . . I ask that the same level of commitment that has been afforded to operation 'Macro' be also afforded to operation 'Bluegum'. A blind man could see the huge difference in resources used in the Claremont case and that of the Hayley Dodd case. An explanation was once given to me by the Police Minister as to why this was the case. 'The business community was outraged that this should happen to one of their own.' Well WA is not made up of business people alone and any decent person would be outraged that these sorts of crimes can be committed against anyone at all, no matter what their social standing was . . .

Continuing a blistering attack on how she regarded the way police had treated the case, she concluded that she wanted an independent review of every detail of Hayley's case. A return letter from the commissioner, dated 24 November 2004 assured Margaret that two internal reviews of Hayley's case had been conducted in May and October 2002 and that the findings were that the police response was both 'appropriate and timely'. The Macro review panel had also, he wrote, been given details of Hayley's case. Margaret fired a letter back.

In five years, she wrote, she had received just one letter from former Commissioner Matthews regarding Hayley. Where was the substantial number of police O'Callaghan claimed had been involved in the first critical 48 hours after her disappearance? Her recollection of the Major Crime Unit was not of a professionally managed team but of one that was inconsistent, frustrated at the lack of resources provided and lacking in either compassion or understanding. Finally, she concluded, '. . . on reading this communication [my family] found it to be constructed in a fashion that is repulsive and bombastic, in fact, it was the most repulsive and bombastic peace [sic] of literature we have ever had the misfortune of reading, it lacked any human emotion, understanding or compassion. And we find it abhorrent that such a letter could be constructed by someone so highly educated.'

Within weeks, Margaret receives lengthy letters from Dave Caporn, trying to placate her. It doesn't work.

59

Already struggling to breathe from the negative publicity surrounding the Mallard case, the Walsham Three case puts further pressure on the WA police. What started as a group of young people – Salvatore Fazzari, Jose Martinez, Carlos Pereiras and a juvenile – enjoying a night out on 27 February 1998 ended with convictions for murder and a verbal brawl between certain members of the media, police and judiciary. The case centres on the death of heavily intoxicated 21-year-old Phillip Walsham, who fell from a pedestrian footbridge over a freeway early in the same morning that Fazzari's group was out partying. What is not in contention is that the group, armed with tyre levers, had earlier attacked Walsham without provocation as he sat alone near a train station, cradling his head in his hands.

But this is where the story veers off. The jury, according to the boys' supporters, got it wrong. Horribly wrong. The girls in Fazzari's group, disgusted at the unprovoked attack, say Walsham was still sitting on the bench after the boys had left. The boys say they went to McDonald's. The police say they returned to the footbridge and either pushed or threw Walsham off of it.

Charged with assault in 1998, the boys thought that was the end of the story. But in 2001 Inspector Scott Higgins reviewed the case. Two years later, the matter was before State Coroner Alistair Hope, who decided Walsham had been beaten and then pushed or thrown off the bridge. The DPP agreed, and in March 2004 the four boys were each charged with wilful murder. Advocacy groups, the boys' families and journalists, including Bret Christian, took up the rallying cry.

Christian shakes his head. 'Look, if they did it, fine. But this case overlooks some basic facts. There are no witnesses to him being pushed or thrown and no forensic evidence that says the boys murdered Walsham. And some evidence is missing. Again.'

What is *not* missing is the crucial evidence of a witness who does not claim to have seen Walsham pushed but who says she saw Walsham backflip off the bridge and bounce onto the road. Just prior to that happening, she told the court, he had been surrounded by a group of men. As the men continue to fight to have their convictions overturned, the police and judiciary are equally adamant that they got it right the first time. This campaign to free the boys, Inspector Scott Higgins told *The Australian*, appeared to be predicated on the assumption that justice in WA is completely rotten. 'It is a symbiotic relationship because the defendants all want to get off, the journalists want a good story and maybe a book or prize and the lawyers want the publicity.'

But mistakes were made. Bad mistakes, including that the four men were charged before a medical report was released as to whether Phillip Walsham was pushed off the footbridge or drunkenly fell over. When they did come in, the results were inconclusive. Neither was there an investigation into whether Walsham was hit by a car after he landed on the road.

In March 2006, after a first trial resulted in a hung jury, the men were each convicted of either throwing or pushing Walsham to his death off the footbridge and are serving 10-year prison terms.

Tom Percy QC, defending the boys, says some of the cases that he has seen over the past 30 years support his contention that Western Australia police simply choose who they will prosecute and then run with it. It is a viewpoint that DPP Robert Cock vehemently rejects, as does Karl O'Callaghan. But O'Callaghan did not avoid the subject of some missing evidence. The system, he admits, needs to do better. Future exhibits need to be more carefully guarded and more carefully preserved.

60

In April 2004 – just months before a state election – WA Police Union President Mike Dean tells the press that it is faster to get a pizza delivered in Perth than it is to get police to attend to serious crimes. Caporn had vacated his position as head of Macro in late 1998, leaving for a promotion, and the taskforce has had several leaders since. In this atmosphere of discontent, the Macro taskforce is now under the stewardship of nuggety Detective-Sergeant Martin Crane, who took over responsibility in October 2003 following Detective-Sergeant Anthony Lee's departure on transfer after a brief four-month tenure.

Crane is standing at Norma Williams's doorstep, flashing a search warrant. She groans. *Not again.* It is now seven years after Ciara was found murdered. When are they going to let up? Resigned to the intrusion, she lets them pass. It's a repeat performance of the first time: the house teeming with officers, drawers and cupboards turned out, the smallest item of interest scoured. In their home for hours, police give her a cursory nod when they have finished. She closes the front door, leans against it and draws a deep, unsteady breath.

Talk of justification for redress or compensation for 'persons of interest' or 'prime suspects' who have been publicly outed is summarily dismissed by Macro insiders. 'The taskforce,' Tony Potts tells me, 'always operated ethically and lawfully within the boundaries of propriety and morality. I do not consider there is any justification or avenue for Lance Williams or anyone else to cry otherwise.'

One of Barry Matthews's last hurrahs before he left office in June was to announce the team that would form the independent review into the Claremont killings. Unless, he said, positive lines of inquiry could be followed, then the taskforce would be disbanded. The decision caused a furore. The inquiry was, in police words, still 'on-going'. How could they collapse a taskforce that had achieved no results?

The review, Matthews announced, would be a 'big bang' to see if anything further could be done to successfully conclude the case. The team: Superintendent Paul Schramm, veteran of more than a hundred homicide investigations, including the biggest serial-killing case in Australian history, the chilling 'Bodies in the Barrels' murders in South Australia where 11 people were murdered, eight of whom were interred in barrels of acid. Hard-nosed NSW Detective-Inspector Russell Oxford, an experienced homicide investigator who had reviewed other serial-murder cases. Dr David Barclay, head of physical evidence at the National Crime and Operations Faculty in the United Kingdom. Malcolm Boots, a forensic expert with vast experience in reviewing homicides. Matthews does not name the fifth team member whom, it transpires, is former international policewoman of the year, Joy Kohout, who has 30 years experience in investigating sexual homicide.

The 'big bang' will start with raids on the property of a high-profile Perth citizen – former Claremont mayor Peter Weygers.

Tom Lawson, a colleague of Weygers, met him in 1999 and since then has become something of an apologist for both the man and his divisive character. In between bites of food at his favourite Indonesian restaurant in Northbridge, Lawson quotes a saying from Kentucky, where he grew up. 'There are them as swear by 'im, and them as swear at 'im.' A high-profile civil libertarian known for his outspoken ways, Weygers has upset many people in powerful places and it is this, coupled with other reasons, that Lawson believes made him a target as the Claremont serial killer. Warned by his lawyer, eminent QC Tom Percy, not to make any further comments in the press – including talking to me – Weygers is now forced into uncharacteristic silence. Lawson chuckles.

'Trust me, Peter finds being quiet harder than anything. Well, almost anything. In a small city like Perth, being a suspect in Claremont was an unmitigated nightmare, and one I believe that was a carefully orchestrated and politically motivated campaign against him. People run on the premise that where there is smoke there's fire, but the point is, who started the fire? He has powerful people against him.'

A former school psychologist in Perth primary schools, Weygers has outraged and ostracised many people with his strident and inflammatory viewpoints. Once his nettle is up, he is renowned for flooding newsrooms with his opinions, not letting up for months at a time. One such issue was the suicide of Penny Easton, which put him on a direct collision course with the government and with Carmen Lawrence, the first female premier of an Australian state.

In 1992, a petition was tabled in WA parliament by a Labor member alleging that Penny Easton – then embroiled in an ugly and protracted divorce settlement with her powerful public servant husband, Brian Easton – had perjured herself in the Family Court. The petition also alleged that then-MP Richard Court had leaked documents to Penny Easton to help her divorce case. The story may have been shelved as just another grubby political exercise but for one tragic fact: four days after the petition was aired, Penny Easton committed suicide. Her family laid the blame for her death squarely on the tabling of the petition and also made explosive claims that Lawrence had authorised it to damage her political rival, Richard Court.

The Easton affair seemed an old scandal when Keith Wilson, a now-retired minister in Lawrence's cabinet, agreed to reminisce about it with a journalist a few years later. While Lawrence had long denied any knowledge of the petition, Wilson insisted she was privy to discussions about it prior to it being tabled. What followed was a political stoush of Shakespearean proportions.

In February 1993 Richard Court won the premiership. In mid-1995 he established the Marks Royal Commission into the saga. In this, he had the full support and assistance of Peter Weygers, a close ally of Easton's mother, Barbara, who had pushed for her daughter's suicide not to be forgotten. Charged with three counts of perjury following the commission's adverse findings against her, at her trial Lawrence claimed loss of memory about the affair so often that the press endowed her with the title 'Lawrence of Amnesia'. Found not guilty, the fallout nonetheless did not help her political career. Viewpoints that Weygers expresses about notorious serial rapist Gary Narkle are not well received either and do little for his mayoral career.

In April 2004, when Narkle was freed on a technicality after his alleged 14th victim was too distressed to testify against him, Weygers supported him. Narkle, he said, should fear women more than they fear him. Comparing Narkle with soccer star David Beckham who, like Shane Warne, was in the limelight as much for sex scandals as sporting prowess, Weygers said the accused rapist is inevitably blamed when women voluntarily have sex with him and later regret it. 'He is a sensitive person; he is an artist,' he said. His statements attracted the ire of community groups, the Education Department and Attorney General Jim McGinty, who described the comments as bizarre and shallow.

'Weygers has that effect on people,' Lawson says. 'Some people think he walks on water, others that he should be taken out and shot.'

Premier Alan Carpenter, formerly the Minister for Education and Training, has been vocal in trying to have Weygers removed from the Education Department on charges of sexual harassment. One of the charges was from his immediate superior, a male, who said that Weygers looked him up and down and made him feel uncomfortable. Lawson scoffs at the concept of Weygers being in any way interested in men. 'He is heterosexual to the core,' he says. 'Men do not appeal to him.' But women do. 'Okay, he has sometimes been guilty of bumbling with women, perhaps saying inappropriate things,' Lawson admits. 'He loves women, but it is a bloody long stretch from that to being a serial killer.'

In his role as mayor, Weygers was highly visible. Everyone knew him. *The West Australian* reported that he trawled the streets at night,' Lawson says. 'It's true; he did. It was called the Mayor's Walk, when he looked into dark corners to see if there was any trouble. We are not privy to the reasons why Macro named him as a "person of interest" but it could almost be funny. He's big and ruddy-faced with a shock of silvery hair. When the killings started he had been mayor for 11 years. Everyone knew him. If he had been skulking in the byways of Claremont waiting to murder beautiful young girls, you can be sure someone would have hailed him and said "Hi Peter! What are you doing out this time of night?" It's simply nonsense to claim that he could prowl the streets for innocent young girls without being noticed.'

Taxi driver Steven Ross, who had volunteered to police that Sarah Spiers was in his taxi the night before she disappeared, lives in a transportable behind a house owned by Weygers in suburban Embleton. He has known Weygers since the early 1990s when Weygers successfully acted on his behalf in a complaint matter laid against him by a passenger. In 2001 financial strife had forced Ross to sell the property he owned at Embleton, and Weygers bought it. Ross had hoped to stay in the house with Weygers but told the media, in his inimitable fashion, that he wasn't welcome. 'They didn't like my smell and reckoned I stunk the house out and they put me out the back. All I do is work and sleep. I eat the wrong food and fart a lot. They found out I was pissing in the esky instead of going to the toilet.'

With the tenth review of the Macro taskforce in the offing, on 25 August 2004, police issue a search warrant against Steven Clegg (Ross). It is specific, citing 'reasonable grounds' for suspicion: 'Clothing and jewellery belonging to Sarah Ellen Spiers, namely tailored Portman's beige shorts, light-coloured t-shirt, black denim jacket and beige suede shoes . . . and a yellow metal keyring in the shape of a sunflower. Clothing and jewellery belonging to Jane Louise Rimmer, namely blue denim Billabong jeans, long-sleeve dark-blue stretch top, short jacket in blue corduroy, elastic-sided black shoes and a small handbag with a long strap.' Ciara's belongings include the fun items she had bought in preparation for her sister's hens night. 'Clothing and jewellery belonging to Ciara Eilish Glennon, namely a black woollen Bracewell suit jacket, yellow metal circular Claddagh brooch, large black shoulder bag, black leather slip-on shoes, brown rimmed sunglasses, a little vibrating Softee vibrator and child dummy in the shape of a penis.'

The warrant also seeks documents and records relating to Spiers, Rimmer and Glennon and fibre, blood and soil samples.

61

In a highly public move, on 5 September 2004 plain-clothed police swoop on the house Weygers owns in Embleton where Ross lives out the back. It is, according to Lawson, a move akin to American wrestling – all choreographed hype and little substance. 'Plain-clothed police jumped over the back fence and scared the hell out of Weygers's tenant,' Lawson says. 'He thought it was a home invasion, with police roaring through doors and swarming all over the place. Weygers rang the local police station and the boys in uniform turned up. They had to tell them that the "thugs" were plain-clothed coppers. It seems the police joined the dots and decided on a huge show of force, with the press watching. But how did the press know about this raid? Did they suddenly develop telepathic powers?'

Asked how they got the information, journalists responded that neighbours had tipped them off. When Weygers checked the veracity of this story, the neighbours all denied it.

The Macro officers seize two vehicles. Accused of being the 'delivery man' for Peter Weygers during a police interview that lasts more than two hours, Ross is also forced to provide a DNA sample. After being brought a pie and a drink, taskforce officers ask him to sign a confession admitting that he had picked up all three girls in his taxi and had delivered them to Weygers's house. Ross baulked. 'I'm innocent,' he spluttered. 'I'm not signing nothing.'

In a lengthy, unsigned statement to the press, formulated in his lawyer's office, Ross details his claims that police had attempted to get him to make false admissions about Weygers the day before the raid on the civil libertarian's home. 'The police made derogatory remarks about Peter Weygers and implied that I was involved in a homosexual relationship with him,' he wrote. 'I denied that I was in a homosexual relationship with Peter Weygers and that he was not my boyfriend. The police alleged that Peter Weygers exerted an abnormal influence over me, which I denied. The police alleged that Peter Weygers gave me orders that I carried out, which I denied. The police then stated words to the effect that Peter Weygers "wanted" young girls.' Approached to make a comment, Crane refused.

'Weygers had cautioned Steven not to put his hand up and say that he had had Sarah in his taxi, but he did it anyway,' Lawson says. 'But instead of being thanked for the information, he got on the Macro taskforce database. That's one free list you don't want to be on. It's easy to get on the list, but bloody hard to get off.' Lawson says it appears that when police gave up on the theory that Weygers may be the killer, it was then they concocted the idea that he was the brains behind the outfit and that there was a 'catcher' involved: Steven Ross. 'When police raided Ross's house, Ross was driving the same car, a Falcon station wagon that he had been using as a taxi when the girls went missing. When the taxi registration ran out, Ross bought the car.'

Lawson looks incredulous when he recounts the theory about how Ross was embroiled in the investigation. 'The thought that this self-confessed grub could somehow entice the girls into his car and take them back to Weygers's house is astonishing. People who know Ross understand there is no way that this bloke in his late 40s could seduce those classy girls into his cab. To say he's not exactly a smooth talker is an understatement.' Told by police that the taxi booking readings on the computer were blank for the nights all three girls disappeared, Ross was refused permission to see the readings. Scared of what may happen, he then beseeched the press for help. 'Police are trying to frame me,' he said. 'If they can't find the killer they are going to put someone away. I want youse guys to protect me.'

A meticulous search of the Embleton house, including the use of Luminol which detects the presence of blood, produces nothing. Throughout most of the search Weygers's stepson cannot leave the property and Weygers, refused entry to the property, impotently watches proceedings from the gate. Soon after the raid, Weygers airs his grievances on ABC radio, denouncing the raid's objective to distract the public's attention from the real issues: the water, power, prison and crime crises, and the dysfunctional health and education systems.

Ten days later, Crane and his sidekick, Detective Cleal, call on Peter Weygers at his Education Department office, seeking a few words. Weygers is not expecting them. 'They just lobbed at his work, unannounced,' his then-solicitor Grant Milner says. 'Refusing to leave, he instead sent out his boss to convey to them the message that he was not coming outside.' Through Milner, Weygers agrees to meet them at his Claremont office. It is a highly inflammatory meeting, with Weygers invoking the spectre of high-profile miscarriages of justice cases in Western Australia. 'He gave the police a mouthful,' Milner laughs. 'Martin Crane is a tough little cookie who looks and acts like something out of *The Bill*, and he warned Weygers he didn't appreciate being spoken to in those terms. But Weygers looked after himself. I didn't need to say much at all.' When the situation calmed down, Milner advised Weygers of his rights regarding the taking of a DNA sample. 'The new law is such that if police require you to, they can insist on taking DNA,' he says. Weygers agreed to have it taken initially but then changed his mind. Milner recalls he asked Crane if they could do it in his presence. 'They didn't give an iron-clad commitment to that, but it was certainly my understanding that I would be there.'

Crane has other ideas. Calling Milner the next day, he tells the lawyer they are going to take Weygers' DNA their way. In a dramatic display of police power, in broad daylight, two unmarked police vehicles sandbag his vehicle at traffic lights. Weygers – extremely well known and with his distinctive appearance – is forced out of his car and his body is spread-eagled against it. Kicking his legs apart at the ankles, he is body searched and told that for the purposes of taking DNA, he is 'being arrested'. But not then, or in the hours that follow, is he *formally* told he is under arrest. Terrified, his girlfriend, Vicky, sits stunned in their car at the traffic lights as Weygers is ordered into the police vehicle and driven at breakneck speed to police headquarters. Detective Symonds sits in the rear of the police car with Weygers. On the way, Weygers alleges, Symonds abused and threatened him, ripping a magazine out of his hands. 'Don't you fucking read!' he yelled. 'Look at me!' Sick with laryngitis, Weygers says he tried to explain he was on his way to the doctor, but he was ignored.

Desperate for help, Vicky calls Tom Percy QC, who advises her to follow Weygers to CIB headquarters. According to Weygers, he is locked in a room and a video camera turns on without his knowledge. With Grant Milner and two Macro taskforce detectives in the room, he is advised that police have an order to take his DNA. On the advice of barrister Ross Williamson, he tells Crane and Cleal that he would happily volunteer a sample of DNA if they tell him why they want it. They refuse to give a reason and tell him they will get a court order and return.

Demanding to see the warrant that shows 'reasonable cause' for taking his DNA, Weygers is shown an internal police memo that they tell him sets out their rights. No memo is attached to the paper. 'I am not going to give you my DNA with consent,' an increasingly belligerent Weygers tells Crane. 'This is body banditry. I will give it to you voluntarily if you show reasonable grounds.'

After hairs are extracted from his arm, Weygers hears a voice he thought was Crane's call out 'Camera off!' from an adjacent room. Moving to leave, he is stopped by two detectives. 'You're not going anywhere yet!' Symonds shouts. After a few minutes, Crane appears in the room. 'We have a search warrant for your Claremont property,' he tells Weygers. 'We're going there.'

Assigned an escort, Weygers is taken out of the building and back to Claremont. Waiting outside the house is a lone reporter, but within minutes the numbers have swelled to represent all media organisations in Perth.

62

Escorted into the house by Symonds, Weygers hears his phone ringing. It automatically switches over to the answering machine and Weygers hears Grant Milner, his lawyer, start to leave a message. He tries to go to the phone but is stopped, he claims, by Symonds who warns him, 'Don't answer that fucking phone!' When the occupant of the other half of the house, Chris, comes over to speak to Weygers, they are pushed apart.

The phone rings again. This time the caller is Robin Napper. Again, Weygers alleges that Symonds prevented him from answering the telephone.

Outside his house, Crane announces to the waiting media that Weygers has been 'taken into custody'. Channel 7 reporter Alison Fan calls out to Weygers, 'You're not under arrest. You can talk to us!' He seizes his chance. Wearing his trademark tie with the Australian flag emblazoned on it, he claims the raid is part of a state government plot to discredit him. 'This is a gross invasion of privacy. This is a gross invasion of rights. I have no idea what their excuse is for this absolutely disgraceful conduct.' Weygers also alleges the raid was motivated as a payback for the suicide of Penny Easton and that he had been used as a scapegoat to prove the government was getting tough on crime. Crane urges journalists to keep pursuing their line of questions to Weygers.

'Keep at him,' he whispers. 'Keep him talking.' More loudly, he rejects the accusation that the raid is politically motivated. 'Police don't take directions from politicians,' he responds, cool disdain evident in his tone. It is, he says, simply a process of elimination; Weygers is a 'person of interest' who had himself attracted the attention of the press.

With a large press contingent watching their every move,

within two hours police have roped off Weygers's Claremont house with crime-scene tape while a forensic team swarms like bees, removing rugs and unrolling them on the driveway and pulling tiles from the roof to examine inside the roof cavity. Press photographers, standing behind the crime-scene tape, click frame after frame while journalists furiously scribble in notebooks. As night falls, police use Luminol in the house and seize items. 'One of the things they grabbed was a laptop that belonged to the student son of Weygers's Filipina girlfriend, Vicky, who he has since married,' Lawson says. 'The lack of computer seriously hindered his studies, and it took correspondence with the police minister to get it back. The other computer contained the records for the Council of Civil Liberties. When his goods were eventually returned, no explanation was given as to what police had or had not found.' In a council meeting, Weygers slammed the police actions. 'The intent has been to terrorise, traumatise and criminally defame me,' he seethed.

A psychic claims credit for the raid, telling the *Post* that she had shared with police a vision that she had of Weygers's and Jane Rimmer's faces. In defensive mode, Martin Crane states that the raid on Steven Ross's house was about the property they seized and was unrelated to Weygers, who did not own the property in the two years that the girls disappeared.

Civil libertarians again join the debate. The raid, one said, is simply an exercise designed to cover Macro's arse. 'It came just a few weeks before the so-called Schramm review in 2004, but you'd have to ask why the bloody hell they hadn't done all this stuff in 1996 if they figured it was so important? The truth is, they hadn't thought about it then.'

Weygers's lawyers also join the fracas. In less than a week, the lawyers have found two more possible suspects. 'If it's taken us only one week, why has it taken police eight years?' one asks. Tom Percy QC, known as much for his utter disregard for political correctness as for his support of working-class Irish ideals, typically does not temper his comments.

'This latest stuff is just a way of police shoring up their own reputations,' he snorts. 'If they want to charge Peter Weygers with murder, then come and arrest him.'

63

Two weeks after the raid, police arrive at the Claremont council offices with a search warrant. It all seems an exercise in futility to Weygers. Following Sarah Spiers's disappearance, he had suggested to the council that they immediately establish a safety and security committee. In a case of bureaucratic buck-passing, they in turn suggested that any committee of that nature was the domain of the police and state government. The exercise then became farcical. Claremont council's then-chief executive officer strolled over to the nearby police station and suggested that police augment the safety council. 'This duly happened,' Lawson recalls, 'but like a lot of things the police do regarding Claremont, it was closed to the public. Police took notes of the meeting, but it wasn't without its drama.' At the meeting, the former owner of Club Bayview seized the opportunity to serve Weygers with a writ for defamation. 'He claimed that Weygers had outed him as being responsible for lack of security in Claremont. Everyone was working to a common goal but the faction fighting was amazing.'

The whole business, according to Weygers, took on an air of high farce when he realised exactly what documents police would have seized when they served a warrant on the council for documents. 'All they are likely to have found is minutes of the safety and security committee that they recorded themselves,' he scoffed. Seeking to obtain the nature of the warrant, and what police were searching for, *Post* newspaper made a request under the Freedom of Information laws for all documents relating to the search. It took 12 months of wrangling to end up with very little: a 14-page decision from the information commissioner denying access to most documents on the grounds that showing the material may prejudice the ongoing investigation. What they did learn was what they already knew: that Macro taskforce officers had executed a search warrant 'for the purpose of gathering further evidence as part of the ongoing investigations into the abductions from Claremont. . .' Bret Christian wrote in the *Post*: '. . . the officer in charge of Macro strongly objects to the disclosure of the specific terms of the search warrant, any material provided by Claremont [council] in compliance with the warrant and any information that would confirm the purpose of the search warrant in respect to the line of inquiry then being conducted by the Macro taskforce . . .'

While Weygers could not provide an alibi for his movements the night Spiers and Rimmer disappeared, he had a watertight alibi for Ciara Glennon. Witnesses verified that he was at a council meeting a distance from Claremont until well into the early hours of the morning. Photographs taken at the time prove it, but they weren't always enough to placate the public. At the height of his dealings with police in 1997, a severed cat's head was left in Weygers's letterbox and death threats on his answering machine when he was taunted to reveal what he knew. 'There are two holes in the ground,' one message said. 'Where is the third body?'

Stories abound in Perth of Weygers's sometimes inappropriate behaviour toward young women; innocuous remarks but ones that are often embarrassing to the women concerned. 'He does things like comment to young reporters on their beautiful eyes when they approach him for a story,' Bret Christian says. 'Things like that are foolhardy for a man in his position but while he is known to be big and brash, he is also committed to helping other people.' Christian believes there are reporters in Perth who wanted Peter Weygers to be the serial killer, because it would make such a good story. 'He's from an old Claremont family, he was mayor, he is highly intelligent and has a reputation as a man who likes women but who is transparently open with them. It's almost the novel you couldn't make up. I don't believe he's the serial killer, no way. He would have to be the world's best liar, to expound like he does on every subject but be able to cover up murders in his conversation.' Bret pauses. 'Imagine if that happened to you, if you were taken down to the police station in such a dramatic fashion and the press films the coppers taking things from your house. That would be the end of your life as you know it, wouldn't it? Look, if a person is guilty, fine. But what if they're not? What if they're not?'

Grant Milner laughs at the suggestion that Weygers could be the killer. 'In my view, there is simply no way,' he says. 'He is absolutely innocent and I have no idea where the police dredged this idea up from. It happened just prior to the external review and I believe it was done as a show, because they needed to be seen to be doing something. It's unlikely there are grounds Weygers could go them for harassment or the like, because everything they do they call being in line with an "ongoing investigation". But it has left a terrible stain on Weygers and his reputation and that is not fair.'

Milner, too, heard the rumours that ghastly things had been done to the girls' bodies after death. 'The rumours didn't come from any official source but they circulated for a long time,' he says. 'The trouble is, these sorts of rumours grow legs of their own. It's impossible to know the truth.'

Ironically, much of Weygers's public railings have been on the subject of the Claremont killings. He was the first civil libertarian to champion Lance Williams's rights against the constant police presence, warning that overt surveillance could drive the already depressed man to suicide. He demanded answers about mass DNA testing of taxi drivers, labelling it a futile exercise if police did not already have the DNA of the offender. If that was the case, he demanded, what was the point of taking DNA to match? 'It must have been awfully embarrassing for police to admit they didn't have anything to match against,' Lawson says. 'It made for a combative relationship with Weygers, who would not back down.'

64

In late 2004 Weygers is confronted by a carload of women who slow down outside his house and yell at him. 'The guy who is the murderer lives here, doesn't he?' one woman screeches before the car takes off. Fed up with the constant intrusion and the smear on his name, he makes a formal complaint to then-Premier Geoff Gallop, demanding both a public apology and a public police clearance. 'Weygers had moved out of the house by then and his tenants were severely traumatised by the whole business,' Lawson recalls. 'They didn't know what was going to happen next, who was going to suddenly jump over the back fence. A cop told one of the tenants that he was being "paranoid" – a bit rich given what they had to go through.'

The nightmare isn't over for Steven Ross, either. In mid-December 2004 police pull him over as he drives to a job and take him to Macro headquarters at Curtin House. Questioned again about what he knows, he is shown an electric stun gun that he once owned to afford himself some protection in the taxi after he was stabbed by a passenger. 'I only used the stun gun once, on a cat,' he told them. 'Then I gave it away because I'd dropped it in water and it didn't work.'

Pictures that Ross took of his former girlfriend lying in bed after she died and photos of her funeral service are placed on the table in front of him. The woman had died at his home while he was at a police station answering questions about a complaint a customer had made about a fare overcharge, later dismissed. 'They reckoned I was a sick sort of bloke for taking those pictures,' he said. 'But I did it because I wasn't with her when she died.'

Asserting that he had picked up Sarah Spiers on the night she went missing and not, as he claimed, the night before – the police also allege that Ross had organised to deliver her to Weygers. 'This is all crap,' Ross said. 'I mean, I didn't own a mobile phone in 1996, so how the hell would I have contacted Peter Weygers? How would I have known where to take the girl to? Until she got in the cab I didn't know myself where she was going. It's rubbish.'

With Weygers's complaint to Premier Gallop now in the upper echelons of government and being dealt with by Police Minister Michelle Roberts, police finally return the possessions they had seized. That, too, is not without its drama. Forensic examination of the two cars seized in the raid had 'yielded items of interest and were being examined forensically,' Crane tells the press. 'At the end of the day, it may well prove relevant or it may prove negative.'

There were few light moments in Weygers's final bid to regain his mayoral crown. Dogged by the smear of being a 'person of interest' in the Claremont case, he fought a hard but unsuccessful fight for re-election in mid-2005. During the campaign, a woman approached Weygers in a Claremont street. 'I'm voting for you,' she whispered to him. Weygers was chuffed. 'Thank you,' he beamed. 'Thank you very much.'

'That's okay,' the woman said. 'If you're the Claremont serial killer, you're very clever, indeed! And Claremont certainly needs a clever mayor!'

Following the Weygers and Ross raids, Bret Christian writes a scathing analysis of the Macro investigation. Why, in light of the imminent arrival of the 11th review team, he asks, are crime-scene samples being re-tested. 'Is this,' he writes, 'a desperate rearguard action to prevent any outsiders seeing, for the first time, the inner workings of the WA police Major Crime department? Are they hiding secrets, like in the John Button case, that will show this has been the most monumental stuff-up in investigation history? So many questions . . . Every single aspect of these murders has been treated as a case-sensitive fact, so is it any wonder rumour has run riot? . . . Perhaps the Perth public are sick of being fed controlled morsels by an organisation they pay for . . . Does anyone really have any idea what is happening, or is this just the last desperate grasping for skyhooks before the drowning man sinks?'

While police defend their treatment of Weygers, citing 'strange behaviour' and other reasons that they 'can't make public', he is still waiting to formally have his name cleared. 'The pressure to "get a result" led the Macro taskforce to deviate from good practice,' Lawson says. 'Rather than quietly building a case for the prosecution, Macro went for the "big bang", naming persons of interest.' He theorises about why Weygers was named. 'The most remarkable thing about the Weygers business is just how ridiculous it is. After reviewing massive amounts of documentation and listening to hundreds of stories, I am inclined to favour this specific hypothesis. While Peter was mayor, he used his then-good relations with the police to get a crackdown on one area in Claremont which was doing a thriving business in illicit drugs. This occurred shortly before the killings started. But others had agendas to protect and one way or another, he was named as a "person of interest", which led subsequently to him being ousted as mayor. The *only* reason he lost the election was because of the "serial killer" cloud over him.'

Lawson, tall when he unfurls from the restaurant seat, stands to leave. 'There is justifiable anguish in this city over the victims of the killer. Everyone would agree with that. But there is little public anguish over the victims of the Macro taskforce. And there should be.'

65

The Schramm review team's work is cut out for them. Beyond 'thinking outside the square', which they pledge to do, visiting the disposal sites and trying to get into the head of the killer, they have a tea-chest size pile of reports to wade through. And a relentless media scrum. Hounded from the time they arrive in Perth, the presence of local, national and international reporters trailing them through Claremont, Wellard and Eglinton slows down their work. It becomes something of a circus, the review team dodging cameras and constantly door-stopped for comment. Schramm quickly sizes up how best to play his hand. Be accessible, but ask they also respect what the team is trying to do.

There are several terms of reference for the review. Its primary purpose is to assist and support the taskforce in achieving a successful conclusion, but of equal importance is the identification of practices and avenues of investigation to assist in future investigations. The specific terms of reference are: to examine the known facts of the disappearance and murder of the three Claremont victims; to examine the investigative avenues explored to date and their outcomes; to review and, where applicable, re-examine all forensic exhibits and other crime-scene materials including the post-mortem examinations; to assess persons of interest investigated by Macro officers and any other persons identified within the review; to assess the potential for other offences to be connected to the crimes linked by Macro; to comment and advise on any potential further investigative opportunities; and to comment and advise on the practices adopted by Western Australia Police and make recommendations for the future conduct of this investigation or any other major homicide investigation.

Collecting DNA samples from bodies is a sensitive, painstaking task, particularly from those long-dead or exposed to extended periods in water or sun. If DNA evidence is not properly documented, collected, packaged and preserved, it will not meet the legal and scientific requirements for admissibility in court. The four criteria are vital. If not properly documented, the DNA origin can be questioned. If not properly collected, unintentional contamination by the investigators can occur and biological activity can be lost. If not properly packaged, cross-contamination can occur later. And if not properly preserved, decomposition and deterioration can and do take place.

In cases where a body is not located for some time, DNA will have suffered deterioration before it is collected. The most common cause is naturally occurring DNA digesting enzymes, from a biological source or associated bacteria. Where deterioration has set in, forensic investigators look to bone and teeth. But there is hope even if that yields little. The use of small stretches of nuclear DNA – known as STRs – in modern forensic techniques can yield clear-cut results even in badly deteriorated samples. Science can provide a means for victims to reach out from beyond the grave. Mitochondrial DNA, used for archaeological DNA analysis, is found in larger initial amounts than nuclear DNA and is more resistant to deterioration. But it has limitations. It is not as individually discriminating as nuclear STR.

In the years since the girls were murdered, there have been remarkable advances in the science of matching DNA with even microscopic samples. The matching of hairs, semen and vegetable matter for identification has also advanced immeasurably. If, as was indicated with Jane Rimmer, the crime scene was 'not fertile', the job of the forensic scientist is difficult. Samples can be taken from inside mouths, from under fingernails or from foreign fauna that may be near the body. But the continuing question is: what have forensic scientists got to compare *against*?

***

The Schramm review team, working out of the secure police academy court building, listens to verbal presentations from police involved in Macro and those who had worked the 24 other unsolved missing or murder cases in Western Australia. Examining profiles developed of the victims against the offenders' profiles, they also have full access to the HOLMES system.

Schramm identifies the enormity of their task. '50,000 calls were logged by Crime Stoppers. 2100 cabbies were interviewed. 50,000 cars were recorded and analysed. We went over all these records again. We interviewed the victims' families at the beginning and the end of the review, read witness statements and crime-scene autopsies. We watched security camera footage.' The forensics area, he recalls, was an enormous juggernaut of information balanced with what was known of the victims. 'We agonised over how those girls were abducted,' he admits. 'And we were always pragmatic. History shows that we can never afford to rule out possibilities.'

Within hours of Jane and Ciara's disappearance, police had doorknocked a five-kilometre radius in the Claremont area. 'The girls would have needed to be controlled quickly,' Schramm hypothesises. 'They would have put up a fight, so it's very possible that they were taken to a safe house in the area. Those doorknocks generated an enormous amount of intelligence which we sifted through.'

I query the number of reviews – 11 – that have been undertaken into the Macro investigation. Is it, I email Neil Poh, standard practice for a taskforce or investigation to have so many reviews or is this figure excessive? The answers to that question are typically brief, a simple reiteration of what I already know with a dash of paranoia. 'Is this a criticism of police?' Poh asks. 'It is standard practice to review homicide and other major police investigations. And as for the number of reviews of Macro: the Claremont case is unique and still ranks as the biggest homicide investigation in WA history. The number of reviews is more reflective of the length of time of the investigation and strong desire by WA police to make sure every investigative avenue is explored and exhausted.'

I also ask that details of all reviews are further fleshed out, to see exactly what has been achieved. The answer is to beat retreat behind police lines.

Poh concludes the email: 'We can't really flesh out the information [already] provided on the reviews at short notice. Also, in some cases to do so would mean revealing sensitive information which we don't want made public.'

66

Margaret Dodd has kept meticulous records of all correspondence, the reams of material she writes, relentlessly
and unashamedly hounding those who deal with missing
persons and homicides. On 11 November 2004 she addressed
this formal request to the Macro Review Panel.

> Dear Sirs and Madame,
> With great insult and disgust I find myself in the position of
> having no other choice and therefore I am putting forward this
> written submission to your panel. Our family has found
> ourselves having to fight and beg (cap in hand) for the minutest
> of input from the WA Police Service in the search and investiga-
> tion of our daughter, Hayley. We desperately seek an independ-
> ent review of Hayley's case, named 'Operation Blue Gum'. We
> have experienced on several occasions information not followed
> up by the investigating team, reluctance to accept any outside
> assistance and a blatant attempt to constantly place Hayley's case
> on the 'back-burner'.

Schramm wrote to Margaret at the end of November 2004 in
response to her letter. 'While it might be reported that we are
solely focusing on the death of three girls from Claremont,
I can assure you that we have sought to widen our search
to include other disappearances such as your daughter's.'
Assuring Margaret that they had met with detectives involved
in Hayley's case, and that they were encouraged by their
commitment, he continued that 'the facts surrounding your
daughter's disappearance will be taken into consideration in
our overall review of various investigations undertaken by the
Western Australia Police.'

***

Days before the review team concludes their month-long investigation, they discover something that was hitherto unnoticed: samples of foreign material taken from Jane Rimmer's disposal site. Well preserved and therefore able to be used for comparison purposes, it had not been compared with any material found on vehicles or suspects. Repeating the words of criminologist Edmund Locard that 'every contact leaves a trace', David Barclay extrapolated on the theory. 'Every contact is an opportunity to transfer saliva, hair, fibres and other material. We haven't anywhere near reached the end of the process in the Claremont investigation.' The murders, he says, could possibly be solved by linking scientific samples to another crime apparently not related to Claremont. But the panel's hopes that the new information could possibly solve the case prove premature.

My request to speak to David Barclay is denied by Deputy Commissioner Chris Dawson. 'We believe that we should leave Supt Schramm, the head of the review panel, to do the talking on behalf of that group,' he writes. 'David Barclay is not authorised to talk publicly about the Macro review.' But Paul Schramm, for all his willingness to help, passes the buck back to Barclay. It is a vicious circle. Why are police hesistant in allowing me to speak with Barclay? Are they concerned he may tell me things they want to keep from the public?

Napper had a package together for the review team outlining his concerns about a person he suspected may be responsible for the Claremont serial killings. 'It took me a long time to prepare the material and I expected that it would be read,' he says. But in 2005 Napper saw Malcolm Boots, with whom he used to work, at a conference in London. 'He told me that he didn't recall seeing my paper or the name of my suspect. He would definitely have recognised my name – Boots is a friend and former work colleague. Perhaps the way the review was structured, Boots didn't get to see all the parts, but it gave me a terrible sense of disquiet. Bottom line is, the police in Western Australia don't have any interest in an outsider like me coming in and maybe, just maybe, solving this case.'

Despite Chris Dawson's edict that Dave Barclay is not to speak to me regarding his forensic findings at the Schramm review, I email a request to speak to him by telephone in Britain in November 2006.

'I don't have any problem talking to you, except that my employers were the WAPS, and I am currently involved in the Mallard miscarriage of justice for them, which is about to come to the Corruption and Crime Commission,' he replies. 'However, I should be able to answer general to *fairly* specific questions, and if you wanted I could also read the relevant sections of the book and suggest additional text or emendations just for your consideration as they might be inappropriate.' Beyond generalities, he says he will have to go back to Dawson for approval but he would like to talk to clear up inaccuracies that inevitably occur in a sensational case of this magnitude. I start with the obvious: what was found at the crime scene?

'Two of the bodies were so decomposed,' he says, 'that the opportunity to get any DNA was very limited. Then there is the compounded problem of Sarah still not found.'

'I have been told that the girls' throats were cut. Can you confirm this?'

'To know, categorically, that a knife was used there has to be a cut in the flesh or bone. Neither of those was evident because of the extent of decomposition. So that is not a hard fact. But the probability from the insect manifestation is that there has been interference to the neck area consistent with their throats being slashed.' He pauses for a second. 'In violent situations, a person does what they have to do to protect themself. If they are desperately fighting back to save their life, the killer's modus operandi can and often does change in accordance with that fight. So if the intention was to cut a throat but the knife is lost, they will settle for suffocation, or strangulation.'

Of the 235 cold-case crimes he has worked on, Barclay admits he can barely remember the names of the victims. His job, he says, is not to look at cause of death but the *lead-up* to it, which gives opportunity to recover evidence. 'Everything is a sequence of events which we piece together. Was a victim held by her ponytail? Then the scrunchie that tied her hair may reveal low-copy DNA. Was she knocked to the ground or did she fall? The scratches on her knees reveal she was knocked down.'

The Claremont case, he says, was always very difficult. 'These girls were abducted from the streets with apparent lightning speed and not quickly found. There was nothing to indicate a dumping pattern by their killer – they hadn't, for example, been tied down with weights. There was no roll of tape or anything similar found at the scene. But investigators may get enough evidence if this killer does something else. They may then be able to find a link.'

Finally, I raise the subject of Robin Napper, who had worked with Barclay in the United Kingdom.

'It's been repeatedly suggested to me by various police officers that you hold a somewhat dim view of Napper's talents. Do you?'

'Not at all,' Barclay replies. 'Not at all. His talents lie in lecturing and getting things done. I think, though, that he takes a black-and-white view of forensics. But he was a very good cop.'

We finish the call with his promise to contact Chris Dawson to see if he can be given clearance to speak to me further. He does not hear back from Dawson.

Eight days before Christmas 2004 Margaret Dodd published this letter in the local Perth paper. It was addressed to the editor, 'in the hope that we may find our daughter, Hayley'.

To whom it may concern.

Dear Sir,
I would not be so presumptuous as to try and analyse you or understand why you took our daughter, Hayley, from us, just as I don't expect you to understand the pain and anguish we live

with every day of our lives. Once again Christmas will soon be upon us, a time of goodwill, peace and joy, a time to give, a time to celebrate, for us another day without Hayley, Christmas is no more. My husband looked into my eyes and asked me what would I like for Christmas; he needed no answer as he too wants the same, neither he nor I have the power to grant each other's Christmas wish, the only one with this power is you. I pray that you will find it in your heart to grant us this wish; by contacting crime stoppers or any media outlet from a payphone or a letter giving them the location where you have hidden Hayley. If you fear that by doing this, your identity may be revealed due to DNA – please have no fear because given the rigors of time the only DNA likely to be found would be Hayley's, as DNA deteriorates and is only likely to remain in bone. Please, please use your power and let Hayley come home; and give us the meaning of Christmas back.

Margaret Dodd, Mother of missing teenager, Hayley Dodd.

Margaret is merciless in her attack on the police, but mostly it is softened by humour, the only thing that keeps her sane. She names two officers whom she respects, but shakes her head about the others she has dealt with. 'I wish I had something good to say about them,' she sighs. 'But I don't.' She cites the way police have handled Hayley's case as best summed up by the way in which clothes that belonged to her were returned to them. 'They gave them back, all right,' she says, her voice dripping with contempt. 'They were in a bag marked "Garbage disposal".' She does not begrudge one cent spent on the Claremont investigation, but seethes with indignation that that case was afforded so much press and financial attention. Why, she asks, is one missing or murdered girl more important than another?

Hayley's father, Ray, a three-time British flyweight boxing champion in the 1960s, can only now mention his daughter's name without sobbing. 'He is a broken man, compared with how he used to be,' Margaret says. 'Hayley's sister, me, Ray.

We're all broken. Our Hayley's been murdered, but we don't know where she is, or who did this to her. Her case is not closed in our minds. It never will be.'

Police shift the focus of Hayley's disappearance back to the girl herself. 'Margaret is understandably distraught and wants to find someone to blame,' one officer tells me. 'But the fact is that Hayley, a slight, naïve girl, was hitchhiking on a lonely country road. She was a gift to her killer.'

67

Catherine Birnie ceased all correspondence with David shortly after starting her sentence, but his sexual violence continued in prison, where he relentlessly preyed on vulnerable, younger prisoners who were incarcerated with him in protective custody. He also helped other prisoners prepare their appeals. One was Robin David Macartney, sentenced to life in September 2001 for the murder of 27-year-old Lalita Horsman, whose remains were recovered from sand dunes two days after her disappearance in Geraldton in December 1999. Macartney, who ran his own appeal, accused police of framing him, claiming DNA evidence – semen found on a singlet near her body – had been planted and that they had refused to investigate other suspects. Critics of his claim argue it is impossible to 'plant' semen that has dried onto a garment.

The appeal caused a public furore when it was revealed Macartney had shown other prisoners tapes, given to him to prepare his case, of Horsman's semi-naked body. Macartney also sent the graphic footage that showed police recovery of Horsman's body to Margaret Dodd. She met him four times in prison in the hope he would admit to murdering Hayley. He never did.

The legacy of the Birnies' killing spree continues to cast a pall over Western Australia. How many women did they actually kill? A class manipulator, Birnie would stop at nothing to get what he wanted. And what he wanted, years into his sentence, was to see Catherine again. On a Saturday afternoon in the late 1980s, Bret Christian took a phone call from Brian Tennant, a self-educated law reformer. Tennant had heard from Birnie: in exchange for a meeting with Catherine, he said, Birnie would confess to other murders that they had committed. 'Here was this bloke wanting to use these unspeakable crimes as some sort of bargaining chip,' Christian says. 'There was no way I was going to get involved with this, beyond alerting police to the claims. But who knows if he was telling the truth?'

Passing the information on to a detective he knew, Christian learned that despite driving Birnie around some areas that he nominated, he was not forthcoming with police with any new information. Birnie whined that the police had not believed him, that they dismissed him as using the information simply to score an outing from jail.

On 23 April 2005 David Birnie was questioned about viewing the Horsman tape but less than six months later, he was dead. In early October he fashioned a crude noose and hanged himself in his cell. The man who had terrorised and tormented women in life, was ignored in death. No one claimed his body and he was given a humble pauper's funeral, for which the taxpayers footed the bill.

Ironically, his death was the same night that his final victim, who had escaped and led police to the Birnies, gave birth to her second child. Catherine's contempt for their victims also returned to haunt her. She was barred from attending David's funeral lest she spit on his grave.

With Birnie's suicide, and Catherine's belligerent, continued silence, the police are now left with little more than speculation and rumour about whether or not they committed other murders. Was he telling the truth? 'Who knows?' Christian shrugs. 'Dead men can't tell tales.'

In late February 2005 a prolific serial killer, who had eluded police for 31 years, was finally arrested in Wichita, USA. Linked with at least ten murders, he penned a terrifying nickname for himself: BTK – Bind, Torture, Kill. He consistently taunted police with letters alluding to his identity.

BTK was 59-year-old office worker Dennis Rader, who was actively involved in serial murder between the mid-1970s to 1980s, when he suddenly, inexplicably, went to ground. Twenty-five years later, he was back, again taunting police with knowledge of an unsolved murder in 1986 and enclosing photos of the victim's dead body and driver's licence. Occasionally he would send jewellery, believed to be trophies taken from victims. Known to neighbours as a belligerent man with an unpleasant personality, he was also a respectable Scout leader and Lutheran churchgoer with a wife and two grown children.

His first victims were a husband and wife and their two children. Later, he murdered only women. But he loved the limelight: when he perceived he was not receiving enough media attention, he grizzled to the local newspaper. 'How many do I have to kill before I get my name in the paper or some national attention?'

While police refused to disclose how they came to arrest BTK, he had a positive DNA match with some of his victims. His modus operandi also changed with his later two victims: their bodies, unlike the other women, were removed from the crime scenes after they were murdered.

Why would BTK resurface after more than two decades? Police chief Richard LaMunyon could only proffer a theory. 'It is possible something in his life has changed. I think he felt the need to get his story out.'

The BTK case, Robin Napper says, points to an undeniable reality; unless a serial killer is caught or dies, the amount of time in between murders is inconsequential. Nothing will stop them.

Nothing.

68

With the rest of the review team, Paul Schramm addresses the press in early December 2004. 'Clearly, there are different views from there being some connection to the offender or offenders to this location, to it simply being a spot that was blindly driven to to leave the body,' he says. They found no major problems with the taskforce work but, he added, 'we still hope this case can be solved and we have not recommended scaling down the investigation. It's not the end of the journey, forensically speaking, which is good news for WA police and of no comfort to whoever is responsible for these crimes.'

The team find that by virtue of the three girls' profiles, they could not rule out the possibility that the killer could be responsible for other murders. But they doubt it. After a detailed review of the 24 other young women either missing or murdered since 1980, they are confident, they say, that there are no definite links to these crimes. 'But,' Paul Schramm cautions in a tone that suggests he is having a bet each way, 'it must be pointed out that links of this nature can never be ruled out.' However, the team does *not* rule out Julie Cutler and the girl who was brutally raped at Karrakatta cemetery as possible victims. 'How do you explain why one woman got away and others are murdered?' Schramm muses later. 'Only the offender can tell us this.'

Trawling information from the 'living witness' project – girls who had been picked up by offenders and survived – proved as lucrative as it did frustrating. 'We could be looking at numerous offenders. We could be looking at just one. The Snowtown 'bodies in barrels' murders taught us this lesson. In that case, there were four offenders working in concert with each other. They exhibited some traits and motivations common to serial killers but by no means all of them. I don't like to refer to criminals as clever or professional. There is always a degree of luck involved in them getting away with murder.'

Joy Kohout speaks about several other suspects. 'They fit the profile pretty well. The conclusion that I reached is . . . these persons of interest or suspects are worthy of the attention they are getting. That isn't to say that there might not be further suspects that develop that are worthy of the same attention.' There is no doubt, she adds, that this is the work of an organised offender. 'This is somebody who's put some planning into these crimes; he's methodical. Probably looks very normal on the surface, might have a steady job, no problems with employment. Many of these organised offenders are very charismatic.'

Malcolm Boots advises that the panel has uncovered several matters worth pursuing. 'We haven't found the big missing bloodstain, the missing hair or whatever – we never expected to. But we have found a few things that are quite interesting.' What are those things? An email from the commissioner's office makes the WAPS position clear. 'Before you ask what they are – we aren't saying!'

That the review team had found areas in which the Macro taskforce could further investigate contradicted Commissioner Matthews's earlier indication that the taskforce would have to be disbanded. 'This has got permanency in terms of the structure we are putting in place,' Deputy Commissioner Chris Dawson commented. 'Quite frankly we have set our jaw and our resolve and we are going to keep going. I'm not prepared to make a decision to park the thing while we've got unresolved matters of inquiry.' In line with the secrecy inherent in the investigation, Dawson refuses to disclose just what those matters are. 'I've got absolutely no intention of giving the direction we will target. I'm not going into details about the unresolved matters of the inquiry but there is sufficient to say, "Look, we need to follow these things through".'

With the benefit of two years hindsight since the review gave its findings, Schramm still believes that it is drawing a long bow to rule anyone identified as a strong person of interest out of the investigation. 'How much weight can be put on profiles?' he asks. 'It is not an exact science. We must keep an open mind.'

Jenny and Trevor Rimmer are decidedly unimpressed with the Schramm review. 'They invited us in to talk to them, saying they might have something we could look at,' Jenny recalls. 'It got our hopes up, but it amounted to nothing. Again.'

Two years after the review, the subject of forensics is still sensitive. When Bret Christian ran a story in the *Post* reporting Commissioner O'Callaghan's decision to change the forensic unit, he claimed that 50 samples had been taken from Jane Rimmer's body.

'Qualified civilians will take over the role from police officers who have moved up through the ranks from other duties to the forensic section,' Christian wrote. 'It was horrified overseas experts inquiring into the disappearance of three women from Claremont in the mid-1990s that triggered the dramatic action. They reported to Mr O'Callaghan in 2004 that forensic procedures in WA were way behind international standards. Among other problems, there were 50 samples recovered from the body of Jane Rimmer that had never been compared with other material.'

Jenny Rimmer is devastated and angry after reading the article. 'What's going on here?' she asks. 'Why haven't the police told us about this earlier?'

I ask Barclay the question. '*Post* newspaper reported that 50 samples were found at Jane Rimmer's disposal site,' I say. 'Is this figure correct?' I have been told in no uncertain terms by the Western Australia Police that it isn't, but want to check again.

'To be honest, I have no idea where that figure came from,' Barclay says. 'No idea at all.'

'That must be frustrating.'

'Yes, it is. It doesn't benefit anyone.'

It certainly didn't benefit Jenny Rimmer, who had asked me to check the information for her. She cried when told it appeared to be incorrect. 'We go on an emotional seesaw every time we read something,' she tells me. The memory of that conversation raises another issue with Barclay. '*Post* newspaper also reported that changes in the forensic section were triggered by the reaction of "horrified overseas experts" inquiring into the Claremont case. Is that right?'

'It's not true that we had a lot of criticism about how forensics was handled at the crime scene. It was how it was organised. In Western Australia there is no integration of forensic laboratories. Chemistry and biology are separate and are funded by different heads. What is needed is one forensic scientist in overall charge working with the police. In Australia, the scenes-of-crime people run the scene and they take and recover material. But they cannot understand all the possibilities for evidence recovery. We were horrified when we found how much was missed because of the moving around of forensic material. Pathologists then take over, and the biologists and chemists are handed the recovered items. This would not happen in the UK. It should all immediately be in the hands of the forensic scientists, who know what they are looking for.'

The police are in no temper to mince words on the accuracy of the *Post* report. 'We have never released that information and never will,' I am told by one incensed former Macro officer.

69

In September 2005 the announcement was made that the Special Crime Squad would replace the Macro taskforce. Under the auspices of the Major Crime Division, the squad's overall brief was to take over the management of cold cases in Western Australia. Heading it up is Detective Senior-Sergeant Anthony Lee, who joined the force in 1988 and became a detective in 1994. He has already had a brief stint as Macro leader in 2003.

The squad, enlarged to 13 members, has a lot to handle. Unsolved murders and serious sexual assaults over two years old fall within its radar. Some cases stretch back 30 years. One of the more celebrated cases is that of flamboyant Perth madam Shirley Finn, whose slumped body was found in her parked car in June 1975. While her murder remains unsolved, it did instigate a review into policing of the sex industry.

The squad is also briefed to investigate murder cases that have been under the microscope for appeal or acquittal. John Button shakes his head when this subject is raised. 'With just that alone – apparent miscarriages of justice – the squad will be flat out.' It is a cosy set-up, investigators moving from the madding crowd at police headquarters into their own offices on Adelaide Terrace. The thinking behind the squad is rational: time may well induce people to come forward with information they had previously been too scared to offer, or to share recollections of suspect behaviour. The squad will also zero in on the transient offenders who blow in across the Nullarbor Plain and blow out again.

With the squad given the seal of approval, Deputy Commissioner Chris Dawson praised Macro's work and insisted that because a crime was unsolved, it was not closed. 'The cases remain under the spotlight and under our notice and if anything additional causes us to take further action then of course we'll do that.' Not everyone agrees. There are perceptible groans from some police officers when the new squad is announced. 'How many more bloody changes of tack are they going to take?' one asks. 'It's becoming akin to changing the deckchairs on the *Titanic*. The perception is that the boat is sinking and there's no rescue in sight.'

Luke Morfesse aired his comments on the formation of the crime squad. For those who had cast a critical eye over the Macro investigation, they were not well received. Praising the decision to keep the investigation open, Morfesse opined that if the case had been referred to a coroner's inquest, that would have exposed 'how thorough and intense the police investigation has been'. 'But,' he continued, 'given that work of the Macro taskforce has been subjected to an unprecedented 11 independent or external reviews that have found little fault, it's almost impossible to mount a sound case against the police handling of the inquiry. The exception has been the odd new chum trying to make a name while at the same time giving a voice to parties with a vested interest in undermining the investigation.'

70

For a moment, Perth held its breath with the announcement that British man Paul Anthony Clare – resident in Perth in the early 1990s, convicted for a rape at Subiaco (near Claremont) and also a prime suspect in a series of notorious rapes in central Kings Park – had been charged over the chilling rape of a 16-year-old girl in England. While British detectives flew into Perth to talk to their Macro counterparts about their dealings with the 42-year-old sales manager's modus operandi over his alleged involvement in the Kings Park rapes in 1989 and 1990, Macro officers in turn gathered beneficial information. His modus operandi – offering to ensure the British girl's safety after she left a nightclub by walking with her and instead raping her behind football clubrooms in Essex – is hauntingly similar to the abductions of the Claremont victims.

Targeted by Macro officers in 1999 as a person of interest, the police were coy as to why Clare was in their sights. But Clare's background revealed an obsessive character who had lived in WA for a time in the early 1990s before returning to his native England, a loner who behaved in a bizarre manner after he separated from his wife and later, his girlfriends. Convicted of the break-in at the Subiaco home of his victim, in which he was armed with sex aids – lubricant, vibrator and condoms hidden in his socks – he became a red-hot suspect for the Kings Park rapes.

Sentenced for the British rape in mid-2005, WA Police told the media in early April 2006 that while Clare remained a suspect in the Kings Park rapes, he had been eliminated from the Claremont inquiry.

It is now almost a decade since the Claremont killings, and with a nose for a topical story, a producer from *60 Minutes* approaches Western Australia police to do a story on the anniversary. The program wouldn't be critical of the police operation, he said, unless it needed to be. But the investigators are in no mood to talk to the media. Frantically putting out fires on the Andrew Mallard front and preparing submissions for the cold-case review and CCC inquiries, their request is denied.

With the serial killings unsolved, satanic believers look to devil worship to explain the terrible murders and the disappearance of young people – especially young women – from Western Australia. How else, they ask, can one explain the crimes that are seemingly perfectly well planned and chilling in their execution?

Infamous satanic serial killer David Berkowitz – the so-called 'Son of Sam' who, in New York in 1976, claimed the lives of six people and injured many others – described the Satanists he was involved with. 'They are peculiar people, but they aren't ignorant peasants or semi-literate natives. Rather, their ranks are filled with doctors, lawyers, businessmen and basically highly responsible citizens. They are not a careless group, apt to make mistakes. But they are secretive and bonded together by a common need and desire to mete out havoc on society.' Berkowitz – nicknamed 'Berserkowitz' in prison – was caught in 1997 after police traced a parking ticket to him that was issued near the scene of the final murder. He had not acted alone, he said, suggesting cult involvement in the murders.

Western Australian Ellis Taylor, who has written numerous books about the occult and published articles on the internet about the Claremont case, warns that to understand these people it is important to listen to cult witnesses without prejudice. 'I have it on very good authority and from more than one source that the police have often been informed about satanic cults operating around Perth,' he told me. 'Yet they failed to give these people any credence. Perhaps it is time this attitude changed. Satanic cults and individuals are a reality. It doesn't matter whether you want to believe it or not. A retired homicide detective with a lifetime of experience assured me that when they came to an impasse they would look at anything and everything. I pray that this is the case with the Claremont case.

'Inevitably,' he continued, 'the Old Bill is provided with all sorts of strange leads by well-meaning people which turn out to be a waste of time. Surely though, the police role is not to prematurely judge the information but to check it out thoroughly, no matter what their personal opinion? It is probable that a group of people are committing these crimes and not impossible that they have links within the police force, government, media and clergy.'

Taylor sends me the transcript of an interview he conducted with a Western Australian woman some years ago. 'It's harrowing and hard to believe if you haven't heard about these things before,' he warned. That was an understatement. The stomach-churning material – pages and pages of it – is unrelentingly bleak, incredibly bizarre and, in parts, highly defamatory. But Taylor wanted me to see a particular section. 'The woman told me that one of the Claremont victims was brought to her home; it was Jane Rimmer, I think. She said she has attempted to tell the police her story but they hadn't believed her. She is definitely traumatised and there is, of course, the chance that she could be making it up, but I don't think so. She is articulate and intelligent.'

In elaborate detail, Taylor outlined complex numerology and other psychic phenomena that he believes are connected with the killings, and sent some of his information to the police. Mindful that his ideas can be misconstrued as the imaginings of a wacky fantasist, he keeps his correspondence with me grounded in fact. 'I spoke at length by phone and in person to a very senior police officer at the time,' he says. 'There must have been something about my information that meant something or he wouldn't have bothered with me, would he? He was very concerned that we used a secure line. I have since been concerned at the shuffling and accusations emanating from WA police. My gut feeling has been that certain people may have got a little too close. Paul Ferguson actually alluded to my accuracy on television once, after Ciara's body was found. Not long after this, he was suspended. I still think he would have solved it by now. There are a lot more victims than Macro is letting on.'

Is the woman to whom Ellis refers mentally unstable, or are her recollections real? I think of the warning he attached to the piece: 'Don't look too long into the pit, lest you become it.'

'This woman described in vivid and horrific detail their abuse at the hands of well-known business people and professionals in Perth,' he wrote. 'She named some of the perpetrators, the dates and the places and also describes how they were present as children at the ritual abuse and murder of others at various locations around the area.' She had come to him, he continued, because she believed that the same people who had ritually abused them were the perpetrators of the Claremont serial killings. He writes of secret societies, of the twilight, dangerous world they inhabit. 'It is all so hard to believe, and I don't want what I'm saying to be taken as the ravings of a conspiracy nut. But I am confident that the witness is telling the truth.'

Stories of satanic worship continue to unfold. A psychiatric patient in her mid-20s, in a secure ward for her own protection, told her psychologist she had lured Sarah Spiers to a car in which her boyfriend was waiting. Driving her outside the metro area, she said Sarah was bashed to death and left at the scene. The patient also claims she visualised where Jane Rimmer's body was found two weeks before the body was discovered. Her story becomes more bizarre. The offender, whom she names, is a police officer who works in conjunction with two other men. The officer took her to where Ciara Glennon's body was lying and warned her that if she didn't shut her mouth, she would be next. The abductions and murders, she claimed, are related to satanic worship activities dating back to an area past Margaret River 20 years ago. The psychologist, who taped a long video session with the patient, called in a colleague to assess the woman's claims. 'She is telling the truth,' he said. 'She is terrified and fears for her life.'

71

In January 2006 I make contact by telephone with the head of the Special Crime Squad, Anthony Lee. Put my request in writing, he advises.

Dear Mr Lee,

Following our recent phone conversation, please find a request to interview Macro officers for inclusion in the book I am writing for Random House Australia, regarding the so-called 'Claremont murders'... I would like to talk to as many officers as possible who have been, and still are, active on this investigation... I understand that as this is an ongoing investigation, many questions will not be answered. I will include them anyway, with the hope that the reason why they cannot be addressed is made clear so I can include in the book... The more police 'voice' in the story, the better the balance will be...

I forward a list of questions.

Two weeks later I prepare to travel to Perth for my first research round, and speak to Robin Napper on the phone to line up an interview time with him. 'Good luck with the police,' he says. 'Listen for their defensive phrases. They will tell you that the review team praised them for having *world best practice.* Yet the crimes are still unsolved!'

Detective Senior-Sergeant Anthony Lee and Senior-Sergeant Ken Sanderson, a forensic specialist, meet me near where I am staying. Forty-year-old Lee, with rugby player shoulders, is imposingly tall and wears a slightly arrogant air. Sanderson – older, ginger-haired and with a gentler attitude – does not appear as hard-bitten. Forensic investigation is a less abrasive field than working the mean streets as a detective.

Sanderson swings the unmarked police car out of South Perth and heads toward the Kwinana Freeway. It will be a long day, starting with the disposal site of Jane Rimmer, moving to Claremont and on to where Ciara Glennon's body was found.

There is a tacit camaraderie between Lee and Sanderson. That's not surprising: police work is tough, the *reason* why camaraderie is so entrenched in the force. They protect each other and protect themselves, as soldiers did in the trenches; part of their mateship ethos. Police work their way up through the ranks, coming into daily contact with the sordid side of life. But it's this that bedevils them most, the murder of innocents and the girls that never came home. Bodies thrown away like trash and the despair on their parents' faces when they knock on the door with the news. *I'm sorry to tell you, we believe we have found your daughter.* Lee is only too acutely aware of it all, and it is in talking about this that his sensitivities show. He uses a well-rehearsed line: 'For the sake of your soul, be careful what you see,' he says. 'Once you see, you cannot un-see.'

We cruise along the Kwinana Freeway toward Jane Rimmer's disposal site, an hour away. With Lee free to talk, it's a good time to start the taped interview. 'Why is this investigation so secretive?' I ask him.

He turns from the front seat. 'If we open up the case to journalists, how does that help the investigation? It doesn't. It just means the paper has got a good story. If they are critical of the police, we're not interested. That's not arrogance – it's just that we've consulted with all the people we should be consulting with.'

Journalists. They are a common theme in Lee's conversation, appearing as the great stitch un-pickers in a carefully woven police garment. 'They are not always fair,' he says, 'not always right'. It sounds like a siege mentality – us versus them.

'The fact is,' he continues, 'with unsolved cases, we're always going to reach a level of controversy. That's the nature of the beast.'

It seems a reasonable point. 'And you've reached it, have you?'

'We've well and truly reached it. We probably reached it after two years in the Claremont case. People are asking, are we competent? Are we good enough to do the job anyway? Are we big enough to handle this? And my answer is I'm confident that police have been innovative in their approach and looked at the case as broadly as we can. And the review came out and said the things we are doing are world best practice. Designed and innovated here in Western Australia.' There it is. He has said it. *World best practice.*

'What sort of things?'

'I'll leave that for Dave Caporn to talk to you about.' Dave Caporn. As the face of the investigation during its most critical period, he is the one Macro officer I am most hoping to speak with.

'Macro has copped a lot of criticism, not least over the fact that these crimes are still unsolved. What is your reaction to that?'

'I think I've just given you an insight into that. The reviews weren't critical.' Those reviews. They rear their heads at every opportunity.

'But isn't that part of the criticism? That the police have been too insular, in waiting too long to look outside Western Australia? Isn't that intrinsic to the criticism?'

He leans around from the front seat of the car again. 'How long's too long?'

'Ten years, probably.'

'It hasn't been ten years!' It is February 2006. The first known disappearance was January 1996. The murders have been unsolved for ten years; the first complete and independent review in 2004 – eight years. He is splitting straws. I let it go.

'I would like to know what has been done, and by whom and when.'

Lee nods. 'It is the public's fundamental right to ask, are they getting the service they pay for from the state?'

'That's right.' I agree. 'Certainly the people I've spoken to in the short time I've been in Perth – general members of the public – say they feel discouraged, ripped off. The attitude is, "why don't the cops do something?" They seem to deeply resent the lack of transparency.'

Lee noticeably bristles. 'Why should we lay bare the facts if it's going to compromise the investigation? Why should we?'

'Because people are saying they feel they have a false sense of security, they are blindly walking around in the dark and that no one, least of all the police, knows who this serial killer is. They want the investigation back on track.'

'How do you know it's not on track already?' He has taken his sunglasses off and is in a half-turn, staring at me. 'How do you know it's not on track already?'

'But it isn't, is it.' It's a statement, not a question. 'You're asking about perceptions, and the answer is that this case is very, very cold. And people in Perth are very, very unhappy.' That is an understatement. The response from almost all victims' families – including those not directly or overtly linked to Claremont – was relief when I contacted them to seek interviews for this book. 'Thank God someone is doing something on this story,' one told me. 'The police would love it to go away, and we need to keep it in the public eye.'

We have passed some of Perth's major landmarks: Kings Park, the Old Swan Brewery and the University of Western Australia, and are now driving parallel along the wide expanse of the Swan River, where ferries lazily cross in the bright morning sunshine and pedestrians stroll along its foreshore. Now we are in the Claremont area, Western Australia's answer to Melbourne's Toorak, where the beautiful people play.

'Does the perception of the community outweigh the needs of the investigation?' Lee asks. He doesn't wait for my response. 'If we did release information, what purpose would it serve and will it help our case? The simple answer, I believe, is no.'

72

Lee talks the talk of a media-savvy officer: about internal mechanisms within the police service; checks and balances; hoops they need to jump through in deciding how to spend money; the actions they are taking. Then he moves to cover the topic so hotly debated in Western Australia: the external assessments. 'The second thing in relation to this investigation is that we invited numerous' – he stretches the word – 'numerous people in to look at the process that we have.' One of those forensic reviews – still ongoing – was started by Senior-Sergeant Sanderson, now attached to the Special Crime Squad. The officer driving the car. 'We don't believe we suffer from short-sightedness, that the reviews are too close. We still have people saying to us, "What you have done is right, justified and at times, best practice."' There it is again. *Best practice.*

'Who said that, particularly?'

'The Schramm review.'

Paul Schramm has a reputation as a highly regarded officer who deftly plays the media. We are only an hour into our meeting and I wonder should I comment. 'With all respect,' I venture, 'as good a police officer as Paul Schramm is by reputation . . .' I don't get to finish the sentence.

'He wasn't the only person involved in the investigation,' Lee interrupts. 'Dave Barclay from the UK was also on that team.'

'Was his response positive?'

'Yes.'

'Everyone was 100 per cent positive about the way the police have run this investigation?'

He nods emphatically. 'Yes. There was certainly no major

criticism amongst those people in terms of how the operation was conducted.'

'Has there been a time when overseas experts, not including anyone from the Australian police service, have looked at the entire case?'

'That happened in the Schramm review.'

'But wasn't part of the criticism, that Paul Schramm headed it up? That he would hardly criticise his colleagues in another state? That it should have been completely independent?' Lee's cool demeanour is changing, his voice harder-edged and louder.

'This is the media's problem. For them the interesting story has stopped and they need to find new angles . . .'

I can see where this is heading. 'But the media represent the community, and the community is unnerved.'

'I do concede that individuals in the community might feel that the police are somehow incompetent, incapable,' he says. 'I can see that there is concern we haven't looked broadly enough, that we've made mistakes.' I nod and Lee starts to generalise about history showing that around the world there have been horrendous errors made in investigations. He moves to bring the interview back onto sure ground. 'You accept that?'

'Yes.'

'Well I don't think this is one of the horrendous errors. If I did, I would certainly be making some noise about it.'

I want to talk about police culture. 'It's known that professionally, officers become very close. So given that, is there room for criticism within your ranks? Is there room for someone like you to say to officers who have previously worked on the case, look, you've really mucked it? How much clout do you really have?'

Lee's sunglasses are again obscuring his eyes. 'How much clout do I have? As much as I dare to take on.' I think about that answer for a moment. Given the hierarchical chain of command in the police service, and the incredible secrecy surrounding Macro's work, it seems a hollow response.

We go through what police have released. Property outstanding. Photographs taken. Lee wishes, he says, that he could publicly release what they have done, their operational techniques. It is, he assures me, outstanding, innovative work. World's best practice. He will talk to Dave Caporn, see what he can organise.

Lee admits that police could have looked in the wrong place for the Claremont killer. He spins the negative into a positive. 'As an investigator, wouldn't it be great if we had looked in the wrong spot; not because of poor police work, but merely because of circumstances? And suddenly, we look in the right place and find all the things we've missed?' He continues. 'What's the best friend of the investigator? *Evidence.* So if we've looked in the wrong spot and then we look in the right place and find the evidence, that would be a good thing, wouldn't it?'

I agree. 'So why, for example,' I ask, 'would you stay on overt surveillance of Lance Williams for years and years, the community knows you're looking at him, he knows you're looking at him . . .'

'Yep.'

'He's never charged . . .'

'Yep.'

'Bucketloads of money have gone into it . . .'

'Yep. Relatively large amounts of money . . .'

'Which the taxpayer is funding . . .'

'Yep. Fair enough.'

'So the community has a right, doesn't it, to demand to know why you did that. Where their money has gone? To ask what has it achieved?'

'Yep.'

'So what has it achieved? Anything?'

'I don't know,' he smiles. 'There hasn't been a murder since then.' Now I am finally getting what he is saying without him articulating it.

'Right. So there apparently hasn't been a murder for ten

years. If you take that by extension then it could be Lance Williams, but you just don't have enough to charge him with?' Now I'm laughing. 'It does sound a little like, "We let John Button go, but we still know we had the right bloke."'

'How do you know we don't with Claremont?' he asks, before turning back to look out the front window.

We move to another topic. 'Why won't the police release modus operandi?'

This time, Lee's answer is swift. The nature of police work demands confidentiality. Persons of interest – that ubiquitous police term – should not be targeted by the media and held up to ridicule or criticism by the public. Trial by media is unfair. His voice rises. 'And who says that members of the community need to know how Ciara Glennon was found, and all the nice sordid details that make for an interesting read? A large percentage flick to the next page and Ciara Glennon will mean nothing to them other than a story to debate in the office. They don't know her, they don't care about her. All they care about is themselves, that they have had an interesting read and they hope it doesn't happen to them or their kids. All the public need to know is, are the police doing their job?'

The modus operandi, he says, needs to be kept secret so that in the event of someone coming forward and making admissions about a murder, police can verify and validate that admission. 'And as for suspects: a number of people in Perth, by virtue of their odd behaviour, have been extensively investigated, in effect creating a database of information about their activities.'

I ask if they have investigated a particular individual, whom I name. 'No comment,' he says. 'You'll have to talk to Dave Caporn about that.' Caporn. I am starting to feel as if I am shadow boxing with a silent partner, a phantom. He concedes the individual I have named is known as a character in Perth, that he is a possibility. But he wants to return to discussing miscarriage of justice cases in Western Australia; he can't understand their relevance to the Claremont story. I can't understand why he needs to even query *why*.

'Because,' I remind him, 'people are scared. If police can get it wrong in other cases – and there is no doubt they have – what does that say about how they have handled Claremont?'

We discuss Bradley James Murdoch, now serving time for Peter Falconio's murder and the abduction and assault of Falconio's girlfriend, Joanne Lees. 'He's someone we are now looking at, trying to work out where he was at particular times.'

'He was in jail for one of them, wasn't he?' There is a long pause. 'It was a question,' I prompt. Another long pause.

'Yes, records show that he was. But we need to check that that was the case.'

'Do you mean he could have had early release?'

'We want to prove there was no discrepancy in the record-ing process.'

Murdoch had spent time in Claremont as a child. When he was nine years old, his brother died of a brain tumour. He became a Gypsy Joker bikie member but was in prison between November 1995 and February 1997. Unless the prison records are wrong, that makes it impossible for Murdoch to have abducted Sarah Spiers in January 1996 and impossible to have taken Jane Rimmer in June the same year. He is a possibility only, perhaps, for Ciara Glennon in 1997.

'Is it likely,' I ask, 'that these girls would have willingly got in with Murdoch? His car was spotless, but he's hardly the classiest man around. Sure he knew Claremont, but what are the chances, really? Can people really change their pattern?'

'It's highly unlikely, I'd say. But you sound more sure of things than we are.' He has adopted a mocking tone, the one police often use to put a curious journalist back in her place. His sunglasses now rest on his forehead and his eyes have a flinty expression. He looks hard at me. 'I'm not sure of any-thing,' he says. 'But I do know this. The public is lucky that the final siren hasn't been blown on this case years ago. And I know this, too: that anything is possible. Given the right set of circumstances, anyone will do anything. Anything at all.'

73

We come upon it, suddenly, a white cross on the verge of this overgrown rural track. No lilies now in the scorching heat of this summer day, but trees that grow wild, their branches entangled as if united in prayer. A freight railway line is close, rusted iron sheeting abandoned on nearby slips and horses graze in paddocks high with brambles. Woolcoot Road at Wellard is still and quiet, even in the prime of the day. Still and quiet, even as the softest breeze whispers that we should step carefully, here in front of the cross that marks Jane Rimmer's disposal site.

I close my eyes and try to imagine what had happened ten years earlier. A car creeping along this track under cover of darkness and crawling to a halt, just here. The driver checking there are no signs of headlights from an approaching vehicle, no one watching his furtive movements as he drags Jane's lifeless body out of the vehicle and down into this lonely verge. He would be hurried, perhaps now slightly panicked, as he covers her with light foliage. Bidding farewell to his quarry – what would he say? – before he scrambles back into his car and drives away, his dreadful night's work done. It is obscene to imagine that the Rimmers' beloved daughter and adored sister was picked up and tossed away like human trash, used as a macabre toy for her killer. This awful place doesn't fit the smiling young woman whose photos adorn laminate surfaces in her family home, whose spirit lingers over all her parents' conversations.

A decade on, there is still little here but brambles, a dirt road and the overwhelming sense that here was visited an obscenity. The police car turns slowly at the end of the road, returning to drive once more past her site. I look back through the rear window and imagine that the trees, swaying in the slight breeze, seem to be waving me goodbye. And the haunting words of Mary Frye's bereavement poem suddenly come to me:

> Do not stand at my grave and weep
> I am not there; I do not sleep.
> I am a thousand winds that blow,
> I am the diamond glints on snow,
> I am the sun on ripened grain,
> I am the gentle autumn rain.
> When you awaken in the morning's hush
> I am the swift uplifting rush
> Of quiet birds in circled flight.
> I am the soft stars that shine at night.
> Do not stand at my grave and cry,
> I am not there; I did not die.

The highway leading to Eglinton is ringed with houses now, but it wasn't always so. In 1997, when Ciara Glennon was in the vehicle in which she travelled to this place, it was a long, lonely stretch of emptiness. To travel through the city traffic from Claremont, stop at red lights, cruise through the suburbs and head out to the bush, would then have been a one-hour drive. A high-risk drive, with a young woman in the car who was either scared for her life, or already dead. One mistake and a police car could have pulled the driver over. Just one error of judgement, the smallest slip. Or was her killer so confident, so psychopathic, that nothing bothered him?

The police car turns off Pipidinny Road and turns left into a rough dirt track before it comes to a stop. From this vantage point, the killer could have seen headlights approaching; fishermen or sporting enthusiasts on their way to the sea. It is an uncomfortably hot day and Lee advises I take care as I follow him and Ken Sanderson through the scrub to Ciara's disposal site. The area, he warns, is teeming with ticks that latch on like leeches and which can cause a nasty infection if not carefully dislodged. I gingerly pick up my feet as I follow Lee off the track and into deeper scrub. Stupidly, I had not anticipated a walk and am ill-prepared in sandals and loose pants. Then, suddenly, there it is.

A white cross, placed by the police as a sign of respect and as a marker for future officers who need to find the site. A terrible reminder of a life cut short. I stare down at the cross and feel a roiling somersault in my gut. Ciara Glennon – brilliant, young, vibrant – dumped out here like human refuse where she would lie for 19 days before she was discovered in this godforsaken, remote place. God only knows what was done to her before her killer wrenched the claddagh brooch from her as a trophy, a memento.

Crows wheel overhead, their harsh caw piercing the still air and the cloudless sky offers no protection from a fierce sun. It feels like we are in Hades. Anthony Lee, privy to the terrible facts of Ciara's murder, has set his jaw hard, and grimaces. Sanderson shakes his head, staring down at the cross.

I realise I am crying, turn from this desolate place before they notice and stumble back to the car. There is a bleak silence before any of us speak again, nothing to say of any consequence: nothing, except to speak of the futility of it all; the terrible, tragic futility. How *dare* this killer selfishly take the lives of these beautiful young women, ending their youthful dreams with senseless, sudden violence, condemning their shattered families to an endless grief from which they will never recover?

Ken pulls the police car off the track, gripping the steering wheel hard as he drives. When he speaks, his voice is barely audible. 'It could have been anyone's daughter,' he says. 'Anyone's daughter.'

It has been a long, sultry and emotional day. My understanding is that the next morning Lee will facilitate interviews with other officers who had worked on Macro and furnish material to me that I had requested. It isn't to be. Instead, I am afforded only a telephone call. 'You're not going to like this, Debi,' Lee begins with a hint of genuine apology. 'No police officers are allowed to speak to you.'

I am stunned. 'Why not?'

'Sorry, I can't tell you that. I am not at liberty to discuss it with you any further.'

'Why wasn't I told this before I came to Perth?'

'Sorry.' I sense that he is. Younger, less entrenched in the patronising attitude often afforded the media by older officers, Lee can see the benefits of a healthy relationship with the press. But his hands – despite the clout to which he earlier boasted – are tied. 'I can only advise you to put your grievance in writing to the commissioner, Karl O'Callaghan.'

Bewildered, I take his advice.

74

8 March 2006

Dear Mr O'Callaghan . . .

It is with some concern I write to you . . . I accept that this case
is still operational and therefore delicate, but I would ask that
the decision for these officers not to speak to me be reconsid-
ered, I travelled to Perth in good faith, believing I would be
afforded some interviews and was disappointed to find this was
not the case on my arrival. I also desperately need the material
promised me and am still waiting for a response to my last
email . . . This book will go ahead but without the voice of WA
police, it will not have the balance I require . . .

Shortly after, an email is sent from the commissioner's PA,
confirming that I will not be afforded police cooperation in
writing this book. No reasons are given.

I want to know why, beyond the case being 'operational',
police are not allowed to talk to me. Or why they won't talk.

A former police officer with his ear to the ground vents his
opinion. I am 'not very popular' with the WA police, he says.
'Why?' I ask him. 'I've only met one, Anthony Lee. What's all
this about?' He agrees to try to find out, on the proviso that his
name is not divulged.

'I would call what I have heard about you as Chinese
whispers,' he writes a few weeks later. 'Who knows where it
started, but it seems a lot of people have heard you are up to
something, but they aren't really sure how it will affect things
for them. This is all about police culture. They never like
an outsider looking in their dirty laundry, or potentially

critiquing police work. Despite the fact that most of your book is about Macro, this actually goes right to the top. This whole Claremont thing was about image, about demonstrating how effective their new style of policing was.'

I have asked for information on other missing and murdered girls. I do not get it. Can I at least have press releases that have gone out to the media in the past which relate to the case? No. Verification of facts to avoid possible repetition of error? No. Lists of clothing and jewellery taken? No. I will be given nothing at all. Instead, part of the information I need is supplied to me by the sole, independent volunteer operator of the Australian Missing Persons website. It is important this story is told, she tells me. She will help all she can.

It is tempting to walk away from the story, to admit defeat. But I think of what some journalists have told me: *Good luck getting anything out of the West Australian police. You'll need it.* I think about what Jane Rimmer's mother, Jenny, said to me when I made contact with her again after a few months. *I thought you may have given up, changed your mind about writing this book. I'm so glad you haven't.* And I read the words taped to my desk, spoken by Dr Christopher Waddell in 2003 at an international conference on policing and security: '. . . the healthy distance that a democratic society requires between police and the media is narrowed . . . [when] police and the media can see themselves as working together for the benefit of the community. That compromises and in some cases eliminates the media's ability to fulfil its role of holding public institutions up for scrutiny and accountability.'

I keep writing, and the stories of alleged bungles by Western Australia police or judiciary keep making headlines.

In February 2006 Canadian police officer Joe Slemko was asked to have a look at the evidence in the Mallard case. His expert opinion on blood splatters in the celebrated murder case of Susan Christie was partly responsible for Rory Christie's release from prison. Working from photographs – a fact criticised by beleaguered police who claimed he did not have the Mallard case knowledge to which WA police were privy – Slemko was blunt in his assessment. 'I would stake my reputation on the fact that another man and not Mallard was responsible for Lawrence's murder,' he said. That statement, too, would come under scrutiny and attract no little scorn. 'He didn't directly name the man he was referring to,' police sources told me, 'but it wasn't the man he was hinting at.'

The same month – almost 12 long years after his conviction for murder – DPP Robert Cock withdrew the charge against Mallard. He is a free man, but with a catch. Mallard, Cock says, is still their prime suspect.

75

Neil Fearis, a decent, conservative man, offers to drive me to a trendy eatery on the riverbank in South Perth on a Saturday afternoon in early February, almost ten years to the day after Sarah Spiers vanished. Tourists and locals wander the foreshore, eating ice cream under an unblemished azure sky, the air pregnant with humidity and the soulful sounds of live jazz. I have been in the city only a week, seduced as I am each visit by its languid charms, its sensuous, laidback air. But on this trip, paranoia and a heightened sense of personal safety have firmly kicked in. The trouble with this story, a Perth colleague warns me, is that no one knows who's who. No one knows who they can trust.

Fearis, casually dressed in shorts and loafers, graciously agrees when I ask if he minds if we talk instead in the restaurant where we have met. I don't tell him the real reason I decline to get in his vehicle. Beyond the two police officers from the Special Crime Squad and my colleagues, whom I know, I will not get in *any* man's vehicle here, regardless of who they are. I spend much of my working life either chasing, interviewing, researching or writing about killers, but I don't take unnecessary risks unless they are unavoidable.

Don Spiers has earlier invited me to talk to him at his apartment in Darkan where his shearing company is based and where he works during the week. I decline for the same reason, offering the spurious, though true, excuse that I am allergic to spiders and that Darkan is a distance from medical care. His poignant response makes me feel ashamed of my lack of trust. 'There are more poisonous spiders in the city than the bush, Debi,' he says.

I avoid taxis here, too, if possible. Who knows who's who? Since the Claremont murders, taxi companies boast that they have cleaned up rogue drivers, that women are safe. How then to explain the behaviour of the driver on my first day in the city, who put his hand on my knee as I paid the fare, accompanied by a running commentary on what he would like to do to a pretty young thing like me if he got the chance. 'I am neither pretty, nor young,' I responded, nervously slapping his hand away and fleeing the cab. It is broad daylight and I shudder at what may have happened had it been deserted and dark.

Fearis swivels his cold drink with a spoon and reflects on Ciara's murder. Nine years later, the subject is obviously still raw for him. Guilt that he did not see her home safely weighs heavily on his conscience. 'Traditionally, men are the hunter gatherers who look after women. We are the ones who offer shelter and protection. It is ironic that had we been out having a drink with women 30 years ago, there would be no question that we would see them home to safety. But the world has changed,' he sighs. He ruminates on how unbelievable her murder is. 'This wasn't 3 o'clock in the morning at a place like Redfern in Sydney. This was 11 at night, in a classy, safe suburb of Perth.' *Safe?*

'Two girls had already gone missing from there,' I remind him. 'One had been found murdered. How can it be regarded as safe?' Fearis nods.

'That's another irony, isn't it,' he says. 'Ciara hitches in some of the most unsafe areas in the world, and she comes home to Claremont. Comes home for a wedding, and ends up going to a funeral. Her own.'

Sarah Spiers's birthday, 12 September, comes and goes, the day passing in a sombre blur for her family. A decade on, the years of searching and finding nothing have ground them down, made them wary of the world. Don, fatalistically resigned to perhaps never knowing where Sarah is, does not dress his heartache in fancy words. 'I feel as if someone has got a scalpel and cut my guts out,' he says. His brooding eyes, set in a rugged bushman's face behind large glasses, are ringed with black from years of little sleep and he has the curt, no-nonsense air of the wounded. Sound sleep eludes him:

nightmares haunt his rest and he nominates to meet me at a South Perth café at 6 am. Dawn has only just nudged out the moon, the sun only now on the rise, but already he has been long awake. Despite this, he is uncharacteristically late; almost an hour. There is very little traffic at South Perth this time of morning, near the trendy Windsor Hotel where Sarah Spiers was dropped the night she disappeared. I feel vulnerable, vaguely unnerved and conspicuous, sitting alone on a wooden bench waiting for him to arrive. So few people around, save for the young, sleepy man behind the cash register at the service station opposite, and the occasional vehicle that pulls in for petrol. How easy, I think; how frighteningly easy for a car to pull up, with one or more passengers, and to be forced or lured inside. No one would notice. It could be all over in a matter of seconds.

Be gentle with Don, I was warned before we met. *He is so heartbroken.* He is more than heartbroken; he is stricken and tormented. His huge hands strangle the coffee cup, as though he may crush it when he says his daughter's name and grief slices through his sentences like a knife. Tired of talking to the press and getting nothing back, he seesaws between quiet and reflective to loud and aggravated, punching his fingers on the table to make a point.

There is a solitariness to Don Spiers that is impossible to penetrate, an emotional drawbridge that he never lets down. Shattered hopes for Sarah's safe return have frayed his edges, robbed him of joie de vivre, and he wanders off mid-sentence when a memory of his daughter suddenly threatens to over-come him. He is savagely critical of me when he thinks I may in some way be censuring the police, and I feel his verbal sting. 'I want to know where my daughter is,' he says. 'You are only writing this book to make money.' Grief has robbed Don Spiers of gentle tact. He lives only for one purpose: to find Sarah.

A decent man who follows the Ten Commandments, Don has been dogged by depression and numerous nervous break-downs in the past ten years, and works obsessively to keep from sliding into that dark mental abyss from which he may never return. He pushes himself hard to keep his demons at bay. Up before the sun, working until 8 o'clock most nights. His marriage to Carol is strained by emotional fatigue and the inconsolable bleakness under which the family labours. He is tired of life; sorrow and dread have stripped him of the will to continue. Carol, the older image of Sarah, shies from the media, battening down in an emotional fortress.

Don doesn't trust the press, either. Not long after Sarah disappeared, he and Carol wrote a letter to the local newspaper on Mother's Day, a heartfelt re-creation of a conversation between Carol and Sarah. But the published result was so changed, so distorted, that Don developed a rancid distrust for the fourth estate. But still he courts the press; it is a pragmatic solution, for how else to get his messages to the public? 'Will the man who called me in the week that Sarah disappeared and who told me she is at Gnangara Pine Plantation, please call me back?' He wants to hear that yuppie, educated voice just one more time. Just one more time.

No one calls. Silence is his enemy.

But even if that voice was captured on tape, what good would it do? Even if Don Spiers instantly recognised it, what would it achieve? It is not evidence that could be used in court; and even if it were, it is inadmissible. Even if it were, the defence would decimate it as the hopes of a grieving father clutching at straws. What good would it do? None, except to stir up emotions that are already raw and bleeding. Inadmissible in court, and so nothing to stop the caller ringing back just one more time.

A decade after she vanished into the night, Sarah would be 28 years old. Don is now 57. The search for her, for this young woman full of uninhibited love for her family, has cost almost a quarter of a million dollars, including medical bills, research and time off work.

Don is certain Sarah would not have willingly got into a stranger's car. He can't bear to articulate what may have happened in her final hours. It is an obscenity to even have to imagine.

76

Karrakatta, a vast cemetery on more than 400 hectares of land, is two kilometres long. Opened in 1899, the headstones offer a peek at lives long gone, of suicides, murder, old age, illness. Without a reference to gravesites, it is impossible to find where Jane Rimmer and Ciara Glennon are laid to rest. It is empty, eerily quiet here in the dying hours of this Sunday afternoon as I begin the lonely trek to locate their headstones. The office is closed and my footsteps echo on the winding pathways as I peer down at names etched in marble and stone. I shiver. It is unbearably warm, but I have an uneasy sense that someone may be lurking behind me. I keep turning to check I am alone. A woman is fussing over her brother's grave, and stands up as I draw near.

'Hello,' I say. 'Sorry to disturb you. I wonder if you could tell me where I might find Jane Rimmer's gravesite?'

Her hands fly to her mouth. 'My brother was obsessed with that girl,' she says. 'He often commented on how tragic it was for such a beautiful young woman to be murdered. He died fretting about her. If Jane were near this site, I would know. I know all the graves near here. You will need a reference guide to find the site. The office is open tomorrow.'

The next day, reference in hand, I find it. Jane Rimmer's memorial plaque, in the old part of the cemetery, is protected by tall pine trees and dainty flowers. 'In loving memory of Jane Louise Rimmer. Taken from us on 9th June 1996, aged 23 . . .'

It is here that Jenny comes to celebrate her daughter's birthday on 12 October, serenading her with pink blush champagne and cake. Here, where Trevor makes the sad pilgrimage each Saturday, brushing stray leaves from the plaque, replacing fresh flowers and talking quietly to his daughter. Here where leaves fall like teardrops, marking the changing seasons of the years. All the years that Jane has been denied.

I locate Ciara Glennon's gravesite. Number 231, behind the desolate children's memorial garden dotted with heartbreaking tiny graves and headstones hugged by teddy bears. 'Gone but never forgotten, our precious daughter and sister, Ciara, born 20th November 1969. Taken from us 15th March 1997. The mercy of God will gather us together again in the joy of his kingdom.'

I bend down to touch the headstone, tracing the letters on it and think of two days earlier, when I had stood above the cross symbolising the end of her tragically short life. That ghastly place of ticks and snakes, her disposal site at Eglinton. Here at least she has dignity. I recall what Ken Sanderson said: 'It could be anyone's daughter.' And it is now that it really hits home. It could be anyone's daughter. It could be my own. I speak softly to Ciara before I turn to leave. 'I'm sorry, Ciara. Who did this to you? Who did this?'

The thought occurs to me as I walk back to the car. Would the killer have stalked the girls' gravesites, silently gloating that he had not yet been caught? There is a groundsman near me, and I nod good afternoon. 'Do you know if any security cameras have ever been put on the gravesites of Jane Rimmer or Ciara Glennon?'

He shakes his head. 'Don't know. But there are plenty of places here to hide them.' I tell him I have felt a sense of danger walking around the cemetery, a feeling that someone could be behind me. 'Females aren't allowed to work after hours on their own here anymore,' he tells me. 'Karrakatta is close to Graylands Psychiatric Hospital and there have been some nasty incidents. It's certainly not the place to wander about on your own.'

The elevator in the apartment block in which I am staying is frighteningly small and even worse, hellishly slow. A claustrophobic, I decide on day one to take the stairs instead. All 12 flights of them. With interviews stretching from early in the morning until late at night, by day four my thoughts are cluttered and dark. Different people have put forward names of individuals whom they suspect may be the Claremont serial killer, and it is hard to know who I am dealing with. I can hear my footsteps echoing on the empty concrete stairwell and am spooked by what I may encounter around the blind corners. It is irrational I know, but the fear that has pervaded Perth residents for years is now seeping into my consciousness. From this point on, I will constantly look over my shoulder whenever I am working.

77

In March 2006 it was announced the Corruption and Crime Commission – an independent and impartial body responsible for overseeing and if necessary investigating complaints against WA government departments and the Western Australia Police – would hold public hearings on the Mallard case, to investigate allegations of misconduct by those involved in the investigation and prosecution of Mallard. Intense media scrutiny ensured the story continued to be a pot-boiler.

By mid-April 2006, a cold-case review was announced. Chaired by Deputy Commissioner Chris Dawson and with the assistance of Professor David Barclay, former head of the UK Forensic Services Institute and known to police through his work on the Claremont case, it found a startling new piece of evidence – an unidentified palm print found at the scene of the murder. In legal terms, it was late evidence: half past eleven and the clock was ticking. Evidence of this print had not been given to Mallard's lawyer at the time of his arrest – the same legal aid lawyer who also worked for convicted killer Simon Rochford, an English tourist in Australia serving life for the murder of his girlfriend, Brigitta Dickens, in 1994. The modus operandi of Dickens's murder was hauntingly similar – though not identical – to that of Pamela Lawrence. Both women were bludgeoned to death in the first half of 1994 in classy Perth areas and both were blonde. Hunted by his girl-friend's parents, one of Rochford's arresting officers was working on the Macro investigation. Rochford readily confessed to killing his girlfriend, a confession taken down in 1994 by one of the detectives who had been party to the Mallard interview a month before.

This time, the reaction was swift: the print was proven to

belong to Rochford. But if he had readily caved in on his girl-friend's murder, he took knowledge of his guilt or innocence relating to Lawrence's murder to his grave. The man who had once shared a remand yard with Andrew Mallard in the 1990s slashed his wrists in his cell just nine days after the police interviewed him, his death adding another twist to an already tortuous case.

British detectives had already had Rochford in their sights before his trial. Prior to travelling to Australia, he had stayed at the same hostel in London where a German tourist had been murdered. 'You've got to ask yourself,' Quigley tells me, 'in light of what was known about Rochford and the time frame, why there was such a narrow focus on Mallard? This whole case is a litany of disasters.'

On 12 May, despite his earlier declaration that it was not necessary, Commissioner Karl O'Callaghan stood down, on full pay, the five senior officers involved in the original investigation into the Lawrence murder pending the results of the CCC investigation into the case. Dave Caporn. Mal Shervill. John Brandham. Alan Carter. Mark Emmett. Keeping a cool head, O'Callaghan described the decision as being about 'good governance'. He added that he had no information to suggest misconduct or that the officers had acted maliciously.

If O'Callaghan showed confidence in his officers – who said they welcomed the inquiry – it was not reflected in the public perception. Between them, the five officers had worked on hundreds of cases, including Claremont. If the CCC findings were adverse, what did that say about other cases in which they were involved? Particularly Macro. Director of Public Prosecutions Robert Cock is blunt in his appraisal of the case. 'The question is, why wasn't the palm print checked against Rochford's?' he asks. 'Why do we have to wait until technology is available and as an extension of that – is there material that can be checked for the Claremont case?' Cock believes that independent audits and scrutiny of investigations are vital. 'Who is marking Macro's report card? If that is done internally, it is not open to the scrutiny it requires. And therefore not good enough.'

John Quigley agrees, and makes no bones about it. Formerly energetic and super-fit, cancer and chemotherapy have debilitated his frame, sneaking up to waste his muscles and rob him of hair, his scalp now as bare as a winter tree. His loud voice still commands attention, as though he is seducing a jury. In remission, the man who was once the saviour of Western Australian police in need of legal advice is now regarded by many officers as a traitor and loose cannon. Between the two sides, it feels like a war. But he takes no prisoners. 'I look at certain sections of the police force today and it looks like a long conga line of suck-holes. They act like the slogan on my Bali T-shirt – "Admit nothing, deny everything. And then make counter allegations" – is a line from the police handbook. It's tragic.'

Finally, in mid-September 2006 there is a breakthrough in my relations with police. The commissioner's media adviser, Neil Poh, has agreed to approach Karl O'Callaghan with a request to allow some officers involved with Macro to speak to me. For eight months I have been frustrated by their stubborn silence. Poh, a former journalist who reporters joke has now 'gone over to the dark side', is canny about the media. It is better, he reasons, for police to defend possible criticisms now, than to wait until the book is published and then enter into a siege mentality.

His rationale is given voice in this email which read, in part: 'I suppose in fairness it was WAPOL's fault for not engaging you earlier, which meant you had mostly been speaking with the naysayers, the likes of Quigley, Napper and Christian, all people with personal vendettas or vested interests, and importantly no REAL knowledge of the inner workings of Macro.'

Poh calls me. Deputy Commissioner Chris Dawson, he says, has agreed to give clearance to certain people to talk to me. But there are caveats. Anthony Lee needs first to complete writing up the findings of the cold-case review into the Andrew Mallard case before he will have time to give me a full interview. He will see who else is willing.

Neil Poh and the Special Crime Squad's media officer, Jim Stanbury, meet me at the squad's office in the centre of Perth. The office is sterile, locked down. They run over my questions with a critical eye.

78

After repeatedly asking when and if Dave Caporn will contact me, I make the decision to call his mobile number in early November. Warned that he is under pressure from the Mallard case, I have until now resisted calling the number that I have had for months. His voice is clipped and professional.

'May I speak to Dave Caporn, please?'

'Speaking.'

Finally, I have made contact with the man who can answer most of the big questions about the investigation into the Claremont murders. Although he can have a smooth tongue, he is not known for his patience with journalists and I cut to the chase. Introducing myself, I tell him I would like to talk to him regarding his role in Claremont and his perceptions of the investigation's successes and failures. How had it affected him on a personal and professional level?

'How did you get my phone number?' he brusquely demands. It is an inauspicious beginning and I push past his question.

'You were the face of the investigation, Mr Caporn. I would really appreciate if you would share some insights with me.'

'Why are you asking me this? I haven't been involved in that case for years. It is an ongoing case and I can't comment on it.'

I tell him that I have been given verbal clearance to speak to him and that he may talk to me if he chooses.

'I haven't been informed of this. Who gave you this information?'

'Interviews have been facilitated with many former Macro officers,' I tell him. 'But you headed the investigation through its most critical period. I know you can't give me details of the investigation, but I would really like your personal perspective. What it was like to head up this terrible case? The pressures must have been enormous. I can call you back after you have checked I've been cleared to speak to you, if you prefer. Is that okay?'

'I'm not prepared to speculate on whether I'm permitted to comment or whether I will comment.'

'But if you are satisfied that you are cleared to speak, will you then talk to me?'

'This is all just conjecture. I can't speculate on that.'

I suppress an exasperated sigh. I have been writing this book for eight months and have been told many times from Neil Poh that it is in the best interests of the Western Australia Police if Dave Caporn talks to me if he chooses to. Given his elevated role in this story, I am confident that Caporn knows that there is a book being written on the case. I give it one last tactful shot.

'I will call Neil Poh to get the appropriate person to confirm with you that clearance had been given and I will call you back. Is that okay?'

'This is all just conjecture. I can't speculate on that.'

It is starting to sound like a scene from *Yes, Minister*. Deflated that I have gained so little from an interview for which I have waited for so long, I realise there is no point in continuing the conversation. One of us is about to hang up. I get in first. 'Thank you, Mr Caporn.'

I call Neil Poh to advise him I have contacted Caporn with no success.

'No wonder,' he says, more than a hint of chagrin in his voice. 'The cold-case review Mallard findings only came out twenty minutes ago. I told you they were being released today. You could have picked a better time to contact him.'

He is right, but I don't recall knowing when the findings were to be released and doubt that regardless of when I had called Caporn it would have made any difference. Shortly after, I receive an email from Chris Dawson.

Dawson – with whom I have never spoken – responds negatively and in full defensive mode to my request to interview Dave Caporn. 'I have determined that I will not permit Assistant Commissioner David Caporn to comment about the Macro investigation,' his lengthy reply begins.

That investigation remains live and unresolved. My overriding priority is to ensure that the integrity of the MACRO investigation is not compromised. For that reason, I will not risk the release of information that may alert a suspect to a particular line of inquiry or the adoption of an investigative strategy or technique. The effluxion of time alone cannot be used as a valid reason to reveal operational matters and techniques, while the murderer remains at large.

Secondly, I understand your intention is to criticise the MACRO investigation and in particular, Assistant Commissioner Caporn. Because of the integral role this officer undertook in this investigation, I am of the view that this officer cannot meaningfully respond without recourse to information which remains confidential. It would be most unfair for me to permit Assistant Commissioner Caporn to be placed in a position where he is pressured to respond to allegations when he is bound by confidentiality.

Furthermore, I am also led to believe that you intend to draw parallels between Assistant Commissioner Caporn's involvement in the MACRO investigation and his involvement in the Pamela Lawrence homicide investigation. As you are aware, the Pamela Lawrence homicide investigation is the subject of a Corruption and Crime Commission hearing. Until that hearing has concluded, Assistant Commissioner Caporn is precluded from making any comment. Indeed, all of the original investigation team have been denied access to the cold-case review report into the Pamela Lawrence homicide. Therefore, those officers cannot comment on reports they have not seen. I wish to reiterate that this officer is not in a position to defend his actions, although I am certain he would want to do so.

Whatever comment you intend about the MACRO investigation or the Pamela Lawrence homicide, in fairness, you should make it patently clear to your readers that Assistant Commissioner Caporn has been prevented from responding for the reasons I have provided. There will undoubtedly be parallels drawn between a number of Western Australian homicide investigations. While the full details of the MACRO and Pamela Lawrence homicides cannot presently be published, any publication will necessarily be limited and therefore open to uninformed and incomplete interpretation. The fact that many reviews, the most recent headed by an internationally respected team of homicide and forensic experts [the Schramm review], gives me confidence in stating that the MACRO investigation has undoubtedly been one of the most thorough, complex and detailed investigations into homicides in Australia. The Western Australian Police will continue to protect the integrity of the investigation, which I have placed into the carriage of the Special Crime Squad, with the strong desire to resolve these homicides.

If Dawson's views were not abundantly clear before, they certainly are now.

Whilst many of the questions I sent through to the police were answered quickly and at length, some were not. How has the investigation affected Macro officers, personally and professionally? Anonymous stories of people who have come forward with false confessions or information? The difficulties in dealing with the parents, year after year, when no one is charged? Who are the heroes of this story to date? Comment on Peter Weygers complaining about police harassment? A comment on the perception that good people were driven out of the force when they did nothing wrong? What has happened to the DNA supplied by the cabbies? What is the police line re Robin Napper? Some, such as the last question, were met with outright indignation and either completely ignored or greeted with mirth. Others I was advised simply would not be answered and no reason given as to why.

But the police service wanted me to provide answers for them, such as why this story also concentrates on miscarriages of justice cases. What is the relevance of these, Neil Poh demanded to know, in a book about the Claremont serial killer? I replied, 'I have had police silence for eight months and am now have only six weeks until deadline. As we discussed on the telephone, I am not here to be critical of police simply because I can be, but nor is it my role to play police PR, as you understand. Re miscarriages of justice: I know they happen in all states and that Western Australia Police have got it right thousands of times (as Poh had pointed out to me). But the reality is that in cases like Andrew Mallard, that's what people remember and that is very often how sections of the force are judged, particularly if the feeling is that other cases may have been compromised as well. I appreciate the opportunity to even up the ledger and will do the best I can with the time I've got to do that.'

Amongst carefully worded police-speak, Paul Ferguson is a breath of fresh air. 'I've gotta say straight up,' he tells me, 'that I'm not talking to you to save anyone's arse. I'm blunt, and I tell it like I see it.' Now based in the Kimberley as a superintendent, Ferguson was surprised by the phone call a few days earlier from police hierarchy asking him to contact me. 'I wanted to talk to you eight months ago,' I tell him, 'but I was warned there was no way you would speak to me. Weren't you informed?' He is taken aback. 'No. Never heard anything about that. I never knew you were writing a book on Claremont. We courted the media for help all the time. It defies logic that we would pull the shutters down now.'

Ferguson is adamant that neither blame nor praise can go to one particular individual in the Claremont case. 'Caporn led Macro through its most critical phase, when the girls were missing and found murdered. But no one person solves a crime or comes to a conclusion. It is a combined effort by a group of people. The evidence draws a picture and people act on that picture.'

***

Months before the CCC handed down its findings into the Mallard case, the five police officers that were stood down early in 2006 – Caporn, Shervill, Brandham, Carter and Emmett – were reinstated. There was no evidence, according to O'Callaghan, of misconduct or corruption by any of them. Amid mounting speculation that the cold-case review would clear Mallard of Pamela Lawrence's murder, the commissioner reminded Western Australians about why they had been stood down in the first place: to avoid a perception they could interfere in any way with the cold-case review. The Corruption and Crime Commission, it appeared, had other ideas. Much to the Western Australia Police's chagrin, officers were gagged from talking about the review findings, and the CCC issued a request to further restrict access by the officers to certain documents and reports.

The reinstatement of Caporn and Shervill was short-lived. They were each put on 'special regional projects' pending the outcome of the CCC findings. 'Special projects' in police terms is often nothing more than a euphemism for 'appearing busy in purgatory'.

The police are circumspect in answering any questions regarding the CCC, refusing to speculate about the hearings or the possible findings. Their assessment is blunt. 'We don't see any relevant connection between the Mallard case and the Macro investigation,' Neil Poh writes to me after passing the questions to Anthony Lee. But the connections are obvious: that some of the same police officers were involved in both investigations and the outcome of the CCC hearings may reflect on their investigative techniques. But there is little point in pushing further: the drawbridge has gone up. I recall what Lee said to me during early conversations in Perth when I asked questions that police do not want to answer. 'We won't be bullied. There is no point being a white knight. It will only get people's back up.' In other words – back off.

Trevor Rimmer, already fed up with the lack of resolution to his daughter's murder, awaits the CCC findings with more than a passing interest. 'We've been told time and again that the cops have done a wonderful job. But it certainly doesn't inspire confidence in us to to see Caporn's name in the CCC list. Maybe everything will be fine when those findings are released, but what if it isn't? How can we be sure about the people who were investigating Jane and the other girls? How can we trust that everything was done exactly the way it should have been, that the wrong people haven't been hounded and the real killer has got away with murder? How can we be sure?'

After much ado, in October 2006 the Special Crime Squad released its cold-case review findings into the murder of Pamela Lawrence. For Andrew Mallard, it spelled complete and long-overdue exoneration. Eliminated as a person of interest in the murder of Pamela Lawrence, the evidence points to Simon Rochford as being her real killer. It also found that Pamela Lawrence's husband, Peter, who found her dying at the jewellery shop, had no part in her murder. The Special Crime Squad, O'Callaghan emphasised, was not tasked with examining the conduct of the officers involved in the original investigation. This is a matter to be considered by the CCC inquiry. Full details of the cold-case review report are to be kept under wraps until the CCC completes its inquiry.

While a beaming Andrew Mallard and a grim Peter Lawrence were issued with apologies, Mallard's lawyers renewed the cry for compensation.

John Quigley, awaiting the CCC findings in 2007, shakes his head about the Mallard debacle. 'It appeared that Caporn had solved that most difficult murder in about 12 days. This, despite not finding a murder weapon, no forensics, no eye-witnesses, no clues – just a meticulously documented dossier that claimed Mallard did it.' He is in high gear. 'What did they do then? They looked at Macro. Paul Ferguson hasn't made an arrest yet, and the commissioner is under the pump to find the killer. Ferguson is taken off the case and is soon under arrest himself – though they later found nothing against him – and he's replaced by Caporn and Shervill. They have a coterie of people underneath them who are taken up in their vortex, the people they want around them. And the wagon keeps rolling.'

79

Just days before the cold-case review findings are released, there is another bombshell: WA Police are set to question Briton Mark Dixie, aka Shane Turner, over the Claremont killings. At first blush, it appears that he could be the person responsible. Dixie was charged in July 2006 with the frenetic 2005 stabbing murder and sexual assault of 18-year-old Sally Anne Bowman, a blonde model whom Dixie stalked as she left a nightclub.

It was his hair-trigger temper that brought him undone: arrested after a post-World Cup pub brawl in Sussex, he gave a DNA sample which matched him to an indecent assault in London in 2001, when he allegedly masturbated in front of a woman who was standing in a public phone box making a call, and to Bowman's murder.

Reports that WA Police have requested Dixie's DNA samples dominate Perth media headlines. The 35-year-old had worked as a chef in Perth and the south-west between 1993 and 1999; the discovery that his visa had expired years before and his subsequent deportation was made only after he was arrested for exposing himself. A charming man with the gift of the gab, young tourists remember him as faking an Australian accent while workmates recall him as reasonably good looking with a fiery temperament.

If Dixie is responsible for Claremont, the modus operandi for his alleged murder of Sally Anne is not consistent with an organised killer nor with the modus operandi the Claremont killer used. She was not abducted and put in a vehicle. Her body was not moved after death. The attack was frenzied, brutal, carried out on the street outside her home where she died. Her body was covered in bite marks and the sexual assault was clumsy, violent. None of the hallmarks of the cool, calculated abductions and murders of the Claremont victims. While Anthony Lee admits only that WA Police are using standard procedures to look at any possible links between Dixie and unsolved crimes in Western Australia during the time he lived there, by October Dixie's news value as the possible Claremont killer has diminished. And it again begs the question why, if there is comparable DNA from Jane and Ciara's bodies, did Dave Caporn admit that the disposal sites were 'not fertile'? And why, if DNA does exist, haven't they tested that against Lance Williams and either exonerated or charged him?

News that Mark Dixie may be in the frame for Claremont precipitated a strong reaction on the 'Gotcha' blogsite. The recipient of three prestigious Walkley Awards for investigative reporting, journalist Gary Hughes is the author of the website, which looks at national and international issues of crime, corruption and law enforcement.

'What would you say if the WA police had suspects and they weren't watching them?' One person writes in with a poignant question: 'How loud would the outcry be if one of these was the murderer and the police had not kept them under observation? It may not be pleasant, but no doubt, it is necessary. All I can think is that if the police checked immigrants leaving Perth around that time the killings stopped & took a close look at why they have left i.e. deported, maybe the life of that young UK girl could have been saved.'

'The primary [sic] suspect seems to have been followed around the clock for a very long time,' another blogger commented. 'His life became unliveable. If it turns out not to be him, we are in for the mother of all compo payments.'

But Williams, according to a Macro insider, has no chance at all if he chooses to sue the WA police department. 'What would he go us for?' he asks. 'His behaviour has put him in our line of sight.'

'Can't he sue for harassment?'

'No, because it isn't harassment. It's an ongoing police

operation and he knows bloody well that there are numerous reasons why we've kept him targeted as a suspect.'

The most scathing 'Gotcha' post is from a former neighbour of one of David and Catherine Birnie's victims. The opinions vented remind me of so many conversations I have had with Perth residents about Western Australia police.

'The WA police force has a deplorable record of investigating the disappearance of and attacks on women in Perth,' the former neighbour starts.

When the Birnies were hunting girls in the '80s, the police, despite credible and consistent reports from families and friends of the missing girls, refused to take the disappearances seriously. I was, at the time, a neighbour of one of the murdered girls and heard first-hand the appalling treatment that her parents received at the hands of police. They accused the missing 15-year-old, a straight A student with no problems and good references, of variously being a runaway, a prostitute, troubled, drug-addled and attention-seeking. All this in the face of overwhelming evidence to the contrary from fellow students, teachers, the parents, various teen counsellors and her neighbours. The police, either too incompetent or too shiftless to act, upped the ante against the teenager, accusing her of being an accomplished scammer and liar, experienced in hiding aberrant behaviour behind an angelic facade.

In fact, this poor young child was an innocent teenager, being brutally assaulted, and latterly murdered, by the Birnies. Young women have been routinely disappearing from Perth streets since the early '80s and the police have resolutely refused to do anything about it. The reason that the police have been brought to account, and their ineptitude exposed, more recently is that two of the parents of the missing Claremont girls had the political clout to compel the police to firstly, act and secondly, tacitly admit that they were, and had always been, out of their depth in major criminal cases.

Whilst no public statements have been issued by the international experts called in to assist WA police, it is well known by journalists that many of these experts were horrified by the lack of police process, diligence and expertise in the early stages of this investigation. The fact that the police continue to dismiss further disappearances of women is not surprising given that at times their desire to cover their ineptitude and plain laziness has by far outweighed their commitment to preventing any further incidences.

If this UK fellow does turn out to be the Claremont killer then the police will have some serious questions to answer, not the least of which will be why they continued to harass and bully suspects long past the date when ANYONE believed the suspects had a case to answer. I fervently hope that the Spiers can bury Sarah, that Julie Cutler's parents find out where she is, that Ciara and Jane's family can at last walk down Perth streets without peering into the faces of every male they pass and that Sarah McMahon's mother can at least know if her daughter is dead or alive.

But one blogger in particular caught my eye. His blog name is Dr Phibes, his real name Andrew.

Dr Phibes is a character in a Vincent Price horror film who is certain that his adored wife died at the hands of incompetent doctors and vows his revenge. He takes inspiration for his murders from the biblical ten plagues of Egypt. The police officer who suspects Phibes to be a killer is initially hampered by the incompetence of the force for which he works but eventually tracks down Phibes. The blogger has chosen the identity of a macabre murderous doctor through which he addresses his thoughts.

Professing that he had met and spoken to Sarah McMahon through friends a few days before she disappeared, 'Dr Phibes' claims that police flew over his property with heat-seeking radar in the search for her body, that they bugged his phone and also took his DNA sample. 'Since they haven't been back, they have discounted me too,' he adds. Jane Rimmer, he says, worked in a day care centre near his workplace and he surmises that Sarah Spiers's body is in water and offers to search the areas that he nominates. 'Sarah McMahon is near Mundaring Wier. Just a feeling i get.' He adds that he has two other lakes that he feels are strongly in need of a search, and that '1 is north near where Kiara was found'. Enigmatically he continues: 'I have had a woman giving me probs for ages. Don't ya hate that ppl accusing you of bopping sum 1 off then annoying you to hell thinking they can do that and sleep OK?'

He offers readers the opportunity to email him directly. I do. We exchange some emails and his full name appears in the address. In the second email, he offers to meet me in Perth – an offer I accept. Trouble is, this book will be published by the time we can meet. Is the name showing in the email address real?

Who is this blogger inserting himself into the case? I call Robin Napper and ask him to take a look at the site. 'The grammar is sometimes poor,' I tell him, 'but it frequently changes to a well-educated style. Do you think this person knows more than he is letting on, that he is mad or just playing a dangerous game?'

Napper gets back to me within 24 hours. 'This is seriously spooky,' he says. 'Whoever this blogger is, he has more than a passing interest in the subject and is teasing us with his knowledge of all three victims. How does he know that some of the areas he talks about are inaccessible and rugged unless he has been there? And if he has been there – why has he?'

Letters regarding the Claremont killings keep pouring into the police. In 2001 barmaid Maree-Ellen Bullard, following a phone call to Missing Persons with information about the disappearance of Sarah McMahon, starts a relentless campaign to have her voice heard, writing countless letters over the years to the premier, police minister and police, raising her concerns about the adequacy of the Macro investigation. A witness in the Susan Christie case, she has, she says, information about McMahon and 'a few other disturbing incidences I would like to tell you about.' One is a person whom she believes police should be treating as a suspect. As polite letters from government departments advise her that her issues are 'being looked into', the tone of Bullard's letters becomes increasingly vitriolic: 'I also in October 2001 voiced my concern over different matters concerning the person I have grave concerns about ... I will forever and a day stand by why I rang and what I am trying to do for these missing women and there [sic] families.'

Bullard and I meet at a South Perth café in 2006. A heavy smoker who runs on nervous energy, she strikes me as manic but determined, a woman who will not resile from her opinions. 'I am so frustrated,' she tells me. 'I can't get anyone in this city, apart from Robin Napper, to listen to me. In all these years, the only time I've ever had an interview with police was January 2002.' She hands me a sheath of papers to read. 'This circus they call the Macro taskforce must end!' one letter begins. 'Who's the next suspect? Bozo the Clown?'

I am startled by the contents of the letters. Her aggressive writing style, I suggest, will win her no friends in the police or elsewhere. This, to Police Minister Michelle Roberts in mid-2005: 'I did write to Jim McGinty with copies I sent to you also. I did not even get the complimentary "who gives a red rats arse" letter back ...' Worse, I warn her, with her continuing use of the word 'youse' instead of 'you', she runs a great risk of being dismissed as uneducated and mad.

'Stuff 'em,' she responds. 'I won't shut up until they start to take me seriously. Writing me patronising letters won't work; I want to see something done about what I'm trying to tell them.' What she is trying to tell them, over and over again, is to look at a person she nominates as a suspect.

One letter, dated 10 June 2005 and signed by Detective-Superintendent Byleveld, addresses the issue of her concerns regarding Macro and the independent review team. 'I must advise that the independent review panel was unanimous in their praise for the professional and exceptional investigation undertaken by WAPOL ...' it reads. 'If you are able to provide relevant information that may assist those investigations, please direct that information to this office so it may be assessed and the appropriate action taken. I reiterate that the information must be more than mere supposition before any investigation is warranted.'

Her response is predictable. 'As for saying they praise your efforts, I personally believe that youse deserve a KICK UP THE ARSE and a CLIP BEHIND THE EARS.' Bullard says she will never give up. 'Look, there are times when I fear for my own safety speaking out like this,' she admits. 'But this whole business is a debacle and someone has got to do something. I won't let it go.'

80

Now almost to deadline, in October 2006 I call GP Dr Andrew Dunn's practice to try to arrange an interview. I want to confirm the story told me by Neil Fearis about the patient who said Ciara Glennon was going to be offered up as a sacrifice; talk about his experience of being a witness in the controversial Christie case and to confirm other details regarding the McMahon family. But Dr Dunn won't take my call. The young receptionist who answers the phone tells me he knows what I want to talk to him about but, he has advised, 'It has nothing to do with him.' *How* does he know what I want to discuss, I ask her? I haven't told anyone. Three times she returns from putting me on hold while she checks again. 'No. Dr Dunn will not speak to you. This has nothing to do with him.'

Finally, the practice manager, Barbara, takes the call. 'What is this about?' she inquires in a professional tone.

'I'm writing a book,' I tell her, 'on the Claremont serial killings and would like to discuss some things with Dr Dunn.' There is a moment's pause.

'Hold the line, please.' Barbara comes back to me within a short time. 'I am sorry. Dr Dunn has advised this has nothing to do with him, and it is his right not to speak to you.' Quietly, she adds, 'I was married to a lawyer, and hope you don't mind me reminding you that it is prudent to be careful what you write about people. It is *so* easy to fall into the trap of defamation.' The message is transparent.

'I understand. Please tell Dr Dunn I was only attempting to check some facts. Thank you.' I hang up.

Detective-Inspector Geoff Ellis, head of Major Crime since October 2004, was present during the original discussions in February 2006 as to whether police should talk to me. It was Ellis's opinion that, from the investigative viewpoint, nothing could be gained from open discussions. He enjoys a reputation as a tough cop who is also somewhat of a 'charmer', skilled in the art of gently pushing even the most cynical toward the police viewpoint. But he doesn't dance around me with his opinions. With only the questions I have sent the Special Crime Squad to go on, he immediately accuses me of both bias and lack of balance. The problem, it quickly transpires, is my use of words and what he perceives as my lean toward Robin Napper's viewpoints. For the first few minutes, it feels like a verbal boxing match.

Ellis is concerned at my use of the term 'trophies' to describe missing clothing or jewellery and demands to know how I have come to that conclusion. As a member of the International Homicide Investigative Association, he says he knows a great deal about serial killers. And what he knows is that they don't always take trophies. It becomes an exercise in banter. 'How do you know they're *not* trophies?'

'How do you know they *are*?'

'What would police prefer they be called?'

'We hesitate to call them trophies because we can't be sure that they are. And we can't be sure because we haven't found them, or the killer.' It is a reasonable point.

'But still,' I say, 'they could well be trophies?'

'Yes, of course. They could be.'

He gives a protracted sigh before admitting that the subject of Robin Napper irks him. 'Mr Napper has never spoken to me with any issues regarding homicides, yet he criticises our techniques,' he says. 'He is not up-to-date with methodology and practice. He advises us to look at predatory behaviour, both historical and present, such as snowdropping and flashing, but we were doing that already. What we didn't have in the early days of Macro was a DNA database where we could match predatory behaviours. That was set up in November 2000 as a result of the Identifying Persons Act, which gave legislative ability to retain a suspect's DNA. Now those historical samples have been placed on a database. But we are legislatively bound to only use the DNA taken from the taxi drivers for the Macro investigation.'

'Have you met Mr Napper?' I ask.

He laughs, one that is laced with scorn. 'No, I haven't. Haven't wanted to and haven't needed to.'

It seems absurd. Napper, a former police officer and thorn in the side of WA Police, is only 10 minutes away from their headquarters.

'I know he pushed for a cold-case review and that the police opinion is that he should accept the umpire's verdict on that, accept that few criticisms were made,' I venture. 'But my understanding is that he is simply bewildered as to why WA Police refuse any offers of his help. He's not angry – just bewildered.'

As the conversation progresses Ellis proves himself to be just as others have described him: reasoned and intelligent. Gone are the aggressive overtones and vague threat implicit in his promise to 'read this story with interest'. He has a genuine concern that I show balance. 'Lance Williams became high profile because of his interest in participating with the media,' he says. 'He was the focus of the investigation and there is significant information to warrant that focus. From a moral standpoint, there are always going to be casualties in this sort of lengthy, tough investigation. I am sorry he feels maligned, but he is not the only focus in this case and to start – or win – any action against the police for harassment he would have to demonstrate malice and forethought. Evil mind, evil act.'

He proffers a grim laugh when I ask if he thinks Williams is guilty. 'Let's just say I wouldn't take bets,' he answers. He won't take bets either on whether the Claremont killer has claimed more than three victims. 'There certainly could be more. There certainly could.' How many more? He won't hazard a guess.

'That's frightening, isn't it,' I say. 'Incredibly frightening to think this person could still be lurking around somewhere but not knowing how many victims he has claimed.'

'It is,' Ellis concedes. 'I wish I felt confident saying something different. But I don't.'

81

Tired of the media beating up the cops, Ellis discusses the 'groundbreaking techniques' shown in the Macro task-force. 'It was groundbreaking for the team to be isolated from other police officers. Confidentiality agreements are signed on every protracted homicide and I have yet to see any other force in Australia so advanced as we are in the West. We assign a team and forensic officer, analyst and data manager to cases. It works.' He concedes that the Andrew Mallard case was 'the pain WA Police needed to suffer in order to get better, a kicking well deserved', and that they are now able to identify a lot of deficiencies from within. 'We've now got a verification process where we bring in a senior officer to sit in on brief-ings. And we're developing a strategy to deal with Macro.'

Dave Caporn, Ellis says, is an outstanding officer who puts things in place and gets things done; a charismatic man who could charm the skin off a rice pudding. 'He's a hard man to work for and he expects high standards. That can come across as arrogance. But while he's demanding, he is not intolerant of someone who is not up to speed on an investigation. He just expects them to get up to speed, fast.'

Ellis points to brain fingerprinting as the way of the future. Based on cognitive recognition, it works by stirring recollec-tions when photographs are seen or voices heard. 'If you're involved in a crime, it will show. And it works the other way as well. Overseas, one person has already been released from prison for a crime he didn't commit. But whoever is respons-ible for Claremont shouldn't think that because it's been more than a decade, we won't get him.'

He adds a postscript at the end of our conversation. He can see some value in approaching Napper for a chat, he says. It makes sense. He will approach him when he gets a chance.

Four hours later when I call Ellis again, he shares some news. 'I don't have to ring Napper now,' he says, his voice betraying more than a hint of mirth. 'He's leaving his job at the university, and that, apparently, is not of his own choice. But,' he quickly adds, 'WA Police had nothing to do with this.'

That Napper had, in his own words, been 'shafted' is old news to me. 'If he stays in Perth,' I remind Ellis, 'it's doubtful he will move far, workwise, from what he does now. So what will change? A meeting could still be prudent.'

He laughs again.

Armchair detectives are still riveted by the Claremont disappearance and murders, and many make spurious claims as to what they believe happened. In October 1980, 12-year-old schoolgirl Lisa Marie Mott was last seen in the south-west town of Collie, near Bunbury, speaking to a person in a yellow panel van after a basketball game around 8.30 pm. While CIB detective Reg Driffill, who headed the investigation into Lisa's disappearance, believed serial killer David Birnie should have been interviewed about the disappearance, both he and Catherine denied any knowledge of her abduction. A former military intelligence agent, on the 'Gotcha' website, made this claim in November 2006.

> As far as I know, the police have NO DNA found on the bodies of the two victims so far found. They have stated that the bodies were in too advanced a state of decomposition to obtain any. But here is something I have suspected for a while. It is based on the fact that the police warrant stipulated that they were searching for human body tissue and flesh when they were searching Mr Weygers's properties. The police have stated that the killer washed his car on site after dumping the bodies. I suspect that the killer only washed the part of the car that may have blood-stains on it. The killer probably drives a utility or station wagon and would have used the tailgate to 'process' the body before dumping them. That is to say, the killer needed to remove body parts that may have got DNA on them during the course of the

murder. Sally Anne Bowman, [the model murdered in Britain, allegedly by Mark Dixie] was found to have bite marks on her body. So it would seem for the murder victims here too. Maybe also the killer's DNA was under their fingernails. So these parts may have been missing from the bodies. They may even have been discarded close to the vehicle . . . I may have some data that ties the murders and disappearances together. Before you ask, no I am not the killer. I was a military intelligence analyst before I retired, so I like to keep my mind turning over by doing some armchair detective work. But I can show . . . that there is a direct link between these killings and the disappearance of Lisa Mott.

The killer washed his car on site? News to me. Removed body parts? Rubbish.

Bite marks on Jane and Ciara's bodies? How would he know? A direct link between these killings and Lisa Mott? The 'link' is so tenuous it is laughable. 'If you draw a line from Ciara to Jane and then continue it south it intersects the town of Collie (where Lisa disappeared), he wrote. 'The distance is exactly 200 kms . . .'

But if this blogger appears way off the mark, still I wonder: who is Dr Phibes?

82

WA Chief Justice Wayne Martin, speaking of the Walsham case, slammed what he called the 'new advocacy role' being adopted by certain sections of the media after high-profile trials. 'Tens of thousands of criminal cases had been dealt with by WA courts, so to take half a dozen cases over 45 years, condemn their findings and then declare they demonstrate a systematic failure of criminal justice in this state fails to put these cases in their proper perspective.'

John Button grimaces. 'It's easy to make these judgements when you've been sitting on the bench. Try making them when you've been sitting in prison for a crime you didn't commit. The whole system is rotten from the bottom up. We want to change it so our kids and grandkids have a decent, safe framework to guide them and work within. The people who have been wrongly convicted are experts in this field, but no one asks us for our opinion. Ever. How can anyone in this state be sure about any investigation – including Macro – when history shows us the mistakes that have been made?'

Former disgruntled police officers describe the tongue-in-cheek past state of affairs in the Western Australia police force as being 'noble-cause corruption'. 'This essentially means,' one says, 'that the police prosecution used to regard it as permissible for an officer to verbal, fit-up, brick-in, roast, pour a bucket of blood over, or otherwise manufacture evidence to suit the occasion. And this was considered all the more acceptable if the intended victim was a police officer, high-profile criminal or a public figure.' If the police culture is changing, he says it is not before time. 'The number plates on our cars call WA, a "State of Excitement". But a lot of us who have been through the system regard it another way – as the "State of Excrement".'

Many doubt that, for all good intentions, the Claremont case can now ever be solved. There are, a former officer who was close to Macro says, just 'too many scratches on the paintwork. The environment in which the Macro officers worked was so controlled it was vacuum sealed. Everything had to be documented, and the entire investigation was steeped in incredible secrecy, rules and regulations. But this approach destroyed morale; officers just tuned out. And it didn't leave any room for police in other areas to add information that may have been beneficial. The consensus is that without a confession, solid forensic evidence that can be matched to a suspect or an eyewitness, police are seriously pushing it to get a result on this one.'

The Western Australia Police remain extremely defensive on the subject of why the case is still unsolved. 'Every state has unsolved crimes,' one officer points out. 'You only have to look at the Beaumont case, where the three children went missing in South Australia in 1966 to know that.' But that case was 40 years ago and science has made huge leaps forward since then. 'Every state has unsolved crimes,' he reiterates, 'and crimes that are unsolvable. The criticism stings. It impacts on the morale of the men, who left their families every day to try and solve a series of shocking murders and who constantly woke the next day to unflattering assessments of their work in the media. It doesn't help anyone.'

Dave Caporn predictably agreed. 'You think about the years that have been taken away from the girls and their families . . . I've had total support from the hierarchy and I defy you to go away and find an ongoing murder investigation anywhere in the world that is continually resourced on a dedicated day-to-day basis where detectives work on nothing else.' But never far from the upbeat tone is the warning Caporn issued in mid-2001. Given the right opportunity, he said, the Claremont killer will strike again. He also sounded a rare note of self-doubt. 'Am I worried that I'll stuff it up? Absolutely.'

Critics of the way the Claremont investigation has been handled scoff at what they perceive as its glaring mistakes and cite the proverb 'every cock will crow upon his own dunghill' regarding the self-congratulatory tone taken by some Macro officers. 'You don't go public and say there will be a break-through soon,' a former officer says. 'It's like a hostage situation, very tense. Deadlines are set and when police publicly miss those deadlines, it's worse than embarrassing. It's like announc-ing the second coming and nothing happens.' He describes the Claremont investigation as amounting to nothing more than 'a lot of crumbs held together by dough. There's an old police expression "Fucked and far from home"', he says. 'In this case, sad as it is, they're fucked and far from a result.'

Former Macro media officer Tony Potts describes Dave Caporn as a 'strategic warrior' – honest and straight down the line. 'He's objective, impartial, determined and able to see all sides of an operation. He's the best investigator I've ever come across.' But who is judging the judges?

'How can you say this,' I ask, 'when the crimes are still unsolved?'

He doesn't miss a beat. 'If an offender runs out with his hands in the air and confesses to police, does that mean it's a more successful operation than one that takes longer to solve? A measure of a successful investigation should be that all procedures have been followed and every avenue to identify the offender is eliminated. It is about thoroughness, not outcome.'

Thoroughness, not outcome.

John Quigley assesses this judgement. 'How interesting. It's a little like the surgeon who says that every one of his opera-tions was technically brilliant, but that it was just a shame that on a mere technicality some patients died.'

Con Bayens doesn't know if the person whose name he gave Macro was ever investigated, but doubts that it was. 'They reckoned that they had their man!' he says. 'So why would they bother?'

Ten years after the first Claremont murder, Paul Ferguson

articulates the pain the victims' families have endured. 'Make no mistake: this serial killer has changed the innocence of Perth. There is a monster out there who has worked up a system to kill vulnerable young women and escape detection. It doesn't get more frightening than this.'

Ferguson was, for the Spiers family, the face of the investigation and their great support. He still thinks about Sarah. 'As tragic as it is, two families have a place to go where they can pay their respects and talk to their daughters. But the Spiers family – the ones who kick-started this whole stinking thing off, the ones whose energies sparked the homicide squad to get going – they don't have that chance. This killer hasn't just robbed Sarah of life, he's taken the lives of her family as well. He has taken the lives of all their families. You only have to look at the enormous emotional and physical toll it has taken to know that.'

Ferguson doesn't like to dwell on murder cases, on the sick psyche of the offenders who treat human lives with careless disdain. For this copper, who himself stared into the abyss during four years of enforced exile from policing, the job is not about politics; it's about the victims and their families. He recounts interviewing a killer many years ago who described in icy, graphic detail what he did to his petrified female victim. 'After he raped her, he asked her how she wanted to die and gave her the options. Stabbing or strangulation?' He pauses. 'Shocking, isn't it. Truly shocking. Partly in light of this, and since the Victims of Homicide was set up in the mid-80s, we know it is critical that families know the most intimate and gruesome details. We have told the parents of the Claremont girls everything we know, so that if it ever comes up at trial they won't be forced to confront it for the first time. But it is always distressing, always disgusting. No matter how much they are prepared, it is terribly painful.'

83

Ten years after the first Claremont murder, all the taskforce members can reel off the mission statement as if it was yesterday. Many describe the feeling of 'emptiness' that the case is still unsolved and others, despite counselling, have symptoms of post-traumatic stress disorder – flashbacks, nightmares – from seeing the girls' bodies, dealing with the families and the intricate details of the case. Tony Potts still maintains that, despite the identity and capture of the killer requiring continued perseverance, there is little doubt that the expertise, innovative approach and dedication of criminal investigators still working on the case will ensure these murders will be solved, one day. It is not an optimism that is widely shared.

At each Friday briefing, as a wind-down, the Macro team had 'fine sessions' where they threw two dollars into the social club account in payment for small errors made during the week. It was agreed from the outset that until the case was done and dusted, there will be no get-together of all the investigators, no back-slapping in the pub to keep up morale. Every year, the social club account relating to Macro grows bigger. Untouched.

Tired of the blood and gore, the murky world that police reporters necessarily inhabit, *The West Australian*'s reporter, Luke Morfesse, now writes a daily column. A journalist since 1986, he cut his teeth on a murder story in 1987 on his first day as a police roundsman. Working *The West Australian*'s Melbourne and Sydney bureaux in the early 1990s, he was the chief crime reporter in Perth, barring a short break, from 1994 until 2006. But his contacts, hard-won and hard-kept, still keep him informed of breaking crime stories. He reflects on the terrible waste of young lives in the Claremont case. 'Sarah was just a teenager, and she would have been no match for whoever did this. Regardless of whether she'd been drinking or not, she would have had little chance. Jane was great fun, loved life and like a lot of people who were out that night, she'd had a few drinks. So if someone had come along and offered her a lift, she would have struggled to put up a fight once in the car. Ciara was known to be very strong-minded, feisty, and she was determined to get home. If she had the opportunity to, she would have fought like a caged tiger.'

Ciara Glennon's memory lives on in the Memorial Law Scholarship in her name at the University of Western Australia, where she was a student. Established in 1998, the scholarship is awarded annually to a law student who demonstrates, amongst other criteria, a need for financial assistance to continue their studies, a caring commitment to others and an active interest in an area outside the practice of law. These criteria, Una Glennon said, capture as closely as possible the characteristics that epitomised the life of her late daughter. The family has also dedicated a shrine to Ciara in a chapel at Notre Dame University in Fremantle and holds a memorial Mass every year at Thomas More Chapel on the anniversary of her death.

Denis Glennon's faith in God is still strong, but his faith in the WA judicial system less so. He expressed concern that even if Ciara's killer was brought to trial, 'the system would fail the expectations of the average Western Australian'.

Like Jane Rimmer's disposal site, the cross that marks where Ciara lay has been repeatedly vandalised and destroyed by fire. It is now made of metal. Many people – friends and family – have made private pilgrimages to both Wellard and Eglinton, to pay respects to Jane and Ciara. In comparison, the Spiers family has no place to go to quietly reflect on Sarah's life. Suburbia has slowly crept into the Wellard area, huge machines clearing the scrub for development. Police ask the developers to keep a keen eye out for any sign of Sarah Spiers's body. The area is subject to feral cats, foxes, kangaroos and high water levels. Ten years after she disappeared, they know her body will be scattered skeletal remains at best. But her family is desperate to find her. So very desperate.

The victims' families can also take no heart from historical evidence from the USA, which points to the phenomenon of serial killing rising in that country. It is likely, analysts say, that Australia will follow suit.

A Macro source, who had offered me information to ensure I did not repeat inaccuracies, denied that Jane's – and probably Ciara's – throat had been slashed when I discussed this with him. 'It didn't happen,' he tells me emphatically. 'Someone has got it wrong.' But they haven't, and he knows it. Two other former Macro sources beyond Jane's family concede it is correct. Dave Barclay also concedes this is correct. The bid to keep secret the cause of death in the guise of checking inaccuracies does nothing but create confusion.

At a police union dinner in 2002, John Quigley was pushed around by police in the men's toilet and called a rat for breaking ranks. The incident followed a television interview where he openly questioned the police investigation into Pamela Lawrence's murder, stating it involved high-level police corruption by senior police. A life member of the police union, Quigley had attended 21 dinners and would continue to attend them. He got a touch-up, he says, but the reasons they did it are their problem, not his.

Quigley nominates the three 'P's that often bring down a copper: Property. Piss. Pussy. 'My first point of call is always cock-up, not conspiracy. The corporate line is, "we don't deny there will be isolated cases of police corruption," but I don't buy that. I usually find that a corrupt officer rarely acts by himself, that the only reason his corruption is able to flourish is because more than one person is involved or people turn a blind eye to it.' There's also a real problem now, he believes, in investigating Claremont. 'Not only do witness recollections become unreliable with the passage of time, but when an investigative team has raked over material ad infinitum, things tend to become confused. And that's not good for an end result.'

In early November 2006 police in Ipswich, England, raise concerns for the safety of 19-year-old missing prostitute Tania Nicol. Within a week, the story had made headlines around the world as a further four women fell victim to a serial killer. The savagery and speed of the murders gained the story grim comparisons with the Yorkshire Ripper and Jack the Ripper cases, and the press sensationally dubbed this killer the 'Suffolk Ripper'. By December, the bodies of all five women – Gemma Adams, 25; Anneli Alderton, 24; Paula Clennell, 24; and Annette Nicholls, 29 and Tania Nicol, whose disappearance first raised alarm – were found in different places in surrounding Suffolk County, around 110 kilometres northeast of London. At the height of the hysteria, 48-year-old forklift driver Steven Wright was arrested and charged with all five murders. Typically of serial killers, he had been living near the area where the girls worked the streets, targeting society's most vulnerable members: drug-addicted street workers in desperate need of fast cash. Advances in DNA and police technology had helped Suffolk police catch the killer, leading to a telling comment from Don Spiers. 'Western Australia Police didn't have this advantage when Sarah, Jane and Ciara went missing. These killers are nothing but predators, waiting for opportunity. When they are caught, we house them in prison at taxpayers' expense instead of getting rid of them. No one will have any argument from me in wanting to bring back the death penalty. Just get rid of these monsters.'

On 7 December 2006 Perth police announce to the media that Mark Dixie has been ruled out as a suspect in the Claremont murders. Their investigations, they reveal, have found it unlikely that Dixie was in Perth when Sarah Spiers disappeared from Claremont and have also found no evidence to link him to any crimes in Western Australia.

With Dixie now officially out of the frame they are, yet again, back to the drawing board.

Ten years on, police are still holding the DNA samples taken from the taxi drivers and the results of the forensic reviews are still not finalised. One of the major forensic issues identified as potentially problematic was the chain of evidence moving through different laboratories and the potential for contamination or loss. The police service is now looking at several options, among them an independent forensic institute which would centralise the work currently being done by Pathwest at the Health Department, the Chem Centre at the Department of Minerals and Energy and some police forensics.

On 10 January, 2007, Bradley Murdoch lost his appeal against his 28-year non-parole jail sentence for killing Peter Falconio and assaulting Joanne Lees. Media interest in his possible involvement in the Claremont killings quickly subsided.

Not everyone in Western Australia is convinced that the murders and disappearance are the work of the same person. Tom Percy QC is one. 'I've acted for a lot of criminals over the years and, to be frank, they're not that stupid. Claremont was crawling with security and we are led to believe that the same perpetrator hit the same street and the same pub on two occasions after Sarah Spiers. I'll believe it when someone confesses and the confession is proven.' Percy says he would be 'astounded' if the killer is Lance Williams. 'There's a culture of police and DPP in this state that categorically likes to win, a culture that goes back at least 50 years. I absolutely fear for anyone who is charged with the Claremont serial killings because the police will run with it with all the zeal of a fifth-century Crusader looking for the Holy Grail. They will be cheered on by the prosecutors and the risk is, that in all the hype that will be generated they could just overlook the fact that they may have charged the wrong man.' Percy compares the WA Police with those in the Canadian Rockies. 'In Canada, they "always get their man". In Western Australia they decide who they want and go after him.'

Percy holds little hope that the serial killings will be resolved. 'At the end of the day, when the mighty drum sounded, did Jack the Ripper stand up? No, he didn't. And there is as much chance now of the Claremont killer confessing as Jack the Ripper. If police can't reach a conclusion, they need at least to be able to say that they chased every rabbit down every hole. Have they done that? Given the resources at their fingertips, if they can't come up with a solid case that invites more than speculation, then there will never be a resolution.'

84

Norma Williams is as bewildered today as she ever was over the police surveillance of her son. She doesn't know what is going on now, what police are doing or planning. 'They still could be around the place somewhere, you just don't know,' she sighs. 'Skulking about, kind of sneaky, you know. People say to me, why don't we sue for harassment, for having our lives turned upside down like this? But the police say they can do anything they like. Anything at all. It's all part of their operational techniques. They are tin gods, with no accountability.' She shakes her head, bemused. 'We've got to try and sort of, you know, get on with our lives, try to get over it. But that's hard to do.'

Lance has hardly left the house since his surveillance was made public, instead staying in his room reading *Reader's Digest* magazines or watching the occasional movie on TV. He has no ambition to go out, Norma says. Why would he, when he was constantly followed everywhere he went? She can't understand why, if they haven't got enough evidence to charge Lance, they don't put him in the clear? 'As far as I know he has never been to where Jane or Ciara's bodies were found. He told me he hasn't been there. It's possible, I suppose, that he could have got out the night Sarah disappeared, but why didn't we hear him? And why didn't the police go public about the other suspects? Who are these people? We never hear anything of them. Never. They're like invisible ghosts.' The Williams family heard nothing of the review team's findings, either. 'They didn't come near us. They just flitted in and out of the place and that was that.'

Does she ever have doubts about her son's guilt, I ask her? Ever wonder if she is blinded by a mother's instinct to protect her own at all costs? That maybe, after all, the criticism that police have worn from the media about the covert and overt surveillance that he is, after all, the Claremont serial killer? Her eyes flicker past me for the briefest moment before they return my gaze. 'Do I ever have any doubt?' she repeats, softly. There is something of a wistful look in her eyes, something hard to define. As though she is in a fugue state, a world of her own. 'Do I have doubts?' she repeats. 'No. No. Not really. Not really.' She bids me goodbye with a wan, faint smile and closes the door.

Epilogue

They still party at Claremont's Club Bayview and Red Rock Hotel, young revellers spilling out into the balmy nights, waiting to get a taxi home. They walk down the street where Sarah Spiers was last seen, high on their youth, giggling from too much alcohol. Sarah's name is only vaguely familiar to them now, just a distant memory of the young, pretty girl whose disappearance changed the axis of their city; just a distant memory of that young, pretty girl who never came home.

Only the occasional car headlight pierces the night's darkness at Pipidinny Road; only nocturnal animals foraging for food breaks the eerie silence. No stars wink in this winter night's sky; there is nothing here to illuminate the blackness. Ciara Glennon's spirit hovers in the chilly air, an unseen presence. *Speak gently, she can hear the daisies grow.*

The lilies still grow at Wellard, peeking shyly from the cool earth in winter, full-blown by spring. Raindrops like tears skate on their green foliage and nestle in the base of their lemon tongues. Like tears, they weep over Jane Rimmer's disposal site, falling bleakly on the sodden ground. Pools of tears in which the death lilies grow.

UNSOLVED, MISSING OR MURDERED

Kerryn Tate, 22, body burnt on tree stump, December 1979. *Murdered.*

Lisa Mott, 12, last seen in Collie, October 1980. *Missing.*

Sharon Fulton, East Perth railway station, 1986. *Missing.*

Cheryl Renwick, 33, disappeared from South Perth unit, 26 May 1986. *Missing.*

Sally Greenham, 20, August 1987, Adelaide Terrace, Perth. *Missing.*

Julie Cutler, 22, last seen at Parmelia Hilton Hotel, 20 June 1988. Car found in surf. *Missing.*

Barbara Western, found in bushland north-east of Canning Dam, Perth. *Murdered.*

Kerry Turner, 18, body found near Canning Dam, July 1991. *Murdered.*

Radina Djukich, 14, last seen at her North Beach unit, 16 May 1992. *Missing.*

Cariad Anderson-Slater, 41, last seen at dawn exiting a taxi, Perth, 13 July 1992. *Missing.*

Petronella Albert, 21, Broome area, April 1999. *Missing.*

Hayley Dodd, Badgingarra, 17, July 1999. *Missing.*

Lisa Govan, 28, last seen at 7.30 am, Kalgoorlie, 8 October 1999. *Missing.*

Deborah Andserson, last seen 25 January 2000. Car found burning with body in front seat at Middle Swan Shopping Centre. *Murdered.*

Sarah McMahon, 20, last seen in Claremont, November 8, 2000. Her car found unlocked in a hospital car park, November 20. *Missing.*

Lisa Brown, 19, street prostitute, last seen on a Perth street at 12.30 am, 10 November 1998. *Missing.*

Darylyn Ugle, 25, street prostitute. Body found at Mundaring Weir, April 2003. *Murdered.*

Acknowledgments

I would like to thank the following people for their enormous help with background research for this book. A special thank you to the heartbroken parents of both the murdered and missing girls who trusted me to tell their stories. To my journalist colleagues, for interviews and for use of the extensive work they have covered on the subject: *Post* newspaper editor and proprietor Bret Christian for your generosity with newspaper clippings and for sharing your overall knowledge of your home city; *The West Australian*'s Luke Morfesse, who is a font of knowledge on the Claremont case and was incredibly helpful; Rex Haw at Channel 10 for trusting me with precious clippings amassed over a decade; and to Liam Bartlett, Colleen Egan and Wendy Page, producer of ABC's *Australian Story*, for general background material.

Thanks to Robin Napper, for all your help and passing on contacts and Thomas Lawson, for countless emails outlining Weygers's story. Thanks to WA Police for use of photographs relating to this story and to those who so generously shared their knowledge in those rushed, last-minute interviews: retired NSW officer Mike Hagan, Superintendent Paul Schramm, Inspector Paul Ferguson, Superintendent Stephen Brown and former Senior-Sergeant Tony Potts.

Thanks also to my 'man in the field', the former police officer who asked to remain anonymous; to the other former investigators who helped me fill the gaps in the puzzle; to Con Bayens, for your support and help; Mick Buckley for information and to Nic from the Australian Missing Person's website, for all your work.

To the lawyers: barrister and MP John Quigley, for your colourful insights; barrister Belinda Lonsdale for the Rory Christie transcripts; lawyer Neil Fearis for colouring-in the

Glennon story; Tom Percy QC and barrister Jonathon Davies for background.

Thanks also to Lance Williams's mother, Norma, for your patience with my questions and John Button, for your wonderful help with this and other projects.

Thanks to Publisher Meredith Curnow at Random House for putting your faith in my writing, again, and courage in bringing this story to the page; Brandon VanOver for your wonderful encouragement and patience in reading and re-reading every line; Louise Sterling, for your fabulous edit and empathy with this tragic story; and lawyer Richard Potter, for your terrific legal advice.

To Michael and Maryanne Wright for the use of your fabulous riverside apartment in Perth; Jane Corten and Geoff Coventry for your company; and Lourette and Brian Neale for your wonderful generosity and for putting up with us.

To my family and friends, for cheering me through this harrowing story – thanks again, as always. To my BSE, William Neale: a rock-solid support through this project and during research trips interstate, who made sure I kept going when I wanted to give up. Thank you so much.

Finally, again, to the special women to whom this book is dedicated: my mother, Monica, a gorgeous friend and support; and my beautiful daughter, Louise, whose life and love I treasure even more after writing this book.

Bibliography

ABC: *Australian Story*, 'Murder He Wrote', 2002

ABC Radio National: *The Spirit of Things*, 'The Una Glennon Story', October 2001

ABC Radio National: *Background Briefing*, 'The Courage of our Convictions – The Claremont Serial Killer', June 2000

ABC: Stateline WA, April 2004

Colin & Seaman, Donald. *The Serial Killers*, Virgin Publishing, 1992

Eggar, Steven A. *The Killers Among Us* (Second Edition), Pearson Education LTD, 2002

Holmes, R. *Profiling Violent Crimes: An Investigative Tool*, Sage Publications, 1996

Napper, Robin. Criminal Case Reviews paper, March 2005. Re-printed (in part) with permission

Ryan, Peter. 'Ripe Justice', *Quadrant*, Vol. 4, No. 5, May 2005

Post Newspaper, Perth

The West Australian